# 35 Strategies for Developing Content Area Vocabulary

**Brenda H. Spencer**
*California State University, Fullerton*

**Andrea M. Guillaume**
*California State University, Fullerton*

**Allyn & Bacon**
is an imprint of

Boston  New York  San Francisco
Mexico City  Montreal  Toronto  London  Madrid  Munich  Paris
Hong Kong  Singapore  Tokyo  Cape Town  Sydney

Vice President and Executive Publisher: Jeffery W. Johnston
Editor: Linda Ashe Bishop
Senior Managing Editor: Pamela D. Bennett
Senior Project Manager: Mary M. Irvin
Editorial Assistant: Demetrius Hall
Senior Art Director: Diane C. Lorenzo
Cover Design: Candace Rowley
Cover Image: Jupiter Images
Operations Specialist: Matt Ottenweller
Director of Marketing: Quinn Perkson
Marketing Manager: Krista Clark
Marketing Coordinator: Brian Mounts

For related titles and support materials, visit our online catalog at www.pearsonhighered.com

Spencer, Brenda H.
    35 strategies for developing content area vocabulary / Brenda H. Spencer, Andrea M. Guillaume.
        p. cm.
    Includes bibliographical references.
    ISBN-10: 0-13-175015-1
    ISBN-13: 978-0-13-175015-9
    1. Vocabulary—Study and teaching (Elementary) 2. Vocabulary—Study and teaching (Secondary) 3. Language arts—Correlation with content subjects. I. Guillaume, Andrea M. II. Title. III. Thirty-five strategies for developing content area vocabulary.

LB1574.5.S67 2009
372.44—dc22                                                                                          2008025619

Printed in the United States of America

4  5  6  7  8  9  10  V092  16  15  14  13  12

For Jay, Jay, and Jennifer
—BHS

For Zachary
—AMG

# Contents

# Preface

*35 Strategies for Developing Content Area Vocabulary* is a supplemental text for preservice and practicing teachers in grades 4 through 12. It is useful for preservice teachers who are enrolled in content area literacy courses or in general methods courses. It is also a valuable professional text for practicing teachers and teachers pursuing alternative certification who wish to boost their students' vocabulary knowledge in ways that are likely to translate into higher achievement and literacy levels.

Unlike other vocabulary texts, *35 Strategies for Developing Content Area Vocabulary* is organized according to a sequence akin to the learning cycle, *helping students prepare to learn words, build word knowledge, apply word knowledge,* and *learn words independently.* Each of these stages ensures that students build deep and rich understandings of content area terms and develop the motivation and skills to continue learning words throughout their lives.

The strategies are written in clear, reader-friendly language and are organized according to the following format:

- Background (including related research)
- Purpose (with information on why to employ the strategy)
- Procedures (step-by-step directions for using the strategy)
  - Getting ready (preparing before class)
  - During class (interacting with students)
- Modifications (including alternative uses of the strategy)
- Troubleshooting (tips for avoiding potential pitfalls)
- Next steps (ideas for where to go next, including many ideas for relating to other strategies in the text)

Many of the strategies include A Note for Your English Learners, which offers tips specific to supporting students who are acquiring English. Many strategies a so include Tech Connect notes that present ideas for integrating technology into vocabulary teaching and learning. Each strategy includes at least two sample applications, and many include work from actual students. Classroom examples cross the 4–12 grade span and address a broad range of curricular areas such as auto shop, photography, cooking, weight training, and economics, in addition to core areas such as science, social studies, mathematics, and the language arts.

## Acknowledgments

We'd like to acknowledge the contributions of a number of individuals whose thoughts and efforts strengthened this text. Thanks go to the students who allowed us to include their work. Among these students, we recognize in particular Alex, Zach, Nolan, Eva, and Tiffany. We appreciate the early input of upper elementary teacher Carol Watts for the perspectives and samples she shared with us. Our thanks go also to colleagues who served as reviewers of earlier drafts: Jackie Glasgow, Ohio University; A. Waller Hastings, Northern State University; Margot Kinberg, National University; Ann A. Wolf, Gonzaga University; Scott Popplewell, Ball State University; Doug Fisher, San Diego State University; and Ann Harris, Austin Peay University. Our heartfelt appreciation goes to Linda Bishop, whose invaluable guidance shaped the project and whose continued support saw it to fruition. Thanks, too, go to Demetrius Hall for his help facilitating the production of the text, and Mary Irvin, Project Manager. Finally, we appreciate the gracious and insightful assistance of Carol Singer at GGS Book Services PMG, for final editing and production of the work.

# Introduction

*"Words are vehicles that can transport us from the drab sands to the dazzling stars."*

—M. ROBERT SYME

The more words your students know and the better they know them, the greater the range of their travels. This introduction argues the importance of content area vocabulary knowledge, explores the complexities of vocabulary development, presents principles of effective vocabulary instruction, lays out the framework of this text, and gives guidelines for selecting content area target terms.

## WHY CONTENT AREA VOCABULARY?

Whether you teach students in an elementary classroom, a middle or junior high school, or a high school, you have the critical job of helping them learn a multitude of important ideas about the world and the human experience through the windows of your content areas. Each content area—from the arts to zoology—has vital contributions to the development of well-educated individuals, and content mastery entails students learning hundreds of new words. A successful theater performance, for example, depends on students knowing and effectively using specialized meanings for words such as *block*, *strike*, and *cheat*. The solution of a calculus problem depends on students applying terms such as *central limit theory, derivative*, and *integrand*. A delicious soufflé prepared in cooking class rests on students' accurate demonstration of terms such as *whip, fold*, and *separate*.

Clearly, content area achievement depends closely on students' mastery of specialized vocabulary. Vocabulary knowledge is important for a number of reasons. First, it is highly correlated with comprehension (Anderson & Freebody, 1981). In most content areas, students are expected to be effective consumers of textbooks and other print sources that contain a large number of specialized terms. Students' knowledge of these words affects how well they are able to learn new concepts and make connections to what they already know.

Second, many of the words students encounter have high utility in that they represent complex concepts that serve as building blocks to other learning. For example, in biology, a thorough understanding of the term *respiratory system* requires more than having a definition for the term. It also requires knowledge of the process of respiration and the biological contexts in which it might appear. Instruction that helps students learn high-utility terms such as *respiratory system* and the ways in which they link to other related words enhances students' conceptual understanding and makes it more likely that students will apply what they know to subsequent learning (Nagy & Scott, 2000).

Finally, every content area has words that are part of the discipline's academic discourse. These words are a part of a complex integrated network of knowledge that mature learners develop for the discipline. Being a member of that discourse community requires being able to communicate effectively both orally and in print using the words that signify membership. In the case of content area achievement, *word* knowledge is power.

## THE COMPLEXITY OF VOCABULARY LEARNING: THE TOUGH JOB AHEAD

Content area vocabulary development is a tough job for students and teachers alike. English has a huge number of words—many more than languages like German, French, and Spanish. Some estimate that children typically learn 3,000 words each year between grades 1 and 12 (Nagy & Anderson, 1984). A substantial amount of that learning occurs not through instruction but through oral language and wide reading (Nagy, Herman, & Anderson, 1985; Stahl, 1999). However, because of the heavy concept load and a structure that many students find difficult, students are *only half* as likely to learn words from reading content area texts as they are from other types of texts, such as narratives (Anderson & Nagy, 1992). Thus, it is unlikely that many students will acquire the essential vocabulary necessary for school success without their teachers' help and solid instruction.

Another complexity of vocabulary learning is understanding what it means to *know* a word. Knowing a word is not an all-or-nothing proposition. Students' knowledge of a word can range from recognizing a word to being able to give a definition of it and understanding how it is related to other information on the same topic (Nagy & Scott, 2000). For example, one student in a geometry class may recognize that he or she has seen the word *radius* before but not know what it means. Another student may be able to give a definition for *radius* but not know how to compute the radius of a circle. Even students who have demonstrated a good understanding of *radius* in geometry may need to develop a new meaning for it when they encounter it in a different content area, such as the study of human anatomy in biology.

In addition, the vocabulary instruction that you provide will vary depending on the level of understanding that is required of the term, its importance to the topic, the background of your students, and the instructional task your students are engaged in (Blachowicz & Fisher, 2000). For example, in a government class, students might encounter this sentence: *One of the major responsibilities of any state is to make and administer laws and to punish people for infractions of those laws.* Consider the words *infractions* and *state* in this sentence. To support students' understanding, it may be sufficient for you to give a synonym for the word *infractions*. The majority of students have sufficient background knowledge to understand an infraction if told that it refers to breaking or not obeying laws. And, most likely, it is not necessary for students to remember the term *infractions* because it is not strongly related to the topic. On the other hand, the word *state* is a core concept in the study of government. Students will need to develop a specialized definition for it, remember its meaning, learn its major attributes, and explain how *state* relates to other words in the same category. It is unlikely that students will develop this rich level of understanding without your careful attention.

Additionally, a large percentage of U.S. students experience financial hardship, and that number is on the rise (Douglas-Hall & Chau, 2007). Recently, one-third of U.S students were eligible for free or reduced-price meals (National Center for Education Statistics [NCES], 2006), and 16% lived in poverty (NCES, 2007). Students who experience poverty have reduced access to resources and experiences that foster the development of academic language (Marzano, 2004). Some estimate that, by age 4, children who experience poverty may have been exposed to 30 million fewer words than children from more economically advantaged homes and begin school with smaller vocabularies than their economically advantaged counterparts (Hart & Risley, 1995). Worse yet, because background knowledge predicts achievement, students who come to us knowing fewer words are less likely to learn new words (Baker, Simmons, & Kame'enui, 1997). Thus, the gap in vocabulary knowledge can persist through high school (Hart & Risley, 1995).

We also teach high numbers of English learners (approximately 10% of our K–12 population nationwide, with many states having higher rates; NCES, 2006). English learners work double duty to acquire English (with its huge lexicon) while simultaneously studying our content areas and their myriad of specialized terms. Specialized terms in the content areas often have specific meanings in one content area that do not generalize to other subjects. And the meanings often differ from the general meanings of the same terms. Perhaps it is for these reasons that the achievement gap found between English learners and native English speakers is largely a vocabulary gap, according to Carlo et al. (2004).

As a result of these factors, our responsibility to help students learn content area vocabulary terms—and strategies for learning words independently—looms large. This responsibility must be carried out teacher by teacher, content by content, and classroom by classroom so that students have control over large stores of specialized vocabulary terms and can use the terms powerfully to accomplish their purposes.

**VOCABULARY INSTRUCTION: WHAT *DOESN'T* WORK AND WHAT *DOES***

Current classroom practices and plentiful research provide insights into both what *doesn't* work for vocabulary development and what *does*.

## What *Doesn't* Work for Content Area Vocabulary Development

Schools can—and do—make a difference in students' vocabulary development (Marzano, 2004). Unfortunately, because time is short and lists of words to master are long, a number of instructional practices that don't work well in fostering vocabulary knowledge seem to seep into classrooms. What *doesn't* work in vocabulary development is to confine instruction to students copying dictionary definitions. Definitions often offer *more* unknown words to define the unfamiliar target term. What *doesn't* work in vocabulary development is to give skimpy definitions of numerous words one day and then develop related concepts the next. Definitions have little meaning if students have limited conceptual knowledge from which to draw, and conceptual knowledge develops over time and in context. What *doesn't* work in vocabulary development is to photocopy and distribute a lengthy list of new words on Monday and then give the test on Friday. By doing so, students often develop sparse word knowledge, and the teacher abdicates responsibility for helping students learn words deeply. Fortunately, the research on what *does* work in vocabulary instruction is clear.

## What Works: Four Principles for Vocabulary Development

The research in vocabulary learning indicates that to be effective, word learning needs to be integrated into the class curriculum so that it becomes an intentional part of instruction. We offer four research-based principles that have wide applicability. You can use these principles as a guide to spur your effective vocabulary development program, and you can see these principles come to life in the 35 strategies found in this text.

### Principle 1: Provide a learning environment that is rich in oral and written language.

To learn content vocabulary, students need to be immersed in words (Alvermann, Swafford, & Montero, 2004). In a language-rich environment, students engage in word learning both incidentally and intentionally, and word learning is part of the fabric of the classroom (Blachowicz & Fisher, 2006). Figure I.1 summarizes tips for creating a language-rich environment.

Much of our general vocabulary knowledge is developed through incidental encounters with language. For example, wide reading of narratives (stories and personal accounts) has been shown to be a major source of incidental word learning for students of all ages. In a summary of their work, Anderson and Nagy (1992) concluded that if students are given texts that they can comprehend, they will learn approximately one word for every 20 unfamiliar words they meet. Because the average fifth grader reads approximately 1 million words a year, with 20,000 or so of them being unfamiliar, we can expect that students will learn 1,000 words simply through their independent readings. As you might expect, students who read more experience substantially higher gains in both vocabulary growth and world knowledge than their peers who read less (Stanovich & Cunningham, 1993).

## Figure I.1 Tips for creating a language-rich learning environment

- Encourage wide reading of narrative text.
- Encourage wide reading of challenging text.
- Lead content-based discussions.
- Foster student-student interactions and discussion.
- Provide access to lots of print and to many kinds of print.

Reading to students from challenging texts is another important source of vocabulary knowledge (Stahl, 2005). Challenging texts can be narrative or informational but are generally too difficult for students to read on their own. Thus, they contain words and require world knowledge that it is unlikely students would encounter independently. When teachers engage in read alouds systematically and provide opportunities for discussion of important vocabulary and ideas, they provide students with an important source of new word and world knowledge.

Language-rich classrooms also provide many opportunities for teacher-led and student-led discussions. Vocabulary instruction that makes use of discussion is more likely to result in the deep, rich understandings of terms needed for school success. Discussions help students activate their prior knowledge and make connections between what they know and what they are learning (Nagy, 2005; Stahl & Clark, 1987). It also allows them to pool their knowledge, to challenge and refine their understandings, to deeply process words and word meanings, and to practice words in a variety of contexts. According to Nagy (1988), opportunity for meaningful use of new terms is an essential component of effective vocabulary learning. In sum, student interaction, including content-driven discourse, fuels students' academic success.

Language-rich classrooms also include many kinds of printed materials and virtual text. Magazines, newspapers, signs, poetry, reference works, primary sources, student writings, bulletin boards, murals, computer software, and the Internet all can provide text in the language-rich environment. Texts can provide additional exposures to terms introduced initially through teacher talk and classroom discussion. They can serve to extend firsthand experiences, providing opportunities for instruction and discussion of new and related terms that deepen students' knowledge and understanding (Spencer & Guillaume, 2006). They can provide opportunities to meet words in other situations, serve as a source for new and interesting terms, and provide reference resources for students to discover word meanings. Finally, student-written texts provide opportunities for sharing new words, exploring their uses, and applying them in personally relevant ways. In sum, a language-rich learning environment immerses students in contexts for speaking, hearing, reading, and writing the language of our disciplines.

### Principle 2: Different words require different instructional strategies.

Different kinds of words present different demands and thus require that you employ a range of instructional approaches (Stahl, 2005). Note that each approach requires students to be actively engaged in word learning (Alvermann et al., 2004). At times, a *definitional approach* is appropriate. One way of using this approach is for you to provide a quick definition or a synonym for unknown words either before or during reading. This approach works best when the unknown words are relatively unimportant to the topic or are words that students will rarely encounter. Another variation of the definitional approach requires that students look up terms in a dictionary, often copying their definitions and engaging in related activities such as writing the terms in sentences. This approach is useful when students already have some background knowledge about the topic in which the words appear. Dictionaries present specific, succinct, and useful information about a word, and they give clues about related words and contexts of use. Thus, looking words up in a dictionary can help students understand the meaning of new words and how they are related to what they already know. However, using the definitional approach alone is likely to result in superficial word knowledge because it is unlikely that the definitions will be well integrated into what students already know (Nagy, 1988). Therefore, it is most useful when students require only limited information about a word.

In the *contextual approach*, students learn to infer word meanings by studying the contexts in which the words are used. They examine the surrounding sentences (and related graphics) to check the clues related to meaning and part of speech of the target terms. This approach provides more information than does the definitional approach about how words are used, but it has other drawbacks. Factors such as text density and student ability affect students' success in learning from context (Swanborn & de Glopper, 1999). Another drawback is that the context clues may provide only partial—or even misleading—information about the term.

The *concept development approach* is most appropriate when students have limited grasp of the concept or concepts underlying the term. In this approach, instruction focuses on the development of concepts and on making rich connections to what students already know. Many concepts are abstract and take considerable time to form. Techniques such as inquiry, hands-on learning, and class discussions are useful in building deep understandings of concepts. Later, instruction can easily help students attach labels—vocabulary terms—to those concepts.

Another important approach focuses on building students' *word awareness* (Blachowicz & Fisher, 2004a; Graves, 2000; Scott & Nagy, 2004). This approach seeks to build students' curiosity and interest in words by creating a classroom environment in which words are valued. One way to promote word awareness is to model your own curiosity and passion for words. You can bring in appealing words to share with your students and invite them to bring in interesting words they find in their reading, conversations, or everyday lives. You can provide opportunities for favorite words to be displayed, discussed, and used in writing and word-play activities. Students' interest in words can also be sparked and expanded through the exploration of word histories and word parts. Thus, an effective vocabulary program involves varied approaches, such as those addressed by the 35 strategies found herein.

### Principle 3: Provide many exposures to words and many opportunities to use the words.

Estimates of the exposures necessary to learn a word vary from 6 to 12 or more (Stahl, 1986). It is only through repeated exposure that students can meet words in different settings, define them, come to understand their shades of meaning, and appreciate their multiple meanings. Because our understandings of terms are gradually shaped over time, repeated exposures are essential.

Additionally, practice is an essential component of word learning. Nagy (1988) urges that practice opportunities be *meaningful*, that is, that they match the contexts and demands under which the students will use the words once they become part of their writing and speaking lexicons. Students should be encouraged to represent their knowledge of words in linguistic and nonlinguistic ways. In terms of linguistic representations, the strategies in this book provide for both oral and written contexts of use. Oral practice is encouraged through increased social interaction, such as partner and small-group discussions and dramatic presentations using target terms. Peer-to-peer discourse-based conversations are especially important for English learners, as they provide increased opportunities to talk, particularly in lower-risk settings. Students' spontaneous use of target terms in their writing may be the true test of deep and rich word knowledge. Strategies in this text include a variety of opportunities for students to use target terms in their writing. Examples include scripts, poems, and reports. In terms of nonlinguistic representations, throughout the strategies, students are encouraged to use graphic organizers, sketches, and reenactments of terms.

### Principle 4: Help students become independent word learners by fostering motivation and teaching metacognitive skills and vocabulary strategies.

Perhaps our ultimate goal as educators is to provide students with the spark and skills necessary to pursue learning far outside and long after classroom instruction. The ultimate measure of success of vocabulary instruction may indeed be that students possess the wherewithal to do the following (Baker & Brown, 1984; National Research Council, 2000):

1. Set their own goals and ask questions
2. Monitor their own thinking
3. Change their behavior when something goes wrong
4. Continue to learn new vocabulary

In order to be successful, independent vocabulary learners, students need to develop the skills necessary to (a) monitor their word knowledge by being aware of the varying depth of knowledge they have for terms, (b) know how to find and use resources to enrich and clarify their knowledge when needed, and (c) reflect on changes in understanding as their word knowledge grows. Teachers can support growth in students' metacognitive skills by providing explicit instruction and modeling, such as in the think-aloud technique, and by providing

**Figure I.2** Four research-based principles of vocabulary development

> 1. Provide a learning environment that is rich in oral and written language.
> 2. Different words require different instructional strategies.
> 3. Provide many exposures to words and many opportunities to use the words.
> 4. Help students become independent word learners by fostering motivation and teaching metacognitive skills and vocabulary strategies.

opportunities for students to use and refine their metacognitive skills. Strategies in this text are meant to encourage a love for language, words, and the power of word knowledge as well as the skills students need to monitor and improve their learning. Figure I.2 summarizes the four research-based principles of vocabulary development, principles that firmly underlay our framework for vocabulary development.

## OUR FRAMEWORK FOR VOCABULARY DEVELOPMENT

How can research-based principles for vocabulary instruction drive our daily teaching? This text embeds principles of instruction into a sequence that ensures a language-rich environment; builds interest and motivation; provides many opportunities for students to see, hear, explore, and use words; and employs a wide variety of strategies to help students learn words. The instructional sequence has three straightforward phases that build teacher guidance into students' arduous yet compelling task of content area vocabulary development:

1. Preparing to Learn Words
2. Building Word Knowledge
3. Applying Word Knowledge

**Preparing to Learn Words** Any new word—or new meanings of a word—that students learn must find a place in the mental networks of concepts and terms they already hold. Additionally, without sufficient motivation or interest, students are unlikely to devote themselves fully to the important task of learning new words. Thus, the *Preparing to Learn Words* phase serves a few important purposes.

First, in some instances, the phase must be used to build concepts to lay a foundation for word knowledge. Because it is much easier to learn a term when the concept is in place, students may need firsthand experiences with events or objects to successfully learn the labels for those phenomena (Spencer & Guillaume, 2006). The richer and more varied students' experience related to particular concepts are, the more finely detailed and precise their understandings of related terms can be expected to be. Firsthand experiences provide a bank of concepts that become students' vocabulary store.

Second, this phase brings students' prior knowledge to the surface, including their potential misconceptions, and thus provides teacher guidance to the process of conceptual change. Effective vocabulary instruction requires the integration of the *new* and the *known* (Christen & Murphy, 1991). Third, this phase draws out students' language related to the topic and, because students are likely to have different amounts and kinds of background experience, builds a common store of classroom language and ideas related to the topic. Finally, this phase sparks interest and builds motivation to learn words. Often, this phase piques students' curiosity and fuels questions about words and ideas that stoke their energy to build word knowledge. Sample activities that occur during this phase include hands-on activities, sketches, predictions, exploratory conversations, and the beginnings of graphic organizers.

**Building Word Knowledge** With concepts budding, prior knowledge at the surface, and interest piqued, the *Building Word Knowledge* phase helps students learn meanings (or specialized meanings) for vocabulary terms. It builds nuances and understandings of appropriate contexts for word use. During this phase, students connect new concepts to known concepts, address misunderstandings, structure their understanding of word networks, and develop rich word meanings. Rather than focusing on memorizing definitions, strategies related to building word knowledge in this text help students analyze word parts, examine word histories, learn definitions deeply, and examine related words within a language-rich environment. Additionally, activities that occur during this phase help students gain skills they will need as independent word learners.

**Applying Word Knowledge** Strategies in the *Applying Word Knowledge* phase address the importance of multiple exposures and opportunities for students to use newly acquired terms. By providing a variety of contexts for use, this phase helps sustain a language-rich environment—through discussion, reading, and writing—and provides occasions for further exploration and use of target terms. This phase also supports student interest and motivation by providing realistic contexts to experiment with words. During this phase, students may make posters, play games, compose reports, or engage in theatrical performances.

**Independent Word Learning** It is impossible to provide instruction on every term students must master. Because the ultimate goal of vocabulary instruction is for students to become ardent word sleuths—independent word learners—outside the classroom and in the future, this text also includes strategies that help students tackle content words on their own. *Independent Word Learning* teaches students to use strategies such as context, definitions, morphemic analysis, word histories, and analogies to further their own word learning.

## Selecting Target Terms for Vocabulary Development

Given the clear relationship between vocabulary knowledge and student achievement, it's tempting to develop long lists of terms to be mastered. In fact, most teachers do select more words than their students can learn. A more effective approach is to select a smaller set of terms and to teach them well. With all the terms that flood textbooks, how can you select the most promising for instruction? Instruction should focus on terms that have a high probability of enhancing academic success. Beck, McKeown, and Kucan (2002) argue that the selection of vocabulary terms is somewhat arbitrary and that teachers should feel free to use their professional judgment in selecting promising target terms. We suggest the following six guidelines to narrow down your list of potential target terms:

1. *Select the terms that students don't know.* Entry-level and ongoing assessment of students' vocabulary knowledge is important. In addition, as you narrow your list, you may wish to delete words that students can easily discern from context or using their knowledge of word parts.
2. *Select the terms that are important for conceptual understanding.* Of the dozens of words suggested in the chapter or unit, it may be that only four or five are truly important for students' understanding of the content. These words might represent critical concepts or might help students develop more precise understandings of related important ideas. A couple sources of information can help you judge terms' importance for conceptual understanding. First, your expertise in the subject matter can provide a strong sense of direction, particularly if you are an experienced teacher and a content expert. Second, your state content standards can provide guidance. Compare your text and other instructional materials to your standards and ensure that they coincide in the priority they place on terms. Consider forgoing the terms that get less emphasis in your state. National content standards can also be consulted as another source of evidence about terms that support critical ideas in your content standards.
3. *Select the terms that are used repeatedly.* There are some terms that students may encounter so frequently that a little instruction can provide lots of mileage. To select high-utility terms, take another look at your text materials and at your standards. This time, examine not just the current unit but the entire text. As you examine your content standards, look up and down the grade levels and across related courses and select words that students will meet again.

You may wish to consult your high-stakes assessment documents and peruse test specifications to ensure that your class has opportunities to learn the terms that may play into their success on these measures. The National Assessment of Educational Progress (NAEP) and some states post released test items on the Web. Check out NAEP items at http://nces.ed.gov/nationsreportcard. As a caveat, although it is important to provide access to terms included in high-stakes measures, it is equally important not to confine instruction to the terms found on tests.

4. *Select terms that may be difficult for students.* Many terms, such as those that represent concepts with which students have extensive experience or that have concrete referents, are relatively easy to learn. For example, many 4-year-olds easily recite with meaning dozens of cumbersome names for dinosaurs. Such terms need not be the focus of instruction. Instead, terms that represent abstract concepts, that are confusing, or that have multiple meanings may instead deserve your instructional intention.
5. *Select terms that are likely to foster students' ability to learn other words.* If, for example, working with a particular term is likely to improve students' ability to analyze context, use reference materials, or develop analogies, the term may deserve to be included on your list of target terms.
6. *Consider differentiating word selections.* After identifying the terms that *everybody* should master, consider attending to words that *some people* may additionally learn. Although they are available to all, these "some people" words may be self-selected by students with particular interests in the topic, out-of-school goals or experiences related to the terms, or a special love of words and word learning.

Applying these guidelines to vocabulary instruction will clearly require advance planning on your part. We recommend that you include target term selection as part of your long-range planning efforts. Working with colleagues to determine target terms is also a valuable practice. By thinking carefully about target terms early in the year or semester, you increase the likelihood that your selections will build important understandings and reinforce each other. As a result, your students are likely to add greatly to their stores of word knowledge and, in the end, use words as powerful tools to understand their world. They may heed the advice of Pulitzer Prize–winning author N. Scott Momaday and change the universe by believing in the power of words.

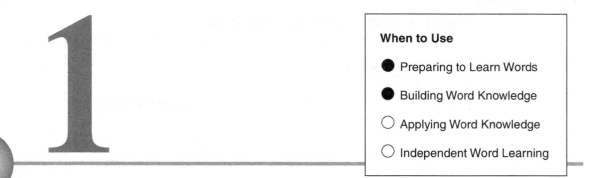

# Concept of Definition Map

Understanding vocabulary in the content areas is a complex process. For example, seventh-grade students studying principles of motion would certainly be expected to provide a definitional meaning of the word *motion*. It would be hard to argue that students know a word if they can't describe what it is (Nagy & Scott, 2000). Being able to define *motion,* however, is only part of the knowledge students need to truly understand a concept. They also need to understand how the concept is related to what they already know and to new understandings they are developing (Blachowicz & Fisher, 2000; Bos & Anders, 1992). The Concept of Definition Map (Schwartz & Raphael, 1985) is a graphic organizer that shows the relationship between a concept's definition and other information about it.

## PURPOSE

The Concept of Definition Map supports vocabulary development by making students aware of the types of information that make up the meaning of a word and how that information can be organized (Schwartz & Raphael, 1985). It displays three types of information about a word: the category to which it belongs, the properties that are related to it and distinguish it from other words, and examples. Concept of Definition Maps encourage students to think critically about the components of words and to consider how these components are related to what they already know.

## PROCEDURES

### Getting Ready

1. Before a unit of instruction, pick the target words. Be selective in your choices. The Concept of Definition Map is designed to help students analyze a word in depth and should not be used with a long list of words. Choose only words that are terms for concepts that are essential for the understanding of your unit of study and are building blocks for learning in the future. The following words were selected by a sixth-grade teacher for the introduction to a unit on Greek mythology.

**A sixth-grade teacher's selection of terms for an introduction to a unit on Greek mythology**

| polytheism | myth | deity |
| --- | --- | --- |

**9**

**Figure 1.1** Concept of Definition Map

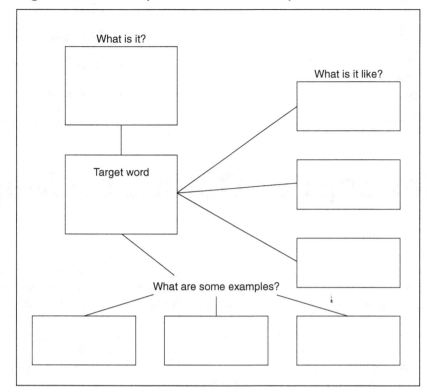

2. Prepare the Concept of Definition Map for students. Figure 1.1 shows a sample. Each word requires a separate Concept of Definition Map. Make a transparency or reproduce the map so that you can record students' ideas. After students are familiar with the Concept of Definition Map you many want to consider having students create their own.

## During Class

Concept of Definition Map is useful both for encouraging students to think about what they know (the *Preparing to Learn Words* phase) and to refine and extend that prior knowledge during *Building Word Knowledge*.

### Preparing to Learn Words

1. Begin the lesson by displaying one of the words you have selected. Provide students with a copy of the Concept of Definition Map. You may elect to have students fill in the map in small groups, in pairs, or individually. However, every student should have an individual copy of the map.
2. Write the key concept in the center of the duplicated map that you will use to record students' ideas.
3. Read the key concept aloud. Tell students that this is an important word in the topic or unit. Have the students write the target word in the appropriate place on their map.
4. Invite students to share what they know about the word. Make a list of their ideas. Ask students to help you group ideas using the categories from the Concept of Definition Map (What is it? What is it like? What are some examples?). Use prompts like the following to guide students in selecting ideas for the categories:
   - Which ideas describe what the concept is? What group or class of things does this word belong to?
   - What ideas tell us what this concept is like? What attributes does it have? Can you think of another object or idea that is similar to our word?
   - Can you provide some examples of our word?

**Figure 1.2** Concept of Definition Map for *deity*

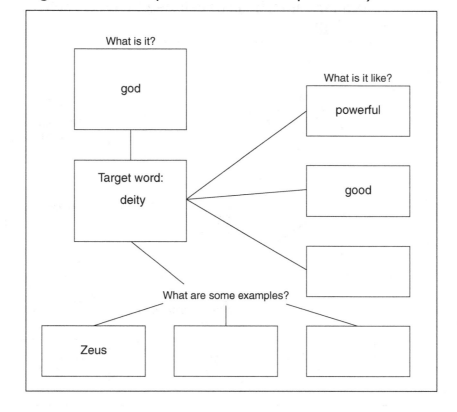

5. Record students' ideas in the appropriate boxes on the class Concept of Definition Map and have students fill in the information on their map. Students are likely to have a wide range of prior knowledge about the target concept, and a class discussion of students' pooled knowledge will help motivate students and facilitate learning new attributes and terms that define the concept. Figure 1.2 shows the partially completed Concept of Definition Map for the word *deity* by the sixth-grade class studying Greek mythology. Note that students suggested the inaccurate term *good* for one of the "What is it like?" attributes. If students suggest ideas that are misconceptions about the target concept, you can either ask questions that will help guide students to a more accurate choice or record the inapt term and return to it after further learning. The sixth-grade teacher decided to record the term *good* without discussion in the *Preparing to Learn* phase of the lesson but returned to it after further instruction so that students could use the new information they had learned to modify the term.

## Building Word Knowledge

1. Provide opportunities for students to add information or make corrections to their Concept of Definition Map as they build new understandings. Explore relevant properties of the concept during instruction by asking questions:
   - How is this idea related to this concept? Which category does it best fit? Is it an example or an attribute?
   - Is this idea relevant to the concept in all instances?
   - How is it related to other ideas that we have already recorded?
2. After instruction, revisit students' individual and class Concept of Definition Maps (from *Preparing to Learn Words*) to add new understandings and make final modifications. Figure 1.3 shows a Concept of Definition Map for the term *proprietary standards* in a high school technology class during a unit on software applications.

**Figure 1.3** Concept of Definition Map for *proprietary standards* developed in a high school technology class

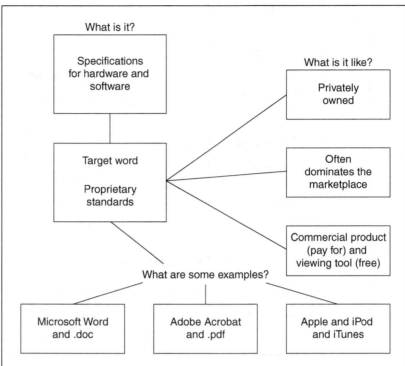

 ## MODIFICATIONS

1. If the words that you select are hard to analyze with the category labels used in the Concept of Definition Map, consider one or more of the following:
   a. Instead of "What is it like?" use "What does it do?" or "What are its attributes?"
   b. Have students draw a picture that represents the term. (See Sketch to Stretch, p. 28.)
   c. Use antonyms and synonyms as categories instead of examples.
2. Once students are familiar with the Concept of Definition Map, consider using the map to assess students' understanding. After a unit of study, give students the Concept of Definition Map with all the category boxes filled in except the identity of the word. Ask students to use the information on the map to identify the word. For more advanced students, try giving them the word and ask them to fill in all the related information.

 ## TROUBLESHOOTING

1. To ensure that your students understand the procedure, provide modeling and guided practice using words they know before introducing new terms.
2. To ensure success and to keep students motivated, limit the number of words you choose to four or fewer.
3. The Concept of Definition Map works best with nouns that are a part of a class of things for which there are multiple attributes and examples. If the words you chose don't work well with the Concept of Definition Map, try using the Frayer Model on page 18.

## NEXT STEPS

The Concept of Definition Map works especially well as a basis for writing activities such as Poetry (p. 149), Word Posters (p. 159), and Readers Theater (p. 140). Consider also activities that encourage students to see the relationship between the words you have targeted for study and other information they are learning in a unit. I-Search a Word reports (p. 163) and Student-Made Books (p. 145) work well for this purpose.

# Possible Sentences

Possible Sentences is a combination vocabulary/prediction activity (Moore & Moore, 1986). It is an easy way to prepare students to read a selection of text because most of the work is done on the board. The strategy introduces students to new vocabulary they will encounter in a chapter or passage and asks them to use two of the words to create a sentence they believe will appear in the text. Possible Sentences has been shown to be an effective strategy for increasing comprehension and for making it more likely that important concepts will be retained (Stahl & Kapinus, 1991).

Teachers can use Possible Sentences in most content areas. This strategy is particularly useful in content areas where concepts and ideas build on one another because you want students to learn new vocabulary that is related to words the students already know.

## PURPOSE

Possible Sentences prepares students for reading and for learning new vocabulary by having them think about the relationship between the words they will encounter in the passage as well as the relationship of the vocabulary to the text as a whole. This strategy provides for multiple exposures to words and for opportunities for students to use the words in written and oral language. Possible Sentences encourages students to use their background knowledge to predict how vocabulary will be used in a passage they will read and to use the information in the text to confirm or modify their predictions. Because students make predictions about the vocabulary they meet in the passage, it is more likely that students will actively comprehend the text.

## PROCEDURES

### Getting Ready

1. Before students read the selection or passage, pick the target words. Choose seven or eight new words (fewer is better) that may be difficult for students. The terms you choose should be words that are central to understanding the topic.
2. Also choose four or five words that are likely to be familiar to the majority of the students. The words should be related to the new words in some way so that students can use them to make logical sentences that might occur in the text they will be reading. See Figure 2.1 for a list of difficult and known words that a teacher chose for a sixth-grade unit on Egyptian tomb art and architecture.

**Figure 2.1** A sixth-grade teacher's selection of terms for a unit on Egyptian tomb art and architecture

The teacher chose these seven new words that were important in the unit and might be difficult for many students:

| | |
|---|---|
| eternity | pharaoh |
| sacred | ka |
| mummy | tomb |
| hieroglyphics | |

She also chose these four words that she believed most of her students already knew:

| | |
|---|---|
| writing | burial |
| ruler | soul |

## During Class

For Possible Sentences, *Preparing to Learn Words* activities build a clear purpose for *Building Word Knowledge* efforts, including reading content text.

### Preparing to Learn Words

1. Write the words that you have selected in random order on the board. You want students to discover the relationships among the words, so it is important not to pair them as you may have done when you selected them.
2. Ask students to write sentences that they believe will appear in the materials they will read. Each sentence should contain two of the words. Requiring students to use two words in a sentence will encourage them to consider how the words are related to one another. Be sure to tell them that words can be used more than once if needed.
3. Write the students' sentences on the board regardless of whether they are correct or not. Continue to accept sentences until all new words have been used at least twice. Because the sentences are predictions of what students think *might* be in their reading material, refrain from discussing the sentences until after students have finished reading.

### Building Word Knowledge

1. To actively engage students in reading, encourage them to think about whether their sentences could be true—or possible—as they read.
2. After reading, direct students' attention once more to the sentences on the board to discuss if the sentences could be true. Ask them to provide evidence from the selection to support their decisions.
3. Invite students to correct the sentences on the board that are not true. See Figure 2.2 for an example from a high school economics lesson.

**Sample Possible Sentences composed by sixth graders during social studies**

Ancient Egyptians thought that making <u>mummies</u> would preserve a person into <u>eternity</u>.

<u>Ka</u> is a letter found in <u>hieroglyphics</u>.

Only the <u>pharaoh</u> had a <u>sacred</u> <u>tomb</u>.

**Figure 2.2** An example of a high school economics lesson on inflation that uses Possible Sentences

**Getting Ready:**

1. The teacher selects seven new words that are important in the lesson that many students may find difficult:

   | | |
   |---|---|
   | *inflation* | *consumer* |
   | *index* | *rates* |
   | *trend* | *goods* |
   | *services* | |

2. Then she selects four related words that most of her students will know:

   | | |
   |---|---|
   | *increase* | *decline* |
   | *price* | *purchases* |

**During Class:**

1. The teacher writes the words on the board in random order. She pronounces them and students repeat.
2. Then she gives these directions:
   - Today we will be studying inflation. Each word on the board is important to this topic. Using these words, you and your partner will write sentences that you believe might appear in our text. Each of the sentences must use at least two of the words. You can use the words more than once, but all words must be used. You can also make a word plural or add *ed* if needed to make the sentence grammatically correct.
   - Before you start to write, discuss with your partner what words might go together. Make certain that you have a rationale for the connections that you are making. Keep writing sentences until you have used all the words at least once. (about 5 minutes)
3. The students volunteer to share their sentences. The teacher records the sentences until all *new* words appear at least twice.
   - One pair proudly shared a sentence that had three of the words (but only one *new* word): *Inflation increases* and *declines*. Another pair contributed: *Consumers decline* to buy things they don't want.
4. After reading the text, the students evaluate the possible sentences and rewrite those sentences that they find are incorrect or in need of clarification.
   - The pair that contributed, "Consumers decline to buy things they don't want" proposed that their sentence be modified to state, "When consumers decline to buy things, it affects the rate of inflation." The teacher said, "Good suggestion. Now your sentence shows the relationship between what consumers do and inflation." Then she asked, "Who can help me identify two of the words we are studying that could be substituted for the word *things*?" Many hands went up, and all agreed that *goods* and *services* could be substituted for *things*.

## ● MODIFICATIONS

1. Provide the definitions for the target words. Even if you have given them definitions, students will have to predict how the words are related in order to make a logical sentence that contains two of the words.
2. Reduce the number of unknown words and increase the number of known words. For example, when you choose the target words, choose six known words and four unknown words.

# NEXT STEPS

Students love to challenge each other. During a unit review, try having students use the target vocabulary they have studied to create new Possible Sentences. In some of the sentences the relationship between the two words they selected should be correct, and in others it should not be correct. Allow students to challenge each other by asking whether a sentence is possible. Students' ability to construct and identify both possible and impossible sentences requires a good understanding of the target words.

## A Note for Your English Learners

If students are English learners or if some students have insufficient background and vocabulary knowledge about the topic, try this idea. Begin the activity with a Semantic Map (see p. 37). Invite students to brainstorm ideas, concepts, and terms related to the key concept. Record their contributions on the board and discuss. It is likely that at least some of the students will have knowledge about the topic. Developing a Semantic Map allows students to learn from each other.

Use the ideas and terms recorded on the Semantic Map as a source for some of the *known* vocabulary you use to develop the pool of words for Possible Sentences. For example, before introducing a unit on government, a fifth-grade teacher had his students brainstorm what they knew about the key term *laws*. From the words and phrases students generated, he chose *laws, judges, government*, and *president* to use as known words and added the new words *legislature, executive, judicial, national, state*, and *mayor*.

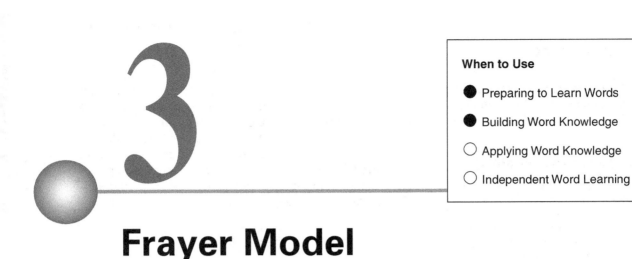

**When to Use**

● Preparing to Learn Words

● Building Word Knowledge

○ Applying Word Knowledge

○ Independent Word Learning

# Frayer Model

In every content area, there are vocabulary words that represent concepts that are so complex that a deep, rich knowledge of the terms is essential for true understanding. Take the word *democracy* as an example. A definition of *democracy* might be "a government by the people." But this definition hardly captures all we need to know to understand democracy. The definition itself raises questions. Who are the people who are governing? Does everyone agree on how to govern? Do some people have more power in governing than others? How do they get their power? Are all democracies the same? How does a democracy differ from other forms of government? Developing a rich understanding of a complex concept such as democracy requires looking at the concept from different perspectives and considering what it is and what it is not (Stahl, 2005). The Frayer Model (Frayer, Fredrick, & Klausmeir, 1969) is a graphic organizer that can be used to help students take an analytic approach to learning words. Frayer et al. found that use of the model promotes the development of deep, rich understandings of terms that represent important concepts.

## PURPOSE

The Frayer Model has several valuable purposes. First, it encourages students to think critically about the components of complex concepts. Second, it helps students activate relevant background knowledge and to consider how new learning is related to what is already known (Knopper & Duggan, 2000). Finally, it provides students the opportunity to self-assess what they know and do not know about a word (Blachowicz & Fisher, 2002).

## PROCEDURES

### Getting Ready

1. Before a unit of instruction, pick the target words. Be selective in your choices. Choose only words that are terms for complex concepts that are essential for the understanding of your unit of study and will be important in other contexts as well. For example, in a unit on early movements in modern art, a high school teacher chose the following three words given in the following figure. The Frayer Model provides a thorough analysis of a word and takes time for completion, so plan on spending one instructional session on each of the words you choose, especially when students are learning to use the model.

**A high school teacher's selection of terms for a unit on early movements in modern art**

| | | |
|---|---|---|
| Impressionism | Fauvism | Cubism |

**Figure 3.1** Frayer Model graphic organizer

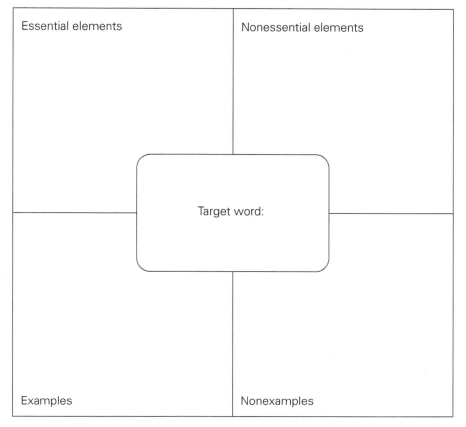

2. Prepare the Frayer Model graphic organizer for students. Figure 3.1 shows a sample. Each word requires a separate graphic organizer. Make a transparency or reproduce the graphic organizer so that you can record students' ideas.
3. After students are familiar with the Frayer Model, you many want to consider having students create their own graphic organizer by folding a sheet of paper into four squares and drawing a circle in the middle for the target word. Or have them create the graphic organizer solely by folding the paper three times, each fold after the other without opening the paper. First, fold the paper in half one way. Second, fold the paper in half the other. Finally, fold the corner that will be found at the center of the paper over with a small diagonal flap. The diagonal fold results in a diamond in the center of the page for the target term. See Figure 3.2 for a graphic depiction of these folds.

## During Class

In the Frayer Model, in the *Preparing to Learn Words* phase, students think about a target term's attributes and in the *Building Word Knowledge* phase they revise graphic organizers.

### *Preparing to Learn Words*

1. Begin the lesson by displaying one of the words you have selected. Provide students with a copy of the Frayer Model graphic organizer. You may elect to have students fill in the graphic organizer in small groups, in pairs, or individually. However, every student should have an individual copy of the graphic organizer.
2. Write the key concept in the center of the duplicated graphic organizer you will use to record students' ideas.
3. Read the key concept aloud. Tell students that this is an important word in the topic or unit. Have the students write the target word in the center of their graphic organizer.

**Figure 3.2** Folded paper for the Frayer Model

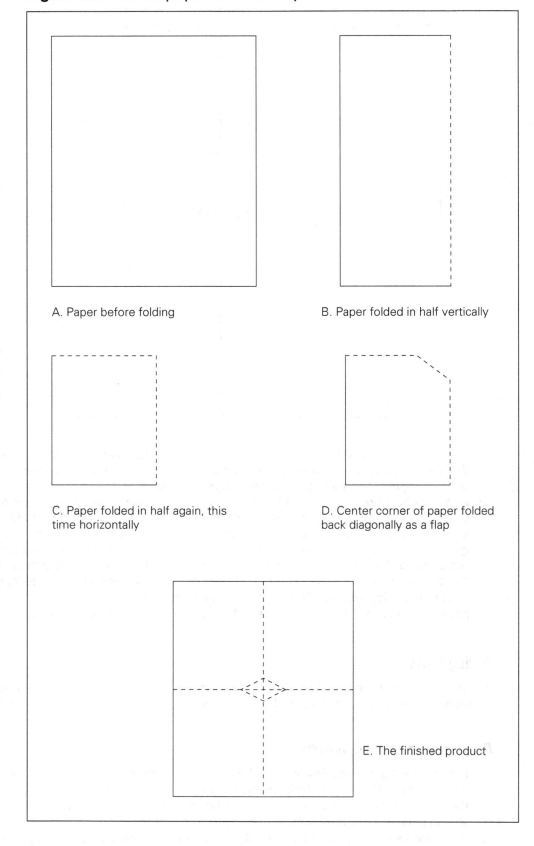

A. Paper before folding

B. Paper folded in half vertically

C. Paper folded in half again, this time horizontally

D. Center corner of paper folded back diagonally as a flap

E. The finished product

4. Invite students to share what they know about the word. Make a list of their ideas. Ask students to help you group ideas, using as categories the headings in the four boxes in the Frayer Model graphic organizer (essential and nonessential attributes, examples and

nonexamples). Use prompts like the following to guide students in selecting ideas for essential and nonessential attributes of the concept:

- What do you think are some ideas we have listed that are essential in all instances of the concept? What can't be omitted if we are to truly understand the concept?
- What makes you believe these ideas are essential in understanding the concept?
- What ideas might occur sometimes or are not important to understanding the concept? Why?
- Do you have other ideas we can add to either the essential or the nonessential categories?

Next, direct students' attention to the categories of examples and nonexamples by asking students for examples and nonexamples of the concept. It is important for students to be able to explain why their suggestions are examples or not by relating them back to the essential and nonessential attributes. Record students' ideas in the appropriate boxes on the class graphic organizer and have students fill in the relevant boxes on their graphic organizer.

Figure 3.3 shows the partially completed Frayer Model graphic organizer created by the high school art students for the concept *Impressionism*. In this case, students suggested *Monet* as an example of *Impressionism* because Monet's paintings use the two essential attributes that were given (*thick paint* and *painting outdoors*), and Monet painted in France, where the impressionist movement started. *Picasso* is a nonexample because although his work represents important principles in modern art, and although he lived in Paris, he did not use impressionist techniques in his paintings.

5. Students will have a wide range of prior knowledge about the target concept, and a class discussion of students' pooled knowledge will help motivate students and facilitate learning new attributes and terms that define the concept. The students in the art class benefited from background knowledge from a class field trip to an exhibit of impressionist

**Figure 3.3** Partially completed Frayer Model graphic organizer for the modern art movement Impressionism

| Essential elements | Nonessential elements |
|---|---|
| painted outdoors | The painters knew each other |
| thick paint | |
| started in France | |

Target word: *Impressionism*

| Examples | Nonexamples |
|---|---|
| Monet | Picasso |
| soleil levant (Impression, Sunrise) | |

paintings. However, if your students have little background knowledge and there are attributes or vocabulary important to the concept that you want students to have before further instruction, it is important that you add them during *Building Word Knowledge*.

### Building Word Knowledge

1. Provide missing essential elements, examples, and nonexamples as appropriate for students' background knowledge.
2. Provide opportunities for students to add or make corrections to their graphic organizer as they build new understandings. Explore relevant properties of the concept during instruction by asking questions:

   - How is this idea related to this concept?
   - Is the idea essential to understanding the concept's properties?
   - Is this idea relevant to the concept in all instances?
   - How is it related to other ideas that we have already recorded?
   - Can you provide an example? A nonexample?

During instruction, revisit students' individual and class graphic organizer (from *Preparing to Learn Words*) to add new understandings. You will want students to be able to provide multiple attributes, nonattributes, examples, and nonexamples in order to demonstrate a deep, rich understanding of the concept. Figure 3.4 shows a fifth-grade example of completed Frayer Model graphic organizer after a unit of study on the math concept *equation*.

**Figure 3.4** Completed Frayer Model graphic organizer for the mathematical concept *equation*

| Essential elements | Nonessential elements |
|---|---|
| equal sign<br>solved in a particular order<br>both sides are equal<br>requires addition, subtraction, multiplication and/or division | may use only letter symbols<br>may use only numbers<br>may mix letters and numbers |

Target word: equation

| Examples | Nonexamples |
|---|---|
| $2+5=7$<br>$a+b=c$<br>$4x-2y=10$<br>$7+3(x-1)=5-(x-1)$<br>$Y=15$<br>$M=3+4y$ | $4y+6w$<br>$3$<br>$=10$<br>$3/4$<br>$7+3$<br>$10<a$<br>$8\neq b$ |

## MODIFICATIONS

1. If the words that you select are hard to analyze with the category labels used in the Frayer Model, consider one or more of the following:
   a. Instead of essential attributes, use facts or characteristics.
   b. Eliminate the nonessential attributes category.
   c. Use "definition" as a category.
   d. Use antonyms and synonyms as categories instead of examples and nonexamples.
   e. Substitute an "illustration" region for one of the others.
2. Once students are familiar with the Frayer Model, consider using the model to assess students' understanding. After a unit of study, give students the graphic organizer with all the category boxes filled in except the target word. Ask students to use the information on the graphic organizer to identify the word. Alternatively, provide a completed graphic organizer with a region other than the target word left blank. Ask students to complete it.

## TROUBLESHOOTING

1. To ensure that your students understand the procedure, provide modeling and guided practice using words they know before introducing new terms.
2. To ensure success and to keep students motivated, limit the number of words you choose to four or fewer.
3. The Frayer Model works best with nouns that have many characteristics that help to define them. If the words you chose don't work well with the Frayer Model, try using Concept of Definition Word Map on page 9.
4. If students demonstrate misconceptions or limited knowledge related to the target term during *Preparing to Learn Words*, emphasize that the initial graphic organizer reflects what students *think* they know before study. Be prepared to respond to misconceptions and to bolster limited knowledge during *Building Word Knowledge*.

## NEXT STEPS

The Frayer Model works especially well as a basis for writing activities, such as Word Posters (p. 159), Vocabulary Graffiti (p. 155), Readers Theater (p. 140), and Student-Made Books (p. 145). Encourage students to create their own quick Frayer Model graphic organizer as they meet new words during independent learning experiences.

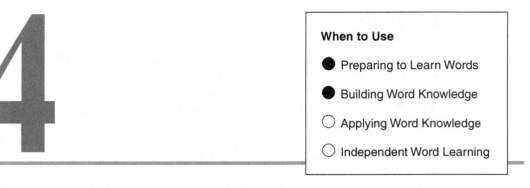

**When to Use**

● Preparing to Learn Words

● Building Word Knowledge

○ Applying Word Knowledge

○ Independent Word Learning

# Semantic Feature Analysis

Sometimes it is necessary to look at a group of events, people, and concepts and consider how they are alike and different. For example, the Iraq War, the Korean War, the Vietnam War, and World War II are all armed conflicts in which the United States played a role. How are they the same? How are they different? What makes each one unique? Semantic Feature Analysis (Anders & Bos, 1986) reinforces essential vocabulary by having students consider the features that differentiate words in a class.

## PURPOSE

Semantic Feature Analysis can be used to help students analyze how concepts are related. It is especially beneficial in units of study in which items, events, or people share some features and differ in others. For example, Semantic Feature Analysis can be used in a natural science class to analyze the features of plants or in world history to explore the features of different types of government. Semantic Feature Analysis can be used to set purposes for reading or other learning activities. It can also be used during and after instruction to build understandings and reach conclusions (Pittleman, Heimlich, Berglund, & French, 1991).

## PROCEDURES

Semantic Feature Analysis employs a grid that students complete by noting whether an item has or does not have a certain feature or characteristic. The strategy can be used successfully by individuals, pairs, small groups, or the whole class. If it is the first time your students have used this strategy, it is helpful to have them work with others to complete a grid before filling one in independently. Figure 4.1 shows a sample Semantic Feature Analysis grid that can be adopted for use across content areas.

### Getting Ready

1. Choose the key vocabulary that will be used to build the grid. Choose vocabulary that represents items, concepts, or people that are of the same type: plants, mammals, land formations, governments, and shapes, for example. List the words that you have chosen along the side of the grid. Choose the features or characteristics that you want students to consider along the top.

**Figure 4.1** A sample Semantic Feature Analysis grid

| Terms representing ideas, items, or people from the same group | Features/characteristics that students will consider as present or absent for each term in the group | | | |
|---|---|---|---|---|
| | **Feature 1** | **Feature 2** | **Feature 3** | **Feature 4** |
| Term 1 | | | | |
| Term 2 | | | | |
| Term 3 | | | | |
| Term 4 | | | | |
| Term 5 | | | | |

2. Create the code that students will use to note the relationship between each vocabulary word and a feature. Consider this widely accepted code:

+ The word has the feature

- The word does not have the feature

? Unsure if the word has the feature

Figure 4.2 gives a sample grid created for the analysis of triangles.

## During Class

Semantic Feature Analysis is useful for both *Preparing to Learn Words* and *Building Word Knowledge*.

### Preparing to Learn Words

1. Introduce the grid to the students by reading aloud the vocabulary words you have selected. Tell the students they will meet the words in the lesson or unit. Ask them to read the words aloud with you.
2. Make connections to the students' prior knowledge by asking them questions like the following:
   - Which of these words are familiar to you? In what context did you meet that word?
   - Are any of the words completely unfamiliar to you?
   - Do you have any ideas about how they might be related to the other words?
3. Point out the features on the grid. Explain to students that each feature relates to one or more of the vocabulary words. Explain that as they read (or engage in some other learning activity), you want them to look for information that will help them decide how to mark each cell within the grid.

**Figure 4.2** Example of a Semantic Feature Analysis grid for triangles

| Terms | Features | | | | | | | |
|---|---|---|---|---|---|---|---|---|
| | **Has three sides** | **All sides are equal** | **Exactly two sides are equal** | **No sides are equal** | **Interior angles = 180°** | **Exactly two angles are equal** | **One angle is 90°** | **No angles are equal** |
| Equilateral | | | | | | | | |
| Isosceles | | | | | | | | |
| Right | | | | | | | | |
| Scalene | | | | | | | | |

**Figure 4.3** Sample Semantic Feature Analysis grid from a middle school science lesson on plant structure

| | Plant 1 Name: | Plant 2 Name: | Plant 3 Name: | Plant 4 Name: | Plant 5 Name: |
|---|---|---|---|---|---|
| **Roots** Fibrous | | | | | |
| Taproot | | | | | |
| **Stems** Herbaceous | | | | | |
| Woody | | | | | |
| **Leaves** Simple | | | | | |
| Compound | | | | | |
| **Flowers** Imperfect | | | | | |
| Perfect | | | | | |
| **Seeds** Gymnosperm | | | | | |
| Angiosperm | | | | | |

## Building Word Knowledge

1. Help students insert the grid. After students have completed the Semantic Feature Analysis grid, discuss the grid with them. Focus on finding patterns that can be used to draw conclusions about the relationships among the vocabulary words you have chosen:
   - Were any of the features found in all the words?
   - What feature was found in the fewest words?
   - Can the features be put into any categories?
   - What big ideas can you identify from looking at the grid?

2. Try using Semantic Feature Analysis after instruction to reinforce learning. For example, after a unit on plant structure, a middle school teacher distributed the Semantic Feature Analysis grid in Figure 4.3 to student groups.

   The teacher asked each group to research new plants that were different from ones discussed in class and to note on the grid whether or not the plants had the features listed. To make certain that students investigated a range of plant types, she required that every feature be represented at least once across the five plants the group chose. After the grids were completed, they were used to draw conclusions about the characteristics of different types of plants.

## ● MODIFICATIONS

For a physical activity, have students sort themselves using results from the Semantic Feature Analysis grid. Follow these steps:

1. Give each student a card with one of the vocabulary terms from the grid listed on it in large print. Two students can pair to hold one card; this allows students to support each other.
2. Then have students stand and, on your cue, sort themselves. Examples from the triangle grid might be, "Go to this corner if you are holding the name of a triangle that

has three sides. . . . Look! That's everyone! Now move to this corner of the room if your triangle has three equal sides and that corner if your triangle has two equal sides."
3. Display your completed grid as an aid.
4. All students can receive a card, or some can watch as a smaller number of students sort themselves.

## TROUBLESHOOTING

1. It is important that students work with the information in the Semantic Feature Analysis grid after they complete it. Otherwise, they may not understand critical attributes and connections among them.
2. Provide opportunities for students to practice using information in the grids.

## TECH CONNECT

Composing your Semantic Feature Analysis grid on a spreadsheet can allow you to sort your terms to display their attributes in different ways. That is, you can sort by one or more columns.

## NEXT STEPS

Have students build graphic organizers to display relationships among concepts. For example, students might build a Venn diagram to display information from a completed Semantic Feature Analysis chart.

# 5

**When to Use**

● Preparing to Learn Words

● Building Word Knowledge

○ Applying Word Knowledge

○ Independent Word Learning

# Sketch to Stretch

In Sketch to Stretch, students create quick line drawings related to the text (Harste, Short, & Burke, 1988; Short & Harste, 1996; Siegel, 1984). Sketches serve as prompts for classroom conversation, and the teacher plays an important role in supporting students' sketches and subsequent discussion.

As originally designed, Sketch to Stretch promotes multiple interpretations of fictional and informational text. The emphasis is often on metaphor (Whitin, 2002), inference, and holistic understandings. In a typical usage of Sketch to Stretch, students record their interpretations of the themes of a text: "Draw a picture of what this passage means to you." However, Sketch to Stretch also has great potential in the content areas. It is a useful tool for exploring and building on students' initial concepts and knowledge of key vocabulary terms. Content sketches can be literal and descriptive, or they can suggest artist-specific interpretations of the content and its concepts.

## PURPOSE

Sketch to Stretch serves no fewer than four valuable purposes. First, it provides an opportunity for *transmediation*, or the translation of meaning from one set of symbols (such as language) to another (in this case, pictures) (Siegel, 1995). According to Siegel, moving into the visual realm from the linguistic one can help teachers shift from the "verbocentric" tendencies of schooling that focus on language as the sole channel for learning. Second, by requiring visual representations of verbal material, Sketch to Stretch supports students in making meaning. It can help students see what they are learning and thus provides a concrete way for students to organize, manipulate, interrelate, and reconsider their developing understandings (Borasi, Siegal, Fonzi, & Smith, 1998). As a result, sketching supports conceptual understanding in content areas such as science (Edens & Potter, 2001). Third, comprehension strategies such as Sketch to Stretch can support classroom talk, most notably peer discussion (Lloyd, 2004). The visual images students produce serve as an intermediary step between reading text and discussing it (Noden & Moss, 1995). Further, discussion of images provides opportunities for students to justify their thinking using specific evidence (Whitin, 2002). Discussion is particularly important for vocabulary development in that it provides rich contexts to discuss new terms, their attributes, and their connections to other ideas. Finally, sketches can support students in writing in clear, vivid, and specific ways (Noden & Moss, 1995).

# PROCEDURES

## Getting Ready

1. Choose the content and related target terms to be addressed through sketches. Figure 5.1 gives samples of key terms considered by a ninth-grade world cultures teacher as she prepared a series of lessons on Buddhism.
2. Determine the type of sketch you will accept. Sketches of a single vocabulary term may be appropriate (e.g., "Sketch what *meditation* means to you"), as might composite sketches that include many related target terms (e.g., "Sketch your understanding of *climate zones*. You'll want to refer in some way to specific zones in your sketch.")
3. As you consider the type of sketch to require, also decide whether you want literal drawings or metaphorical ones. Literal—or descriptive sketches—are particularly useful for helping students learn how a system or process works (Edens & Potter, 1995). In metaphorical sketches, students create visual analogies to help anchor their meaning of new terms.
4. Decide when in the instructional sequence students will sketch. Sketches *before* instruction can help you and the students discover their ideas related to the content and to target terms. Figure 5.2 provides ninth grader Max's preinstructional sketch of one of the terms from the lesson series on Buddhism in his world cultures class: the *Noble Eightfold Path*. (Recall his teacher's ideas of important terms found in Figure 5.1.)

   Sketches *during instruction* can help students correct inaccuracies and add detail during reading and other study of target terms. Sketches *after instruction* can help solidify new understandings. Figure 5.3 shows Max's postinstructional sketch of the *Noble Eightfold Path*.
5. Prepare a couple of contrasting sketches to model the process if students are new to the Sketch to Stretch process.

## During Class

Pre-instructional sketches are useful for *Preparing to Learn Words*, and sketches made or revisited later support *Building Word Knowledge*.

**Figure 5.1** Likely Sketch to Stretch terms from a series of lessons on Buddhism in a ninth-grade world cultures course

Bodhisattva

Buddha

Four Noble Truths

Mahayana Buddhism

Meditation

Nirvana

Noble Eightfold Path

Sutras

Theravada Buddhism

**Figure 5.2** Ninth-grade Max's preinstructional sketch of the Noble Eightfold Path

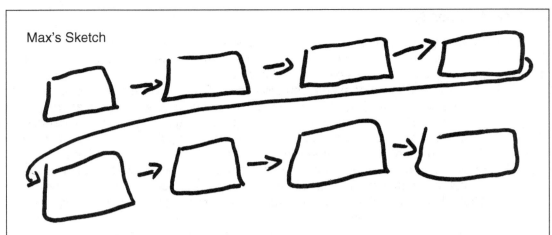

Max's Sketch

Commentary

*(Context: Students sketched what they knew about the Noble Eightfold Path before instruction. T = Teacher, M = Max)*

T : Tell me about your drawing.
M : Well, every religion offers certain advice. I think the Eightfold Path gives Buddhism's rules to live by.
T : Ah! So why the boxes?
M : People usually give advice on charts, so the boxes represent charts.
T : I notice you included arrows.
M : The word "path" lets you know that there are steps to be followed.
T : The boxes are empty.
M : I don't know the advice yet to fill them up.

## Preparing to Learn Words and Building Word Knowledge

1. At the appropriate time during the lesson (before, during, or after instruction), ask students to sketch the target term(s) or larger ideas. You may elect to have students select the term(s) they sketch based on what is important to them.
2. If appropriate, display your sample sketches and discuss them before students begin to sketch.
3. Set a brief time limit (perhaps 3 minutes) and ask students to sketch individually. Request simple line drawings. Other types of pictorial representations (such as crude line graphs) may also be appropriate.
4. In groups of three, have students share their sketches, one at a time. Group members hypothesize about the meanings of the sketches before artists share intended meanings. Discussion that pushes students to make meaning and justify their reasoning is very important. Some prompts that may help students think about their sketches and the content include the following:
   • What are the critical attributes of this term?
   • How does your drawing represent them? What are different ways to represent those attributes accurately?
   • Go back and check your drawing and make sure that it shows what you just learned.
   • Check the highlighted words [in the text] and make sure they are clear in your drawing. (Edens & Potter, 2001)
   • Tell your group members what you *understand* about the concepts, not just what you *memorized*.
5. To close the session, one student can project her sketch for the class using a computer system or an overhead projector, and the class can discuss different interpretations of the target terms and ideas.

**Figure 5.3** Ninth-grade Max's postinstructional sketch of the
Noble Eightfold Path

Max's Sketch

Commentary

*(Context: As the class studied the Noble Eightfold Path through reading and other activities, students revised their original drawings or created new ones. T = Teacher, M = Max)*

T : You ditched your first drawing.

M : I realized from the reading that the Eightfold Path is not a series of steps. All lead to one goal, but not one step after the other.

T : So you placed the one goal in the center?

M : Yes, and I used a web. I also learned that some of the rules are connected together into larger groups.

T : Oh! Got it! How else has your drawing changed?

M : It has more information. Now I have some ideas about each of the pieces of advice that make up the Noble Eightfold Path and how they are related.

*(Teacher's Notes: Max's teacher noticed that Max knew many conventions that are used to represent ideas pictorially. She noticed that Max revisited the text many times in creating his second drawing. She smiled at the connections to his own life that Max considered important. For instance, as a new football player, Max placed high premium on the bulging biceps of the individual displaying Right Livelihood. Finally, the teacher noted that Max spent several minutes contemplating how to represent each specific term pictorially; this task seemed new and a bit uncomfortable for him. She committed to using more sketching opportunities for Max in the future.)*

## MODIFICATIONS

1. Allow students to complete sketches with partners or in small groups.
2. Encourage the use of color in sketches as another way to convey meaning.
3. Consider using alternatives to sketching such as sculpting or pantomiming.

## TROUBLESHOOTING

1. Some students are nervous about drawing. If you share your own sketches that are of less than museum quality, students may feel less anxious.
2. Siegel (1995) cautions that, without support, sketching can be trivialized and thus ineffective at supporting student understanding. Be certain that you scaffold student understanding as they work individually and during discussion. For instance, in the use of Sketch to Stretch for content area vocabulary development, accuracy is important, and detail often is as well. Help students differentiate between details that inaccurately depict the concept and those that are accurate and yet still imaginative (Edens & Potter, 2001).
3. Use the Sketch to Stretch strategy when your focus is on higher-level thinking and conceptual understanding. It appears less effective in supporting factual recall.

## TECH CONNECT

Electronic media allow for easy storage and display of sketches.

## NEXT STEPS

- Use sketches to generate writing and performance. See Poetry (p. 149) and Readers Theater (p. 140) for examples.
- Develop analogies from sketches more fully. See Analogies (p. 111).

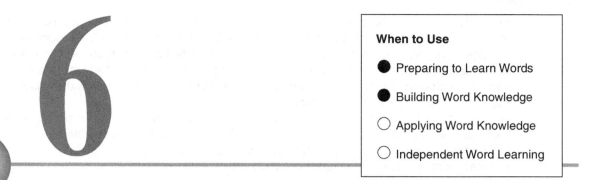

# Ten Most Important Words

One reason students have difficulty understanding content area texts is that the concept load is very dense and numerous vocabulary words are introduced in a small space, many of which are new (Alvermann, Swafford, & Montero, 2004). Students' ability to make decisions about the relative importance of the vocabulary is an important skill in making sense of reading (Harvey & Goudvis, 2000). An activity that requires students to consider their understanding of the importance of vocabulary is Ten Most Important Words (Stephens & Brown, 2000; Yopp & Yopp, 2002).

## PURPOSE

Ten Most Important Words can be used before instruction to help students access what they already know about a topic and to reflect on how it will connect with the new concepts they will be learning. It can also be used after instruction to encourage student reflection of what they have learned and of what vocabulary is most critical to understanding the topic. In addition, words selected from a class's Ten Most Important Words recommendations can be used to restructure or reflect on any graphic organizers or Semantic Maps (see p. 37) developed during instruction.

## PROCEDURES

### Getting Ready

1. Select a word or phrase that best represents the topic for study.
2. Choose your grouping strategy. Will students work individually, in pairs, or in small groups? Consider the level of your students' background knowledge when making your grouping decisions. If students know little about the topic, having them work in pairs or small groups will allow them to pool their knowledge.

### During Class

The Ten Most Important Words strategy can be used for *Preparing to Learn Words* and for *Building Word Knowledge*.

### *Preparing to Learn Words*

1. Introduce the class to the topic and to the resources you will be using for instruction.
2. Invite students to brainstorm ideas, concepts, and terms related to the topic. Have students share their ideas orally during a brief whole-class brainstorming session (no more than 5 minutes).

3. After the brainstorming session, ask students to work in pairs or small groups to list the 10 words they predict will be most important in the topic they will be studying. If you prefer to have students initially work independently, have each student make an individual list of 10 words that can then be shared with a partner or a small group.

4. Ask each pair or group to come to a consensus about which of the words they have suggested will be their 10 most important.

5. Once the pairs or groups make their choices, to motivate students and help them make personal connections, explore some of their selections by asking the following:
   - What word on your list do you think is most likely to be on other lists? Why?
   - What word on your list do you think is unique? Why?
   - Which word do you think is the most interesting word on your list? Why?

6. Invite groups to share their lists by writing their words on the board. Instead of writing identical words again, use a notation system to keep count of the number of times a word is suggested. The figure that follows is an example of a class list of important words on classical Greek theater from a high school drama class.

## Building Word Knowledge

1. After instruction, ask groups to modify their Ten Most Important Words lists to reflect what they have learned. Figure 6.1 is a chart a fifth-grade teacher used for groups to modify their lists. Note that students must provide a rationale for their choices.

2. Have groups share their revised lists by writing the words on the board (see item f above for details). Ask questions that encourage students to reflect on their choices:
   - Which of your words were not on your original list? Why did you add these words?
   - Which words did you not keep? Why?
   - Which words represent big ideas about the text? Which represent important details?
   - How can we organize or sort the words to reflect the structure of what we have learned?
   - Which words are essential for representing what we learned?

**Example of a class important word list on classical Greek theater from a high school drama class**

| Classical Greek Theater | |
|---|---|
| plays ✓✓✓✓✓ | director ✓ |
| stage ✓✓✓✓✓ | curtain ✓✓ |
| script ✓✓✓ | playwrights ✓✓✓✓ |
| actors ✓✓✓✓✓ | costumes ✓✓✓✓ |
| performances ✓✓ | props ✓ |
| drama ✓✓✓ | comedy ✓✓ |
| audience ✓✓✓✓ | old ✓ |

Note: Checkmarks represent the number of groups who nominated that word.

**Figure 6.1** Chart developed by a fifth-grade teacher for students to modify their Ten Most Important Words lists

| | Important words | Rationale |
|---|---|---|
| 1 | | |
| 2 | | |
| 3 | | |
| 4 | | |
| 5 | | |
| 6 | | |
| 7 | | |
| 8 | | |
| 9 | | |
| 10 | | |

## NEXT STEPS

1. Students can be asked to write summary statements about each word or to write a summary paragraph that uses all the words.
2. Have students create Vocab Cards with their words. These cards can be used in sorting activities and in reviews. Look for these and other ideas for using Vocab Cards on page 50.
3. Encourage students to use Ten Most Important Words lists for writing letters, books, or poems and developing multimedia presentations.

### A Note for Your English Learners

1. Use fewer than 10 words for shorter lessons, for times when you hope to direct students toward essential concepts, or for students who are in the early stages of acquiring English.
2. Another way for groups to share is by writing each of their words on a sticky note. Such notes are used to construct a class bar graph. Identical words are placed above each other to form a bar that represents the number of times the word was suggested. Each unique word forms its own bar. This creates a visual representation of the class choices. Try this method with upper elementary students and English learners.

## MODIFICATION

Yopp and Yopp (2007) suggest distributing colored cards printed with questions that help students think about the words they have selected. Cards might direct students to think about how words are related, to use the words in context, and to think of examples of the word.

## TROUBLESHOOTING

Ten Most Important Words is only useful as a *Preparing to Learn Words* strategy when students have sufficient background knowledge. If they have little information about the topic, they won't be able to contribute many words. Instead, try using it only as a closing activity to a lesson or unit to help students pull together the new ideas and reflect on what they have learned.

**Excerpt from students' choices of words related to the lesson
"components of culture"**

| beliefs | food | laws  |
|---------|------|-------|
| dance   | food | norms |
| dance   | food | norms |
|         |      | rules |
|         |      | slang |

## TECH CONNECT

Ask students to compose their lists on a spreadsheet. Place all lists into one spreadsheet, and then sort alphabetically. The words above show some students' choices of words related to the lesson "components of culture." If you like, use analysis tools to count the frequency of each word. This Tech Connect is another way of building a graph to demonstrate word frequency.

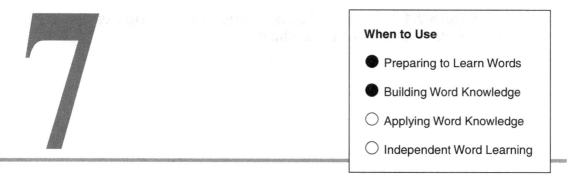

# Semantic Maps

Semantic Maps (Johnson & Pearson, 1984) are a type of graphic organizer. A Semantic Map forms a visual representation that looks something like a spider web. Lines connect a target concept to a variety of subcategories that contain related ideas and events. Semantic Maps allow students to see how words and ideas are related to each other. These maps have been shown to be an excellent strategy to use for improving vocabulary and comprehension (Harmon, 2002).

## PURPOSE

When you are preparing to present a new concept to a class, it is valuable to have an understanding of what students already know about the concept. Semantic Maps are devices that can be used to help students access their existing knowledge and organize it in a way that will help them connect what they already know to the new concepts and vocabulary they will be learning. As students build new understandings, the initial Semantic Map is revisited so that students can extend the map to reflect what they have learned. The maps can also be used to help students organize their ideas for writing and other activities that encourage them to apply new vocabulary and concepts in other contexts.

## PROCEDURES

### Getting Ready

1. Before beginning a unit of study, pick a target word that represents the topic or key concept that will be your focus. For example, near the beginning of an academic year, an auto shop teacher chose the word *engines* as the target word before starting a unit.
2. Decide how you will group students to develop the Semantic Map. Maps can be developed in a variety of ways, including whole group, small group, pairs, and individually. If students are being introduced to Semantic Maps for the first time or have limited background knowledge, consider using whole-group instruction so that you can provide scaffolding and students can learn from each other.

### During Class

In class, Semantic Maps can be used during *Preparing to Learn Words* and *Building Word Knowledge*.

**Figure 7.1** Example of a Semantic Map on *engines* created in an auto shop class

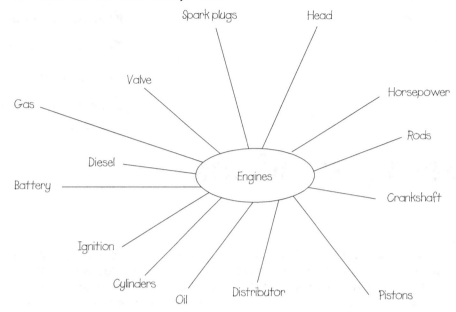

## Preparing to Learn Words

1. Write the key concept in the center of the chalkboard, transparency, or chart paper that will be used to record students' ideas.
2. Read the key concept aloud. Invite students to brainstorm ideas, concepts, and terms related to the key concept. Figure 7.1 is an example of a Semantic Map on *engines* created in the auto shop class mentioned earlier.
3. Record students' responses around the central concept. Ask students to help you group related ideas and terms together to form categories. Encourage students to discuss why the ideas go together and to supply a name for the category by using prompts like the following:
   • Which of these words might go together?
   • What makes you believe that they are related?
   • What term or phrase could we use as a label to describe why they go together?
4. Reorganize information on the map as needed, adding category labels and using lines to connect related ideas. For example, the students in the auto shop class suggested labels such as fuel (gas and diesel) and engine parts (spark plugs, valves, pistons) and related items (oil, battery, ignition, distributor) to categorize their words.
5. Create a class map that can be displayed so that students can refer to it and add to it as new learning occurs. You may find it useful to highlight important ideas by using boxes or color.
6. Discuss the map and how the ideas are related. Students will have a wide range of prior knowledge about the target concept, and a class discussion of students' pooled knowledge will help motivate students and facilitate learning new terms. If there are categories or vocabulary important to the concept not suggested by the students, you can add them to the map during the discussion.

## Building Word Knowledge

Provide opportunities for students to add to the map as they build new understandings. You can use boxes, stars, or different-colored pens to highlight new words and concepts. In the Semantic Map in Figure 7.2, the teacher used color as well as other methods to highlight the ideas the class added to their map during an investigation of isopods (commonly known as pill bugs).

**Figure 7.2** Example that shows how a teacher highlighted new information students added to their map during an investigation of isopods (commonly called pill bugs)

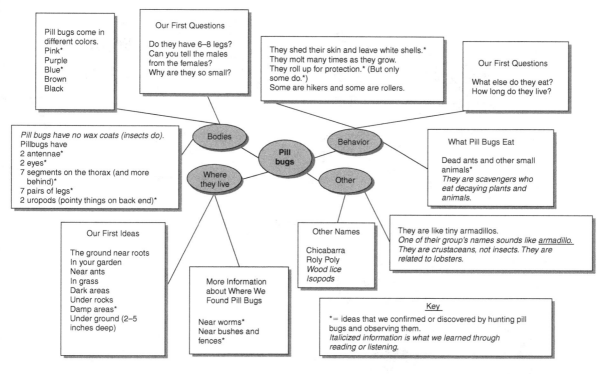

 **MODIFICATIONS**

1. In some cases you may want to have more control over the vocabulary and concepts that will appear on a Semantic Map. One way to do this is to give students a partially completed map and have students generate examples. For instance, cover the class Semantic Map or remove it from students' view. Provide students with a partially filled in version of the map and ask them to use what they have learned to complete it. Have students check their work by comparing their filled in map with the class map.

2. As students become more experienced with mapping, they can be asked to create their own maps in groups or individually.

**A Note for Your English Learners**

Pictures and other visuals can be added to or substituted for print to support comprehension for English learners. Figure 7.3 shows a graphics-rich portion of the auto shop Semantic Map, *engines*, discussed earlier.

 **TROUBLESHOOTING**

1. Semantic Maps are useful only for concepts with which students already have had some experience. If they don't know much about the concept, they will have few ideas to contribute to the map.

2. Sometimes students contribute ideas and terms to a Semantic Map that reflect misunderstandings about the target concept. Accept all responses initially, reminding students that some of the information on the map will change as more information is gathered. To help

**Figure 7.3** A portion of the *engines* Semantic Map, reworked with categories and graphics. This map was created using Inspiration.

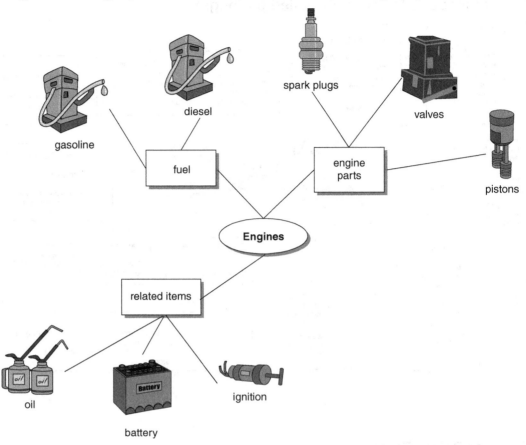

students see the difference between prior knowledge and things they learned during the lesson, you can use two different colors of ink: one for before instruction and one for during and after instruction. A legend can help students remember what the different colors represent. Be sure to discuss misconceptions that were addressed through the lesson.

3. Although a Semantic Map shows relationships among terms, it does not represent well ideas that have a hierarchical relationship. If you want to show hierarchical relationships among concepts, you may want to consider using a different type of graphic organizer.

## TECH CONNECT

Two valuable software resources that can be helpful for you and your students in creating Semantic Maps are Inspiration (6–12) and Kidspiration (K–5). Figure 7.3 was created using Inspiration. Free trials can be downloaded at http://www.inspiration.com. The software allows you and your students to use an interactive white board or other projection device with a computer to add to and refine maps. Symbols can be dragged around to reorganize information, and information can be added from multiple sources.

## NEXT STEPS

Semantic Maps work especially well as a basis for writing activities such as Poetry (p. 149), Readers Theater (p. 140), and Student-Made Books (p. 145). Additionally, students should be encouraged to use Semantic Maps as an independent learning tool as they tackle content area reading materials.

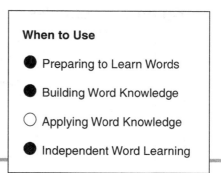
# Vocabulary Knowledge Ratings

"Good learners take control of their own learning" (Blachowicz & Fisher, 2007, p. 184). In Vocabulary Knowledge Ratings, students appraise their preinstructional knowledge of terms they will encounter in a lesson or reading. Students can use a variety of formats, typically charts, to judge the depth of their understanding of target terms. Students reevaluate their understandings of words after instruction.

## PURPOSE

Direct teaching of individual words alone does not reduce the gap between the vocabulary knowledge of students with poor versus rich vocabularies (Baker, Simmons, & Kammeenui, 1995). Instead, students need to be taught strategies for independent word learning. Recent studies suggest that instruction in metacognitive strategies helps students build awareness and control of their own learning and improves their vocabulary knowledge (Boulware-Gooden, Carreker, Thornhill, & Joshi, 2007; Shira & Smetana, 2005).

Powerful word learners are aware of their own word knowledge and its boundaries, and they use this self-awareness to set targets and focus their learning efforts productively. Vocabulary Knowledge Ratings help students gain awareness of the extent and limits of their word understanding and track it over time. Thus, Vocabulary Knowledge Ratings help students develop independent word learning strategies that can fuel learning long after students leave the classroom.

## PROCEDURES

### Getting Ready

1. Select the target terms to be encountered and developed in the lesson or text. Limit the list to fewer than 10 words; five terms may be about right.
2. Think about which strategies might be most useful to teach the target terms should the need arise. For example, will Context Clues (p. 124) be appropriate for one or more terms? Will Morphemic Analysis (p. 106) or perhaps Word Histories (p. 115) work best? Thinking about strategies in advance will also help you later model for your students how they can select strategies for learning words on their own.
3. Place target terms on the rating chart of your choice. Figure 8.1 gives contrasting examples.

**Figure 8.1** Examples of vocabulary knowledge rating forms

| Term | I can use this word. I can explain it in different ways. | I can say a few things about this word. A review would help. | I don't know much about this word. I need to study it carefully. | Description, drawing, or synonym |
|---|---|---|---|---|
|  |  |  |  |  |
|  |  |  |  |  |
|  |  |  |  |  |

| Word | Before Reading | | After Reading | | Notes |
|---|---|---|---|---|---|
|  | Got it! ☺ | Need it! ☹ | Got more! ☺ | Need more! ☹ |  |
|  | ☺ | ☹ | ☺ | ☹ |  |
|  | ☺ | ☹ | ☺ | ☹ |  |
|  | ☺ | ☹ | ☺ | ☹ |  |

Rate your understanding of each term. After the lesson, we'll cross out these ratings and conduct new ratings.

| Word | I can teach it. | I have seen it. | I've got nothing. |
|---|---|---|---|
|  |  |  |  |
|  |  |  |  |
|  |  |  |  |
|  |  |  |  |

**Figure 8.2** A sample rating for a fifth-grade theater lesson

Rate your understanding of each important term: 3, 2, or 1.

3 = I've got it down!

2 = I know something about it.

1 = I have no clue!

| Important terms | Before the lesson | After the lesson | Definition (Give it a try!) |
|---|---|---|---|
| Cue | | | |
| Dialogue | | | |
| Monologue | | | |
| Script | | | |
| Sense memory | | | |

## During Class

Vocabulary Knowledge Ratings are useful for *Preparing to Learn Words*, *Building Word Knowledge*, and *Independent Word Learning*.

### Preparing to Learn Words

Present the rating form with target terms. Ask students to rate their current knowledge level with the terms. Figure 8.2 gives a sample rating form for a fifth-grade theater lesson.

### Building Word Knowledge

1. As a class, discuss ratings to find a few terms rated low by many students. Decide whether you should teach these few terms directly during the lesson—using strategies you anticipated earlier—or whether you want students to learn them on their own through reading. For example, the teacher who created the chart in Figure 8.2 decided to use Morphemic Analysis (p. 106) to teach two words his class rated as low: *dialogue* and *monologue*. Both terms make use of common prefixes (*mono-* and *dia-*) and a helpful root word (*logue*). He anticipated sharing the interesting history of the word *cue*, but students did not rate the word low, so he skipped his Word History (p. 115) minilesson. He does, though, remind students that using an etymological dictionary (such as http://www.etymonline.com) is a useful strategy for learning some words, like *cue*. His students all marked *sense memory* as low, but he knows the text develops the term fully, so he does not address it through instruction.
2. Encourage individuals to pay attention to their own lower-rated terms. Students should seek to develop these lower-rated terms as they engage in the lesson or reading. Remind students that the terms will be revisited later.
3. After the reading or instruction, ask students to conduct new ratings of the terms and to reflect on their word learning: Which terms were particularly easy to learn? Which ones are still foggy and need more attention? What strategies did students use to learn the terms? Context Clues? (p. 124) Analysis of word parts (Morphemic Analysis, p. 106)?

**Figure 8.3** A ninth-grade geography student's self-knowledge ratings, used to focus his final exam studies

```
                          Geography

            Study Guide for First-Semester Final Examination

  + conservation                      √ middle cohort

  + culture                           + monotheism

  − demographic collapse              + neocolonialism

  + desertification                   + nuclear nations

  − ecomigration                      √ preservation

  + globalization                     √ Sepoy Revolt

  + guest worker                      − suburbanization

  + IDPs                              − vernacular

  √ infrastructure

  − irredentism
```

4. Encourage students to reflect on the effects of knowledge ratings as a tool for learning: How did using ratings before and after reading help them learn? How can students use this tool in their independent studies?

### Independent Word Learning

Encourage students to use knowledge ratings as a study tool in reviewing previously presented material. Figure 8.3 gives an excerpt of a list of terms for a ninth-grade geography final exam. To prioritize his studies, a student rated each term with a + ("I can explain and apply this term"), a √ ("I can define this term, but I'm shaky with it"), or a − ("I don't know anything about this term"). After rating the terms, the student focused his study efforts first on the terms he knew the least about: the − terms.

## TROUBLESHOOTING

1. Struggling readers in particular need support in developing *Independent Word Learning* strategies (Harmon & Hedrick, 2005). Because Vocabulary Knowledge ratings are based on self-report, students may need help in building accurate understandings of their own knowledge. Model the self-rating process by thinking aloud as you rate a sample term: "I read the term *vicissitude*. Hmm. It sounds familiar, but I can't really remember why. I can tell it's a noun because it ends with *-tude,* and other words (like *attitude* and *solitude*) with that ending are nouns. But that's all I can say. I'll have to rate my knowledge for this term pretty low." Also encourage students to test their own knowledge of a few terms to ensure that their ratings are accurate: Can they define the term? Provide synonyms or examples?
2. For Vocabulary Knowledge Ratings to be effective as an *Independent Word Learning* strategy, students need to be able to find target terms prior to reading or study. Point out strategies to help students locate important terms in content areas, including

skimming and perusing chapter-end lists of key terms and bolded terms found throughout many texts.

## NEXT STEPS

Students tend to learn words better if they are involved in the selection of those words. See Vocabulary Self-Collection Strategy (p. 54) for a strategy that dovetails with Vocabulary Knowledge Ratings.

# 9

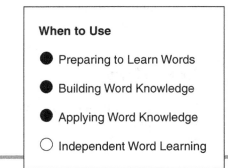

# Concept Guides

Most likely, you will find that some students in your class find information in content area textbooks difficult to understand and to recall. There are several reasons for this. First, these texts are written using text structures that are not as familiar to students as the structures used in stories. Second, students may have little background knowledge about the concepts that are presented in content area materials. Finally, those new concepts are likely to be expressed using vocabulary terms that are unknown to students.

Herman (1969) suggested that in order to learn effectively from text, students must comprehend 75% of the vocabulary. In his theory of verbal learning, Ausubel (1963) argued that using advance organizers such as Concept Guides could help students master content area concepts by presenting them with a structured overview of new information, including vocabulary, which they needed to learn from written text. Concept Guides provide students with guidance on what terms are most important to learn and how the information can be organized to make clear important relationships (Barron, 1969; McCrudden, Schraw, & Hartley, 2006; Wade, 1992). Concept Guides organize information in ways that make clear the relationships among words and promote the development of deeper understandings of content area vocabulary.

## PURPOSE

Research in vocabulary learning supports the use of Concept Guides in vocabulary and concept development (Brookbank, Grover, Kullberg, & Strawser, 1999; Moore & Readence, 1984; Stetson & Williams, 1992). Concept Guides are typically used to support students during independent reading of content materials. They set the stage for learning by guiding students through an instructional sequence designed to help them master content-specific vocabulary (Stone, 1983). They provide opportunities for students to learn vocabulary through meaningful activities, increasing the likelihood of mastery (Pehrsson & Robinson, 1985). A well-designed Concept Guide can help students recognize important vocabulary, see how the terms are related to other ideas, and guide students to applying the new vocabulary in other contexts.

## PROCEDURES

### Getting Ready

1. Choose the text that you will use for instruction and select the target words that label the major concepts that you want students to learn. See p. 7 for tips on choosing words. Be selective and choose a relatively small set of words, no more than 10. Focus

**Figure 9.1** Steps for creating a Concept Guide

*Note:* Concept Guides often have three parts, although they can have fewer. In a three-part Concept Guide, Part I consists of true-or-false statements. In Part II, students complete cloze sentences. Part III asks students to complete a categorizing activity.

**Steps**

1. List the vocabulary terms that you have selected for students to learn from reading the text. These will go in Part II.
2. Select sentences or paraphrase sentences from the text that contain the vocabulary terms. These will be used for the true items in Part I.
3. Write some false statements about some of the terms that sound like they come from the text but are not accurate. Mix these in with the true statements to form Part I of the guide. If you have chosen 10 target words, you should have a total of between 15 and 18 true-or-false statements in Part I.
4. Write directions for Part I that ask students to indicate whether each statement is true or false.
5. Write at least one cloze sentence for each of the target vocabulary terms that you listed for Part II. This completes Part II.
6. Write directions for Part II that ask students to put the correct vocabulary word in the blank.
7. Reread the true statements in Part I and decide on two or three categories that can be used to organize the information.
8. List the categories that you chose in Part III.
9. Write directions that ask students to take each of the correct statements in Part I and place them under the correct category.

     on words that are essential for mastery of the content and that will be useful later in other contexts as well.
2. Develop the Concept Guide. Concept Guides often have three parts, although they can have fewer. In a three-part Concept Guide, Part I consists of true-or-false statements. In Part II, students complete cloze sentences. Part III asks students to complete a categorizing activity. Suggestions for developing Concept Guides (Barron, 1969; Blachowicz & Fisher, 2002; Roe, Stoodt-Hill, & Burns, 2007) usually include some of the steps in Figure 9.1.

## During Class

Concept Guides are most powerful when they are used across many instructional phases and include time for student feedback and discussion.

### Preparing to Learn Words (5 to 10 Minutes)

1. Begin by displaying on an overhead or chart the Concept Guide. Figure 9.2 presents a Concept Guide developed by a sixth-grade teacher for text materials on volcanoes.
2. Present each of the words listed in Part II of the Concept Guide. Pronounce each of the words clearly and ask students to repeat.
3. Build connections to prior word knowledge and build motivation to learn by discussing prompts like the following:
   - Which of these words have you already met? In what context? What did they mean in that context?
   - Which of these words look completely unfamiliar? Any guesses on their meanings?
   - Which two (or more) of these words might go together? Why?

### Building Word Knowledge

1. Provide each student a copy of the Concept Guide. Instruct them to fill out the guide during and immediately after reading.

**Figure 9.2** A Concept Guide developed by a sixth-grade teacher for text materials on volcanoes

Part I: Write true (T) or false (F) for each of the following statements. Some of the statements were taken directly from the book, some are paraphrased from the book, and some are made up.

1. _____ Most volcanic activity takes place along tectonic plate boundaries.
2. _____ Volcanic eruptions can be predicted with accuracy.
3. _____ When magma collapses, it forms a caldera.
4. _____ Lava flows from all volcanic eruptions.
5. _____ A vent or groups of vents form a volcano.
6. _____ The top vent in most volcanoes is shaped like a crater.
7. _____ Fissures in the surface of the earth can allow lava to flow over a large area.
8. _____ The rock of the mantle is usually a hot liquid.
9. _____ Magna is most likely to form when the pressure on mantle rock decreases.
10. _____ Magna is commonly made of solids and liquids.
11. _____ It is easier for magna to travel through the crust where there are tectonic plate boundaries.
12. _____ Lava is made of different elements than is magma.

Part II: From the words listed below, choose the correct word for each blank:

| eruptions | magma | lava | caldera | tectonic plates |
|-----------|-------|------|---------|-----------------|
| fissures | mantle | crater | vent | |

1. _____ is magma that flows onto the earth's structure.
2. The outermost layer of the earth's crust is made up of _____.
3. Volcanoes are created from a hot liquid material called _____.
4. Volcanic _____ can be nonexplosive or explosive.
5. It looks like a funnel-shaped pit at the top of a volcano.
6. Magma rises through holes in the earth's crust called _____.
7. _____ in the earth's crust allow lava to erupt.
8. A large circular depression at the top of the volcano is called a _____.
9. The _____ lies between the earth's crust and its core.

Part III: Place each of the true statements in Part I under one of the categories below. Write their numbers below, under the correct category.

1. Features on the surface of a volcano
2. Features inside a volcano
3. Predicting where and when volcanoes will erupt

2. After the guides are completed, lead students in a discussion of their responses. Ask questions such as the following:
   - How well did you predict the meaning of the words? (from *Preparing to Learn Words*)
   - Which statements were false? How can you correct the statements so they are true?
   - How is this idea related to the information we are learning?
   - Which category does it best fit?
   - Which ideas describe the concept? What attributes does it have?
   - What are some examples of this word?

### Applying Word Knowledge

Use these ideas to practice using the words students were introduced to on the Concept Guide in a new context.
   1. Have students write the words from the Concept Guide on Vocab Cards (p. 50). Encourage students to use open sorts, where students sort by their own criteria, and then try closed sorts, where you suggest the sorting criteria. For an open

sort, have students place related words into groups. For a closed sort, give students the criteria: "Group words together that are related to the features inside of volcanoes and form another group that contains words that relate to the shape of a volcano."

2. Have students write a summary of the reading that includes the words on the Concept Guide or have students try organizing them in an outline form.

## MODIFICATIONS

1. Some students may find it difficult to fill out all three sections of the Concept Guide at once. You can simplify the Concept Guide by creating a guide that has one or two parts instead of three. Or try having students fill out one section after reading and the others as homework.

2. Have students work in pairs or threes instead of individually to complete the Concept Guide. Pairs or group discussions will allow students to pool their knowledge and help motivate students and facilitate their learning the new vocabulary.

## TROUBLESHOOTING

1. To ensure that your students understand the procedure, provide modeling and guided practice using words they know before introducing new terms.

2. To ensure success and to keep students motivated, limit the number of words you choose.

3. Concept Guides take time to prepare. Divide the prep time by working with another teacher in your content area.

## NEXT STEPS

Concept Guides work well as the basis for writing activities such as Poetry (p. 149), Word Posters (p. 159), and I-Search a Word Reports (p. 163).

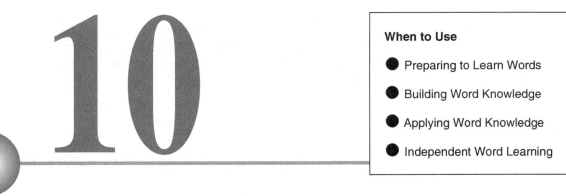
# Vocab Cards

Vocab Cards are a flexible, powerful extension of the ubiquitous flash card. Used wisely, flash cards have been shown to be effective in supporting learning outcomes such as word retention (MacQuarrie, Tucker, Burns, & Hartman, 2002), decoding (Tan & Nicholson, 1997; Wentink, van Bon & Schreuder, 1997), and comprehension (Calhoun, Poirier, Simon, & Mueller, 2001; Tan & Nicholson, 1997). With Vocab Cards, teacher and students create sets of word cards that are manipulated and used repeatedly for instruction and practice with target content terms. Practice periods are short, primarily oral, and enjoyable.

## PURPOSE

Vocab Cards are a simple means to meet major criteria for effective word learning. First, they are an easy way to provide multiple exposures to words (both in print and orally) within a variety of contexts. Second, they encourage oral language and allow students to use and talk about target words many times. Third, they can provide a vehicle for strategy instruction and can build word curiosity and motivation.

## PROCEDURES

### Getting Ready

1. Before a unit of instruction, pick the target words. See p. 7 for tips on choosing words. Remember to be selective and choose a relatively small set of words. Focus on words that are essential for mastery of the content and that will be useful later in other contexts as well. An eighth-grade teacher preparing a lesson on radioactivity, for example, chose these four words.

**An eighth-grade teacher's selection of terms for a lesson on radioactivity**

| radioactivity | alpha particle | beta particle | gamma ray |

2. Transfer words to your choice of cards. You may use 8½ × 11 in. cardstock for your instructional set, for instance, and reproduce students' cards on index cards or on cardstock that is cut into smaller rectangles. Some teachers have students create their own sets by hand. See the Tech Connect for other ideas on preparing Vocab Cards.

## During Class

Vocab Cards are most powerful when they are used across many instructional phases, as shown in the following suggestions. You no doubt can identify many other productive uses of Vocab Cards as well. For any single lesson, select just a few strategies for using the Vocab Cards, as our eighth-grade teacher does during the lesson on radioactivity found in Figure 10.1.

**Figure 10.1** A sample eighth-grade physical science lesson on radioactivity that employs Vocab Cards in a few ways

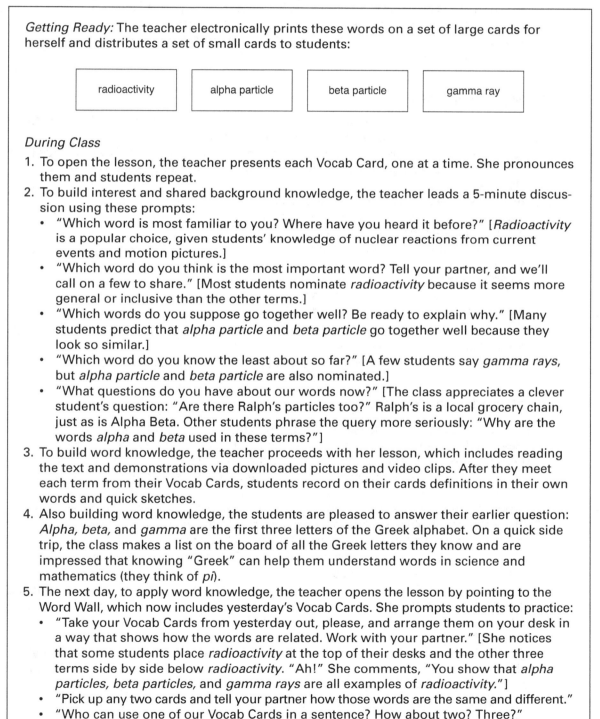

*Getting Ready:* The teacher electronically prints these words on a set of large cards for herself and distributes a set of small cards to students:

| radioactivity | alpha particle | beta particle | gamma ray |

*During Class*

1. To open the lesson, the teacher presents each Vocab Card, one at a time. She pronounces them and students repeat.
2. To build interest and shared background knowledge, the teacher leads a 5-minute discussion using these prompts:
   - "Which word is most familiar to you? Where have you heard it before?" [*Radioactivity* is a popular choice, given students' knowledge of nuclear reactions from current events and motion pictures.]
   - "Which word do you think is the most important word? Tell your partner, and we'll call on a few to share." [Most students nominate *radioactivity* because it seems more general or inclusive than the other terms.]
   - "Which words do you suppose go together well? Be ready to explain why." [Many students predict that *alpha particle* and *beta particle* go together well because they look so similar.]
   - "Which word do you know the least about so far?" [A few students say *gamma rays*, but *alpha particle* and *beta particle* are also nominated.]
   - "What questions do you have about our words now?" [The class appreciates a clever student's question: "Are there Ralph's particles too?" Ralph's is a local grocery chain, just as is Alpha Beta. Other students phrase the query more seriously: "Why are the words *alpha* and *beta* used in these terms?"]
3. To build word knowledge, the teacher proceeds with her lesson, which includes reading the text and demonstrations via downloaded pictures and video clips. After they meet each term from their Vocab Cards, students record on their cards definitions in their own words and quick sketches.
4. Also building word knowledge, the students are pleased to answer their earlier question: *Alpha, beta,* and *gamma* are the first three letters of the Greek alphabet. On a quick side trip, the class makes a list on the board of all the Greek letters they know and are impressed that knowing "Greek" can help them understand words in science and mathematics (they think of *pi*).
5. The next day, to apply word knowledge, the teacher opens the lesson by pointing to the Word Wall, which now includes yesterday's Vocab Cards. She prompts students to practice:
   - "Take your Vocab Cards from yesterday out, please, and arrange them on your desk in a way that shows how the words are related. Work with your partner." [She notices that some students place *radioactivity* at the top of their desks and the other three terms side by side below *radioactivity.* "Ah!" She comments, "You show that *alpha particles, beta particles,* and *gamma rays* are all examples of *radioactivity.*"]
   - "Pick up any two cards and tell your partner how those words are the same and different."
   - "Who can use one of our Vocab Cards in a sentence? How about two? Three?"

*Preparing to Learn Words (no more than 10 minutes)*

1. Begin a lesson or unit by displaying, one at a time, a small set of words (no more than 10; fewer is better). You may elect to have students manipulate a set of the words at their seats, individually, or in pairs.
2. Tell students that they will meet these words in the lesson or unit. Enunciate as you pronounce each word and ask students to repeat.
3. Build connections to prior word knowledge and build motivation to learn by discussing prompts like the following:
   - Which of these words have you already met? In what context? What did they mean in that context?
   - Which of these words looks completely unfamiliar? Any guesses on their meanings?
   - Which two (or more) of these words might go together? Why?
   - Which two words would you and your partner predict to be the most important words in our lesson?

## Building Word Knowledge

For each of the following suggestions, physically manipulate the Vocab Cards to reinforce the printed version of the word and its connection to the spoken version:

1. Teach meanings of selected Vocab Cards directly. Point out root words and affixes (see Morphemic Analysis, p. 106) and words borrowed from other languages (see Word Histories, p. 115).
2. As words arise in the context of the lesson, explore relevant properties of words, drawing from students and providing direct instruction:
   - What is its function?
   - In which categories does it belong?
   - What are its attributes?
   - Which words are related to this one?
   - What is another word that means the same thing?
   - What is an antonym for this word?
3. During instruction, revisit students' predictions on word meanings and important words (from *Preparing to Learn Words*).
4. Have students illustrate target terms by sketching on the reverse of the cards.

## Applying Word Knowledge

Use these ideas to open or close a lesson or during spare moments or practice periods:

1. Have students sort words. They can use the words for the day's lesson, or you can include a selection of Vocab Cards from the chapter, unit, or term. Try open sorts, where students sort by their own criteria, and try closed sorts, where you suggest the sorting criteria. For example, "Put these words into groups that go together" is an open sort, and a closed sort is, "Make two groups: words related to respiration and words that are not."
2. Have students build a graphic organizer such as a Semantic Map (p. 37) using a selection of Vocab Cards. Or try organizing them hierarchically on the board as in an outline.
3. If students have drawn sketches on the backs of their cards, pair students up and have them match terms with pictures.
4. Create content links (Guillaume, Yopp, & Yopp, 2007) with Vocab Cards. Have students each select a Vocab Card, stand, and mingle throughout the room to locate a peer with a Vocab Card that somehow links with theirs. Ask a few partners to explain their links before they mingle again and find new links.
5. Display Vocab Cards on a content-based Word Wall (see p. 81) or pocket chart. Revisit them frequently. For instance, ask students to orally compose a sentence with a term you select plus one (or two) others.
6. Play 20 Questions, with the aim being that students discern the target term from among those displayed by asking the fewest number of questions possible. To make the game harder, require a variety of kinds of questions (e.g., meaning-based and

letter-based questions). Sample questions are "Is your word an action word?" and "Does your word have a suffix?"

7. Give students a flyswatter and ask them to swat the displayed vocab term (perhaps on the Word Wall or whiteboard) that meets the leader's clues. For instance, "Swat the word that means the opposite of *internal.*" Students at their seats can hold up their own Vocab Cards to participate in the session.

8. Use the displayed Vocab Cards as the basis of written and oral practice. For instance, "Tell your partner about different *cooking techniques* using at least three of the words from the board." Or "Write a haiku poem about *heat transfer* using one or two terms from our board."

### Independent Word Learning

1. Distribute one Vocab Card to each individual or pairs. You can assign cards or allow students to select them. To become word experts (Lansdown, 1991), students might create Vocab Cards where they draw a picture, write a definition, use the word in a sentence, and write related words (Richek, 2005). To help students place the words in a broader context, they might investigate, record, and report three things (Schwartz & Raphael, 1985):
   - What is it?
   - What is it like?
   - What are some examples?
2. Invite students to select their own terms for Vocab Cards. Keep extra blanks (and class time) available for this purpose.

## MODIFICATIONS

1. Allow students to nominate some Vocab Card terms. They may find words by flipping through the text during a preview. Discussion related to nominations can build motivation and curiosity both about new words and about the upcoming content.

2. Vocab Cards are sometimes effective in helping older students prepare for exams. Students may elect to write brief definitions or examples on the reverse of their Vocab Cards for this purpose. Ensure that students have had multiple opportunities to learn word meanings before composing definitions. We do not recommend that students copy dictionary definitions.

## TROUBLESHOOTING

To ensure student success and motivation, select a reasonable number of words and use them in quick, meaningful, and enjoyable ways. Otherwise, students may come to see working with Vocab Cards as a chore.

## TECH CONNECT

1. Create electronic Vocab Cards using software available online. Word processing programs or other widely available programs, such as Print Shop, can be used for this purpose. Print the cards out or have students practice on the computer.

2. Free software allows students to download Vocab Cards onto their personal digital assistants and beam them to peers. See http://www.freewarepalm.com/educational/vocabularycards.shtml.

## NEXT STEPS

Vocab Cards work well as the basis for writing activities such as Poetry (p. 149) and for Vocabulary Games (p. 73).

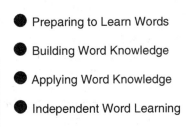
# 11

# Vocabulary Self-Collection Strategy

A large proportion of new vocabulary terms that students encounter in the content areas comes from textbooks and related printed materials. Therefore, it is essential that students master strategies for using the context to identify and build understanding of words that are important to understanding. The importance of word learning from text is emphasized by the National Reading Panel's recommendation that teachers use content area texts as a major source of words for instruction; these texts contain words that are likely to affect student learning, and students will be exposed to target terms often enough to make learning them worthwhile (National Institute of Child Health and Human Development, 2000).

One strategy that promotes the use of the context for vocabulary selection is the Vocabulary Self-Collection Strategy (VSS) (Haggard, 1982). VSS is an interactive strategy in which students select from their texts words that they believe are important for the class to learn. Through discussion and teacher guidance, students narrow down the number of suggested words to five to eight words that the entire class will be responsible for learning. Students record the words and practice using them orally and in writing.

## PURPOSE

VSS serves a number of important purposes. First, it supports comprehension by developing both knowledge of the definition of words and knowledge of the context in which the words are found (Haggard, 1982). Second, it requires elaboration and discussion of words and opportunities for practice, making it more likely that meaningful learning will take place (Beck & McKeown, 1991; Stahl & Fairbanks, 1986). Third, VSS promotes student choice in learning. Student choice has been shown to be motivational and to promote self-efficacy: students' belief that they can accomplish their learning goals (Haggard, 1986; Ruddell & Shearer, 2002). Students who used VSS were more likely to choose more challenging words and to develop their own systematic independent word learning strategies that enabled them to learn more words quickly (Fisher, Blachowicz, & Smith, 1991; Haggard, 1986).

> **A Note for Your English Learners**
>
> Experts suggest that strategies that help English learners select relevant words for study and make use of both contextual information and word definitions are effective in bolstering vocabulary and in improving comprehension (Scott & Nagy, 1997; Stahl, 1983). For these reasons, English learners may find VSS helpful.

# ⬤ PROCEDURES

## Getting Ready

1. Decide on the text you want students to read. Choose a selection that includes a sizable number of vocabulary terms, varying in difficulty and importance to the topic. Providing students with a range of terms from which to choose will help them to think critically about the words they meet in text and to develop criteria for determining their relative importance to the topic.
2. Consider choosing seven or eight target words from the selection that you think are important, especially at the beginning. Choose one or two of the words to share with students. Although you will share only one or two of your choices with your students, having a list in mind can help you guide the discussion and make it more likely that the target words selected for class study are essential to understanding the topic. Figure 11.1 gives the selections made by a high school art teacher from a text selection on color theory. The words in bold are the two he chose to share.
3. Decide how words selected for the class to study will be displayed in the room. They need to be large enough that everyone can see them. They can be displayed in alphabetical order or in other categories, such as semantic groupings, depending on your topic of study and your overall learning goals.

## During Class

The Vocabulary Self-Collection Strategy stretches across all instructional phases and is effective for *Independent Word Learning*.

### *Preparing to Learn Words*

1. Introduce students to the selection they will be reading and discuss how it is related to the topic they will be studying. Ask students to read the text and choose two words (or one word if the number of students in the class is large) from the text using the following criteria:
   • The words must be important to understanding the big ideas about the topic.
   • The words are ones that everyone in the class should learn.
2. Additionally, tell students they should be prepared to share the following information about the words they have chosen:
   • The context in which the word(s) are found, that is, a sentence or a phrase from the text that contains the word(s)
   • A possible definition for the word(s)
   • The reasons for choosing the word(s)

**Figure 11.1** Selection of words made by a high school art teacher from a text on color theory

**primary colors**

**secondary colors**

tertiary colors

analogous colors

complementary colors

tints

shades

## Building Word Knowledge

1. Once you and your students have selected words, model for students the process you used in choosing words by giving one or two examples. Then provide each student with the opportunity to share information about his or her word(s) with the class. Encourage a discussion of the words as they are being presented by referring to your own thinking processes and asking students questions that clarify and extend the meaning of the words they are sharing. Try using questions like the following to guide the discussion:

   * How is the word related to the topic we are studying? Is it related to a big idea or a detail?
   * How does the context in which you found the word help you define it? What clues did the author give you? What other sources could we use to refine our definition?
   * How is your word related to other words we have already discussed? How does it add to our understanding of the topic?

2. After all the words have been presented, invite the class to vote on five to eight words that the entire class should know. Discussion is critical at this stage in helping students make good decisions as they narrow the list. Continue to use questions like those given previously to encourage students to justify their choices and make connections. In Figure 11.2, the left column shows the number of unique words suggested by students in the art class in their study of color theory (expect some students to nominate identical words). The right column shows the narrowed list. Notice that the final list includes most, but not all, of the words the teacher selected, shown in Figure 11.1. However, the teacher chose not to modify students' final list because he wanted students to assume ownership of it to increase their motivation and self-efficacy. Instead, he planned to incorporate omitted words in the unit by including learning activities that provided opportunities to discuss the terms and use them in different contexts.

### A Note for Your English Learners

Blachowicz and Fisher (2002) suggest that VSS discussions can be especially useful for English learners if they include an exploration of synonyms, Morphemic Analysis (p. 106), Word Histories (p. 115), and personal experiences. These discussions help students make connections between prior knowledge and new learning and make it more likely that the new terms will be understood and remembered.

**Figure 11.2** Nominated words and final list choices made by high school students studying color theory

| Words Nominated by the Class | Final List |
| --- | --- |
| harmony | primary colors |
| analogous colors | secondary colors |
| tints | tertiary colors |
| proportion | complementary colors |
| primary colors | analogous colors |
| secondary colors | harmony |
| tertiary colors | dominance |
| color relativity | subordination |
| nuance | |
| complementary colors | |
| shades | |
| dominance | |
| subordination | |

**Figure 11.3** An art student's vocabulary log entry for the term *complementary colors*

> *Complementary colors—contrasting colors across from each other on a color wheel. Examples: blue and orange or green and red. Hint:* **CCC**—*complementary colors contrast.*

3. Have students record the class words in word logs, personal dictionaries, or Vocab Cards (p. 50) and ask them to create some sort of meaning aid (an illustration, a definition, a sentence, a Semantic Map Insert [p. 37] or chart) that will help them remember the terms. Emphasize the importance of making individual choices in vocabulary learning by encouraging students to also record and learn any other words related to the topic they feel are important to their individual vocabulary growth. Figure 11.3 shows an example of a word log entry made by an art student for the term *complementary colors*.
4. Provide multiple opportunities for students to practice using the words by using activities such as the following:
   - Use the words in sponge activities that require students to quiz each other about the meaning of the terms (e.g., "What are the primary colors?" "How are complementary colors different from analogous colors?")
   - Have the students act out the definitions of words. Ask the class to guess the word they are acting out.
   - Choose words from the list and encourage students to compare and contrast them by asking, "How are my two terms alike? How are they different? What other words can you find that contrast?"
   - Select two terms and ask students to tell you how they are related. Have them choose two other words and tell how they are related.

## Applying Word Knowledge

Once students have learned basic meanings for the terms, provide opportunities to use the words in a variety of contexts. Here are sample activities:

1. Build graphic organizers using the words. Have students arrange the words and add annotations such as arrows or other images to clarify meaning and show relationships. Encourage students to use words from their personal lists or other sources to add details and expand relationships. For example, in a health class, students might create a flow-chart or a diagram to show the effect of aerobic exercise on the human body.
2. Encourage students to use the terms in their writing. For example, have students write a one-paragraph summary of a lesson using four words from the class list. Also consider having students compose Readers Theater scripts (p. 140) and Vocabulary Graffiti (p. 155).

## Independent Word Learning

Students can use the principles in VSS to develop independent word learning strategies. For example, try these activities:

1. Encourage students to refer to the context for help in identifying important words and their meanings. See Context Clues (p. 124) for strategies for teaching students to use the context for figuring out new words.
2. Invite students to create personal word lists to explore words of interest and provide opportunities for students to share their words. Consider a bulletin board or other area where students can display interesting words (see Word Walls, p. 81) and related items, such as definitions, artifacts, and illustrations. Take time to have students share their displays and make sure you make regular contributions as well. Word-of-the-day activities in which a student selects a word to share with the class can also motivate students and create an interest in words.
3. Class discussions can invite students to identify words that they found helpful in understanding the text and to explain their reasoning.

**MODIFICATIONS**

1. After students are familiar with VSS, allow students to share their words in small groups. Ask the members of the small group to narrow their selections to two or three words to share with the class.
2. Have students nominate words of a particular type, such as words that describe or are examples of an important concept.

 **TROUBLESHOOTING**

1. Students with little background knowledge about a topic may find it difficult to discriminate among words in terms of their importance. Build background knowledge by using inquiry activities, field trips, digital recordings, and/or class discussions using Semantic Maps (p. 37) or other graphic organizers before you ask students to select words from the text.
2. Students may need support to resolve differences that arise in choosing words for the final class list. For example, some students may vote for words on the basis of their friends' choices rather than relying on their own thinking, or students may have difficulty in narrowing their choices in voting for a final class list. Before students vote on a final list, try having them reconsider their original lists and make any changes in the words they would nominate after having participated in class discussions. Ask them to rank order the words on their revised lists using a gradient scale, with the number 1 and 2 words being the words they feel most strongly should be on the class list and the last words those that they might be persuaded to omit. Use the revised lists to guide discussion and to justify words selected for the final class list. A count of the class rank order of a word can be used to break ties if necessary.

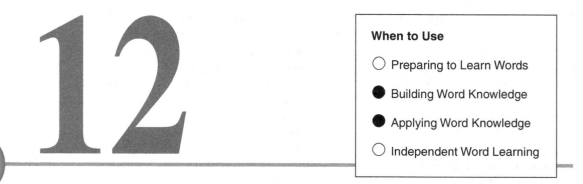

**When to Use**

○ Preparing to Learn Words

● Building Word Knowledge

● Applying Word Knowledge

○ Independent Word Learning

# Semantic Gradients

In order for students to become effective word learners, they need to understand how words are associated with each other. This knowledge helps students develop the word consciousness necessary to learn new vocabulary and to understand how writers and speakers use language effectively (Blachowicz & Fisher, 2004; Graves, 2000; Scott & Nagy, 2004). A Semantic Gradient (Blachowicz & Fisher, 2006) requires students to order words along a continuum, making clear the semantic relationships among the terms. Semantic Gradients are most effective with adverbs, verbs, and other words that can be scaled (e.g., *cool, brisk, cold,* and *frigid*).

## PURPOSE

Semantic Gradients use a graphic to help students focus on the subtle differences in word meanings that can exist among categories of words. For example, if students come across the unknown word *agitated*, we might provide them with a synonym such as *excited* or *nervous*. However, neither the word *excited* nor the word *nervous* has exactly the same meaning as *agitated*, nor does *excited* have exactly the same meaning as *nervous*. Although all these words are clearly related, there are important but subtle differences in meaning among them. Helping students understand these differences enriches their vocabulary and deepens their understanding of how shades of meaning can affect word choice in oral and written communication. Semantic Gradients are valuable because they provide students with the opportunity to order related words along a scale that makes distinctions among them based on shades of meaning. Students must discuss and justify the way they ordered the words. When students are required to justify their choices, they deepen and broaden their understanding of the words they are studying (Greenwood & Flanagan, 2007).

## PROCEDURE

### Getting Ready

1. Before the lesson or unit of instruction, pick the target words. Be selective in your choices. Semantic Gradients are designed to help students clarify the relationships among categories of words that can be ordered across a continuum. You can choose to have students order words that are very closely related. For example, *large, immense, gigantic, colossal,* and *enormous* all are associated with objects that are big, but they can be ordered on a scale of "bigness" from smallest to largest. Semantic Gradients can also be used to order terms that fall between antonyms, such as *peaceful* and *militant* (e.g., *conciliatory, pacifying, placating, assertive, contentious,* and *aggressive*). Figure 12.1

**Figure 12.1** Examples of antonym terms that can be explored on a scale

| **Social studies:** | **Economics:** |
|---|---|
| democracy ↔ dictatorship | patronize ↔ boycott |
| disloyalty ↔ allegiance | independent contractor ↔ conglomerate |
| **Science:** | **Writing/descriptive verbs:** |
| frigid ↔ sweltering | limped ↔ sprinted |
| arid ↔ wet | whisper ↔ scream |
| **Literature:** | **Art:** |
| cowardly ↔ courageous | tertiary colors ↔ primary colors |
| virtuous ↔ corrupt | warm colors ↔ cool colors |

provides examples of other antonym pairs that could be explored using Semantic Gradients. You no doubt will be able to think of additional pairs that could be used.

2. Prepare the Semantic Gradient for students. Two types of Semantic Gradients that can be developed are the Word List Semantic Gradient and the Student Generated Semantic Gradient (Greenwood & Flanagan, 2007):

   a. The Word List Semantic Gradient provides students with a partially filled-in gradient and a word list. Students choose words from the word list to place along the gradient. Because students don't have to generate any words to complete the gradient, it provides the most support. It is an excellent choice for English learners and other students who have low vocabulary knowledge or for any students who would benefit from having the words provided. See Figure 12.2 for an example of a Word List Semantic Gradient that a middle school teacher developed for a lesson on the effects of poverty.

   b. The Student Generated Semantic Gradient provides antonyms at each end of the gradient, but students must generate the words that fall in between. This Semantic Gradient allows students to make decisions about what words to include, promoting creativity and critical thinking. Because the words to fill in the gradient are not provided, it is more challenging than the Word List Semantic Gradient. See Figure 12.3 for an example of a Student Generated Semantic Gradient a sixth-grade teacher used after a unit on climate.

**Figure 12.2** Example of a Word List Semantic Gradient from a middle school lesson on poverty

**Directions:** Arrange the words in the list from those that describe the poorest people to the wealthiest.

**Word List:** salaried, insolvent, affluent, destitute, prosperous, jobless, indigent, comfortable

Wealthiest

_____

_____

_____

_____

_____

_____

_____

_____

Poorest

**Figure 12.3** Example of a Student Generated Semantic Gradient from a sixth-grade unit on climate

**Directions:** Arrange climate words in order from arid to wet.

Wet

_____

_____

_____

_____

_____

_____

_____

Arid

## During Class

Semantic Gradients are useful for *Building Word Knowledge* and *Applying Word Knowledge*.

### Building Word Knowledge

1. Present the Semantic Gradient. Discussion is essential to the success of this strategy, so you will want students to work in pairs or triads. Encourage students to discuss and justify their ordering as they fill in the gradient.
2. As a class, discuss the choices students made in ordering the terms, paying close attention to those words for which students most often had divergent points of view. Ask students to defend their decisions by explaining how the meanings of the target words are related and how they are different. Help students explore relevant properties of the terms by asking questions:
   - How is this word related to the word that you listed before it? After it? How does it differ?
   - Why do you think it goes in that place in the order? Could it possibly be placed somewhere else? Why?
   - When might you use this word? What is its purpose? How does its purpose affect its placement?
3. After discussion, allow students to make any changes to the order of their words. If you are using the Student Generated Semantic Gradient, encourage students to expand their list to include other words that were introduced during discussion.
4. If you are using the Semantic Gradient before a unit or lesson, have students revisit their gradient after instruction and include new related words that they learned. Have them reflect on their choices.

### Applying Word Knowledge

1. To ensure that students fully appreciate how shades of meaning affect comprehension, try combining Context Clues (p. 124) with Semantic Gradients (Greenwood & Flanagan, 2007). Figure 12.4 shows two Semantic Gradients and cloze-type sentences that a fifth-grade teacher used as part of her instruction on word choice in narrative writing.
2. Have pairs of students create their own cloze sentences for the words after they have completed a gradient. Students can use the cloze sentences to quiz each other.

**Figure 12.4** Example of Semantic Gradients and cloze-type sentences used by a fifth-grade teacher in instruction on word choice

---

**Directions:** Choose the best word from the gradients to fill in the blank. Be prepared to justify your choices.

**Laughed**

giggled _____

chuckled _____

snickered _____

tittered _____

sniveled _____

whimpered _____

wept _____

sobbed _____

**Cried**

**Hard**

tough _____

solid _____

firm _____

delicate _____

feathery _____

cozy _____

**Soft**

1. "Watch, Adam," Joe _____. "He is so clumsy. He's going down for sure."
2. "Please let me go with you, Mommy," the child _____ in a barely audible voice.
3. The principal told the students in a _____ voice that she would not tolerate their behavior.
4. The baby's _____ skin was bruised when he hit his hand against the crib.
5. Ana and her friend, Jen, _____ with delight over the possibility that they might win.
6. The old lady's _____ touch tickled Carla's arm.

---

## TROUBLESHOOTING

1. To ensure that your students understand the procedure, provide modeling and guided practice using words they know before introducing new terms.
2. Encourage students to use resources such as dictionaries, thesauruses, and content materials as needed.

## TECH CONNECT

The Internet provides a number of sources that are valuable for teachers and students in searching for antonyms, synonyms, and definitions. Try the following: *Synonym Thesaurus with Antonyms and Definitions* at http://www.synonym.com, Thesaurus.com at http://thesaurus.reference.com, *Free Online Dictionary* at http://www.thefreedictionary.com, and OneLook Dictionary Search at http://www.onelook.com.

## NEXT STEPS

Semantic Gradients will help students succeed in other strategies such as Analogies (p. 111), Vocabulary Games (p. 73), and Content Area Read Alouds (p. 135). Consider also using other activities that are described in Context Clues (p. 124) to deepen students' understanding of the meaning of the terms they have used in the Semantic Gradients (p. 59).

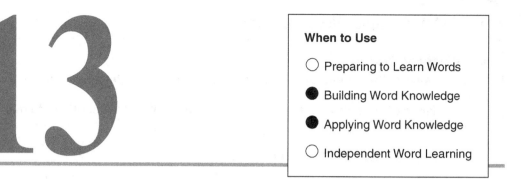

# Word Decisions

Is your dentist likely to warn you about *irredentism?* People who are involved in *ecomigration* are environmentalists, right?

In Word Decision activities, students make choices about the ways that words can be used in multiple contexts and justify their decisions. For students to have real ownership of new vocabulary, they must have somewhere between 7 and 12 encounters with the target words in contexts that are different from the original (Stahl, 1986). Activities that require students to actively process the meaning of words across contexts and to make connections with prior knowledge are most likely to produce the powerful learning needed to promote a deep understanding of new vocabulary (Beck & McKeown, 2007; Stahl & Fairbanks, 1986). Thus, Word Decisions encourage students to interact with the meaning of words in various contexts to promote word learning.

## PURPOSE

Word Decisions are used with words that students have encountered through reading, discussions, or direct instruction. Word Decisions promote the development of word knowledge because they require students to make choices about previously instructed words as they interact with them in new contexts. Word Decisions can be an effective learning tool because they require that students make connections with their prior knowledge. In addition, repeated experiences with the words in context make it more likely that the target words will be recalled and understood in the future (Beck & McKeown, 2003, 2007; Bransford, Brown, & Corking, 1999).

## PROCEDURES

### Getting Ready

1. Select the words. Choose terms that you have previously taught or that students have experienced in print and in discussions. Limit the number of terms to between 6 and 10 words. You want to provide a rich context to reinforce and extend word meanings, so fewer words is better.
2. Choose the kinds of tasks you will provide. In general, Beck and McKeown (2003) recommend Word Decision tasks that require students to do the following with target terms:
   a. Answer direct questions and give reasons.
   b. Recognize examples.
   c. Use related words.
   d. Use words in the same context.

## Figure 13.1 Sample Word Decision activities

---

**Questions and Reasons**

- If you were in the Sahara Desert, it would be *arid*. Why? What are some other places that might be *arid*?
- What kinds of animals might you find in a *savanna*? Why? What other life might you find in a *savanna*?

**Recognizing Examples or Characteristics**

If any of the things I say are characteristics of a *democracy*, say "democracy." If they are not, say "no."

- People have the right to vote.
- One person holds the power.
- People have access to diverse information sources.
- Laws apply equally to all people.
- The government owns most factories.

**Words That Are Related**

- If you scratch your arm, would you rather have the scratch injure your *dermis* or *epidermis*?
- If you met an angry animal in the forest, would you hope that the animal is a *carnivore* or an *herbivore*?

**Using the Same Context**

- If you have a cold, do you have *a communicable disease*? Why?
- Is your cold caused by *bacteria* or a *virus*? Why?
- How would *nasal congestion* make you sound?

---

From these general tasks, Figure 13.1 provides a list of sample activities that allow students to interact with target words in different contexts.

Thinking of new contexts and examples for words is not always easy. Try brainstorming ideas for new contexts in which the words might be found. Grouping words that are related can also be helpful. Figure 13.2 shows a teacher's partially completed planning sheet using instructed words in a unit on fitness.

3. Decide on the format you will use in presenting the Word Decisions and prepare materials. Following are some choices for you to consider:
   a. Have students answer orally as a class.
   b. Have students use an active participation technique. For example, have students hold up "yes" and "no" cards, use unison response, or use thumbs up/thumbs down.
   c. Have students work individually, in pairs, or in small groups to fill out a worksheet.

### During Class

Word Decisions can be used for both *Building Word Knowledge* and *Applying Word Knowledge*.

### Building Word Knowledge

1. Introduce the Word Decisions and explain how students are to respond. Model how to complete some examples to ensure that students understand the process.
2. Have students work as a whole group, individually, in pairs, or in small groups to make their decisions.

**Figure 13.2** A teacher's partially completed planning sheet for instructed fitness words

| Word list | Contexts |
|---|---|
| *aerobic exercise* | *running, swimming, jumping rope* |
| *anaerobic exercise* | *lifting weights, golf, sprinting* |
| *agility* | *mind, body, limbs, dogs* |
| *flexibility* | *a gymnast, in bending, in getting through a tiny space* |
| *maintenance* | |
| *commitment* | *goal setting, to another person* |
| *discipline* | |
| *energy* | |
| *endurance* | |
| **Related words** | |
| *energy and endurance* | |
| *aerobic and anaerobic exercise* | |
| *agility and flexibility* | |

3. Ask students to explain their answers. For example, you might have students write a brief explanation, draw a picture, act out the meaning, or justify their answers orally to other groups.

## Applying Word Knowledge

1. Have students develop their own Word Decisions using a different list of instructed words. You can either select the words for students or let them select words from their class notes, texts, or other instructional materials. Ask students to quiz each other using their word questions. Figure 13.3 shows the word questions that a student developed using words from *The Giver* by Lois Lowry (1993). Notice that she used two question types for her Word Decisions. To quiz each other, students might also write their Word Decisions in plastic baggie books (see p. 145) and have their peers write their responses using dry-erase markers.
2. Play Word Decisions games. Divide the students into teams and give them points or some other reward for giving the correct answers. For added fun, ask students to act out the answers or draw pictures when appropriate.

## ● MODIFICATIONS

Consider reteaching words students have difficulty using appropriately. Semantic Maps (p. 37), Concept of Definition Word Maps (p. 9), and the Frayer Model (p. 18) are good choices for reteaching a small number of words.

**Figure 13.3** Student-developed Word Decisions using vocabulary from *The Giver* by Lois Lowry

1. Should a mayor have <u>integrity</u>? Why? Who else should have <u>integrity</u>?
2. Does taking a test make you <u>apprehensive</u>? What other things make you <u>apprehensive</u>?
3. Would you rather have a friend who is <u>indolent</u> or <u>diligent</u>? Why?
4. Would a <u>meticulous</u> friend like being in a <u>disorderly</u> classroom? Why?

## TROUBLESHOOTING

If students are working in small groups, in pairs, or individually, be sure to check their work to ensure that the answers and examples that they describe are accurate. Require students to consult a dictionary or their class materials when they miss questions about a word.

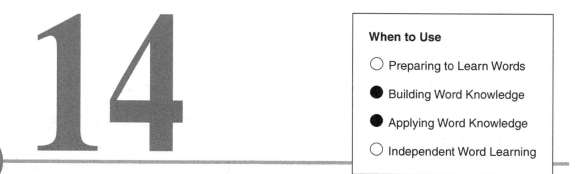

**When to Use**

○ Preparing to Learn Words

● Building Word Knowledge

● Applying Word Knowledge

○ Independent Word Learning

# Word Chains

Understanding a word involves connecting it to other words and building a conscious aware-ness of its connections. In Word Chains (Stephens & Brown, 2000), students link terms in sequence based on meaningful connections among the words. Students can generate the 5 to 10 terms themselves, or you can supply them. Figure 14.1 shows an Algebra I student's Word Chain and her explanation of its links.

## PURPOSE

Vocabulary development requires the related tasks of establishing associations and devel-oping conceptual knowledge (Baumann, Kame'enui & Ash, 2003). Word Chains supports both of these tasks by extending students' understandings of concepts and by encouraging students to explore concepts in relation to each other, thus helping to develop semantic relationships among words (Blachowicz, Fisher, Ogle, & Watts-Taffe, 2006). Word Chains can also support metacognitive awareness as students justify the links they form between terms. Word Chains is a low-preparation strategy that encourages students to think about how words they are studying are related. It also gives them practice in using the words.

**Figure 14.1** An Algebra I student's Word Chain and her explanation

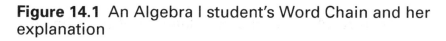

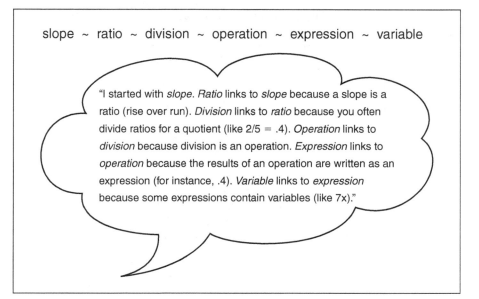

slope ~ ratio ~ division ~ operation ~ expression ~ variable

"I started with *slope*. *Ratio* links to *slope* because a slope is a ratio (rise over run). *Division* links to *ratio* because you often divide ratios for a quotient (like 2/5 = .4). *Operation* links to *division* because division is an operation. *Expression* links to *operation* because the results of an operation are written as an expression (for instance, .4). *Variable* links to *expression* because some expressions contain variables (like 7x)."

# PROCEDURES

### Getting Ready

1. Decide whether you will select the terms or have the students select them.
2. If desired, select the terms. Remember that students will use between 5 and 10 words in their chains. You may either assign all the terms or select a large number of terms and let students choose a set number from among them. Your Vocab Cards (p. 50) will serve useful if you've developed them.

    If students are to develop the terms, choose a strategy to support them in selecting words. You may plan, for example, for them to use Ten Most Important Words (p. 33) or Vocabulary Self-Collection Strategy (p. 54). Alternatively, plan to lead a brief brainstorming session for students to list terms.

3. Decide on the physical format for the chains and prepare materials. Some choices follow:
    a. Have students simply write the words on paper.
    b. Have students manipulate small Vocab Cards (p. 50) at their seats.
    c. Duplicate a template such as one of those given in Figure 14.2.
    d. Have students write the words on strips and later staple them together into actual chains.
    e. Use diagramming software like Inspiration to create the chains.

### During Class

Word Chains are useful during *Building Word Knowledge* and *Applying Word Knowledge*.

### Building Word Knowledge

1. Display a Word Chain and discuss how each term is related to its neighbors. Complete one Word Chain as a class to ensure that students understand the process.
2. Display the terms or support students in developing a list of terms.
3. Have students work individually, in pairs, or in small groups to develop their chains.

**Figure 14.2** Sample templates for Word Chains

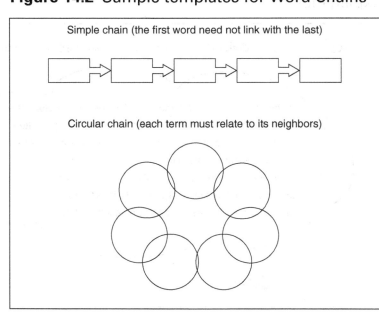

**Figure 14.3** A different Algebra I Word Chain (created using Inspiration)

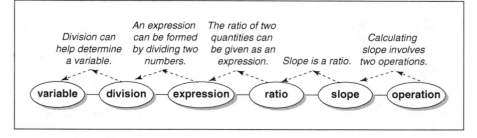

*Applying Word Knowledge*

1. Ask students to use their chains' terms and relationships in another form. For instance, you might have them write a brief paragraph, draw a Vocabulary Graffiti (p. 155), or explain them orally to other groups.
2. Have a few minutes before the bell rings? Play Word Chains as a game that encourages students to stretch the number of words they know related to specified categories. This game uses spelling as an additional criterion. Specify a category of words, such as "things you find at the beach," "color words," or "things you might see in an auto shop." Teams alternate, contributing a word to the chain. Words must fit the category *and* begin with the last letter of the previous word. Here's a chain for "things related to football":

blocking → goalpost → tackle → end zone → extra points → snap

## MODIFICATIONS

1. To encourage flexibility in their thinking, ask students to form more than one Word Chain using the same terms. Figure 14.3 displays another Word Chain using the same Algebra I terms as in Figure 14.1.
2. Distribute a different list of terms to each small group and ask them to form small-group Word Chains. Then form a whole-class Word Chain by linking each group's chain to the others.
3. Simplify Word Chains by requiring students to link only two words in a strategy called Connect Two (Richek, 2005). Present two columns of terms on the board and ask students to link a term from column A with one from column B.
4. To encourage independent word learning, urge students to use the dictionary in building their word chains. Dictionary use can sensitize students to listings of words with multiple meanings (Thornbury, 2002).

## TROUBLESHOOTING

Be sure to check students' work to ensure that the concepts and connections they describe are accurate. Otherwise, students might reinforce misconceptions through their Word Chains.

## NEXT STEPS

See Semantic Gradients (p. 59) for a strategy that requires students to order terms according to a specified semantic category.

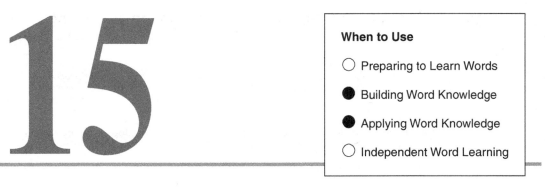

# Clues and Questions

In Clues and Questions, students work with vocabulary terms in a game setting (Readence, Bean, & Baldwin, 1998). On cards, they write questions or clues that will allow other students to guess their term, and then they trade cards and try deducing each other's words. Figure 15.1 gives a Clues and Questions card from a science class.

## PURPOSE

Clues and Questions gives students practice in formulating productive questions, a skill of all good readers. Creating clear and specific clues requires students to think carefully about attributes of terms, and it encourages students to think about their terms in different ways. This can support development of the shades of meaning that are associated with deep knowledge of a word (Nagy & Scott, 2000). Clues and Questions also provides for practice (both written and oral) with the target terms, important because meaningful practice is essential for lasting word knowledge (Flynt & Brozo, 2008; Nagy, 1988). Finally, Clues and Questions gives students a reason to revisit content texts and reference materials for a purpose they are likely to find meaningful.

## PROCEDURES

### Getting Ready

1. Select a set of content terms with which students have had plenty of experience.
2. Collect index cards, enough for one card per term. Write one term at the top of each card or, later, have students do so. Each card, then, requires a different term.
3. Decide which types of clues students will be required or encouraged to write. Figure 15.2 gives some sample types of questions and clues.
4. Place students in small groups, each with an assigned partner within the group.

**Figure 15.1** A Clues and Questions card from a science class

| Circuit |
| --- |
| 1. Analogy: *Horses are to racetrack as electrons are to _____* |
| 2. Definition: *The circular pathway of electricity.* |
| 3. Context: *The lights wouldn't turn on, so I went out to check the _____ breaker.* |

**Figure 15.2** Kinds of clues for Clues and Questions

| Type of clue | Example |
| --- | --- |
| Analogy | awake: asleep :: peace: _____ *(conflict)* |
| Context | One witness reported that the robber wore a baseball cap, but the other witness saw a ski mask. Their reports _____. *(conflict)* |
| Definition | What is the military term for a prolonged and bitter but sporadic struggle between opposing sides? *(conflict)* |
| Etymology (word history) | This word came from the Latin for "to strike together." *(conflict)* |
| Cognates (words that sound similar in other languages) | In English, how do you say the Spanish word *cronómetro* and the Danish word *kronometer*? *(chronometer)* |
| Compare-contrast | Although they serve similar purposes, a watch and a _____ are a bit different. The latter is more precise. *(chronometer)* |
| Conceptual approach | What device did sailors in the 1700s and 1800s use to determine longitude when at sea? *(chronometer)* |
| Morphemic analysis (word parts) | Which word is made of two word parts, from ancient Greek, meaning "time" and "measure"? *(chronometer)* |

## During Class

Clues and Questions is useful during the *Building Word Knowledge* phase. Building word knowledge doesn't always mean learning new words; it can also strengthen knowledge of words that students already have. Clues and Questions also helps during *Applying Word Knowledge*.

### Building and Applying Word Knowledge

1. If students are unfamiliar with Clues and Questions, tell them they will be playing a word game, and they will write the clues. Show them a sample card (perhaps from Figure 15.1) and talk about its attributes.
2. Explain the game:
   - Each group will receive a set of Clues and Questions cards.
   - One person in the group will select a card and, without reading it, show it to the group members.
   - Group members will read aloud the clues and questions on the card, and the individual who drew the card will use the clues to guess the term.
   - Decide whether you will use points. Students might, for example, obtain 3 points if they guess the term with one clue, 2 points if they use two clues, and 1 point if they use all three clues.
3. Explain how students are to construct the cards, perhaps using these directions:
   - Work with your partner to create a set of three clues that relate to the target term. Write them on scrap paper.
   - Use your textbook and reference materials, including online materials.
   - Place the most difficult clue first and the biggest hint last. Be sure to include a variety of clues.

- Have your clues checked by the teacher for accuracy and clarity.
- Beneath your target term, write the clues on your index card.

4. When cards have been written, collect them from each group and redistribute to other groups.
5. Have groups play Clues and Questions with their newly received set of cards.
6. Afterward, discuss the attributes of productive Clues and Questions. This can improve students' questions for the next time they create clues.
7. Store the cards nearby for cumulative review. The cards can be placed in a learning station, for instance, for partners who finish work early. They can also be used as a sponge or a quick and productive way to begin or end a class. When using the cards as a sponge, the teacher or a student can draw a card from the stack and read the clues aloud to the whole class. Or the class can be divided into opposing teams who take turns guessing terms.

## MODIFICATION

Although much of the richness of Clues and Questions comes in devising careful clues, students can also practice asking good questions in a related 20 Questions word game. One person (teacher or student) selects a target term. Students ask yes-or-no questions to guess the term ("Does your word have common Latin word parts in it?"). The goal is to guess the word in as few questions as possible.

## TROUBLESHOOTING

1. If you discover that students don't know the terms well enough to succeed with Clues and Questions, put the cards away until students have more opportunity to learn word meanings.
2. Support beginning English learners and struggling readers by pairing them with other students judiciously. Consider choosing with special care the terms for which they are to create clues.
3. Similarly, you can differentiate level of difficulty by providing different levels of terms to different groups of students. The difficulty of the clues can also be modified to adjust for student readiness.

## NEXT STEPS

1. Many other strategies in this text can form the basis of students' clues. Examples include Semantic Feature Analysis (p. 24), Sketch to Stretch (p. 28), and Semantic Gradients (p. 59). You can encourage practice of these word learning strategies by requiring students to use them in writing clues.
2. See Vocabulary Games (p. 73) for other ideas on practicing terms in game-like settings.
3. Send home cards for students to play with family members. This is especially easy if students type their cards and you print multiple copies. See Home Connections (p. 98) for more ideas for involving families in vocabulary learning.

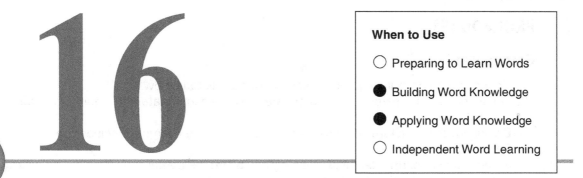

# Vocabulary Games

Girls aren't the only ones who want to have fun. The need for fun, according to Glasser (1986), is basic to all humans. Many games support vocabulary learning in an enjoyable setting by encouraging students to learn new words or to extend meanings for words they already know. Some classics, like charades or crossword puzzles, are readily available at no cost (many online), and there are plenty of commercially available board games that foster word learning. Figure 16.1 lists a number of board games that build word knowledge; all can support a positive attitude toward words and general vocabulary knowledge, and many can be modified for classroom use to support development of specific content vocabulary.

## PURPOSE

Games add to the linguistic richness of a learning-centered classroom (Blachowicz, Fisher, Ogle, & Watts-Taffe, 2006). Fisher and Blachowicz (2007) support the use of games to encourage word play. They note that students tend to be motivated to learn through games and that games can support metacognitive understandings of words. Further, games can be used at home to extend students' learning beyond the school day.

**Figure 16.1** Commercially available games that build and extend vocabulary knowledge, some with junior editions

- **Apples to Apples** (Play the card deemed the best match with the target term.)
- **Balderdash** (Give a definition for the obscure target term: Are you bluffing?)
- **Buzzword** (Guess your team's 10 words, given clues and a buzzword.)
- **Catchphrase** (Follow your teammate's clues to guess the term while the timer ticks.)
- **Cranium** (Guess words that your teammate sculpts in clay, draws, or acts out. Work with words in other ways, such as guessing definitions too.)
- **Lexogon** (Find a word that uses the clue letters in order but arranged in special ways.)
- **Password** (Guess your teammate's word given a single clue word.)
- **Pictionary** (Guess words that are drawn by your teammates.)
- **Questionary** (Ask yes-or-no questions to guess your teammate's word.)
- **Scattergories** (Fill out a category list, such as "animals," with words that start with specified letters.)
- **Taboo** (Describe the target term so that your partners can guess it, but don't use the five taboo words on the card.)
- **Outburst** (Guess as many words as you can on the card, all related to the same topic.)
- **Word Sweep** (Guess three words in a row that are consecutive dictionary entries.)

## PROCEDURES

### Getting Ready

1. Choose your vocabulary game. (Many options are listed below.)
2. Obtain necessary materials. If appropriate, prepare game materials required for your content.
3. Decide on the structure you'll use for game play. Some examples include the following:
   a. Individual or partner learning station (perhaps on the computer)
   b. Small-group learning station (A few students—perhaps early finishers—play while others engage a different learning activity.)
   c. Small groups all at once (All students play the same game in small groups, or each group plays a different game.)
   d. The whole class plays a game, perhaps as two opposing teams.

### During Class: Examples of Games That Support Word Building and Word Play (Applying Word Knowledge)

1. *Old favorites.* Traditional games like hangman, 20 Questions, and charades require little preparation and can easily be used with your content area vocabulary terms.
2. *Online vocabulary games.* A myriad are available at no cost. Promising sites include: http://www.vocabulary.com. Grade-level interactive word puzzles
   http://www.vocabulary.co.il/index_main.php. Learning Vocabulary Can Be Fun; interactive word games
   http://www.gamequarium.com/evocabulary.html. Vocabulary games
   http://www.crossword-puzzles.co.uk. Crossword puzzles from many sources
   http://www.quia.com/pages/worldowords.html. World of Words
3. *Game show vocabulary games.* Use your content to create versions of popular game shows such as Jeopardy and Who Wants to Be a Millionaire? using templates available online free. See examples available at Teacher Tools, http://www.internet4classrooms.com/teachertools.htm.
4. *Content-specific word puzzles.* Create crossword and other word puzzles with your own content using online puzzle creators. One site is http://www.crosswordpuzzlegames.com/create.html. Crossword puzzles are a great opener or sponge for spare moments. Online tools allow students to create their own puzzles quickly, focusing on the content instead of the format.
5. *Content vocabulary Apples to Apples.* In Apples to Apples, individual players are awarded points if the term on their card is judged as most closely matching that of the target term. Figure 16.2 shows how a sixth-grade teacher made her own social studies vocabulary version of the game.
6. *Vocabulary Taboo.* Prepare a set of cards. Each needs a target term and a few terms that may not be used in describing the target term. For example, one target term might be *oligarchy*. Taboo terms might be *rule*, *few*, and *king*. Players work in teams, with one person giving clues to help teammates guess the target term.
7. *Six-Word Memoirs.* Smith and Fershleiser's (2008) text, *Not Quite What I Was Planning: Six-Word Memoirs by Writers Famous and Obscure* can be used as a pattern for an intriguing exercise with words: Can students capture their stories in just six words? Which six words best explain their lives to date? Would it be "Not quite what I was planning?" or "Played all night. Slept through morning?" In a content vocabulary twist, students can create six-word memoirs of major target terms. A U.S. history student chose *conflict* as the target for her six-word memoir: "Sought freedom, clashed violently. Struggling still."

**Figure 16.2** Content vocabulary Apples to Apples: Ancient civilizations

---

**Preparation:** Use a flash-card template online or index cards to make two sets of word cards. Students can add to the stacks over the year.

- Set A: Approximately 200 cards, each with everyday nouns and adjectives (examples: powerful, salad plate, bumpy, and Sponge Bob).
- Set B: Approximately 30 social studies terms, printed on a color different from set A (examples: Hunter/gatherer, monotheism, oligarchy, silk roads).

**Play:**

1. Individuals play in small groups of approximately five or six.
2. Each player receives seven cards from set A. They don't show their cards to others.
3. During each round, one person acts as the judge. The judge rotates.
4. The judge turns over a card from set B.
5. All other players place one card from their hand face down in the center. They individually choose the word they feel most closely links with the set B target card.
6. The judge reads all cards and chooses the one he or she feels matches the target term best. The player who played the best-matching card receives 1 point. Play continues until a predetermined point value is reached. [See sample hand and sets below. The judge chooses "brash" as the winner because he reasoned that oligarchs would need to be brash to maintain their rule.]
7. Modifications: The judge can call for a word that matches the target term the worst.

**Sample Hand:**

Set B target term: Oligarchy

Set A cards played: Brash, Purple, Extinct, Powerful

---

 **TROUBLESHOOTING**

1. Steer clear of word searches; often more time is spent looking for letter combinations than in learning about words. If you do use word searches, make them available as one option rather than assigning them.
2. Many games rely on speed, and students with larger vocabularies are more likely to win. In addition, not all students respond positively to competition. For these reasons, set teams up carefully and be sure to vary the type of games you offer. No one likes every game.

## NEXT STEPS

Make at-home versions of your vocabulary games. Send home materials too. Rather than assigning questions at the end of a chapter, have students play Vocabulary Games with their family members. See Home Connections (p. 98) for other ways to involve families in Vocabulary Games.

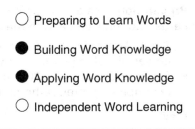

# Word Trees

New information is much easier to learn and often more interesting when we can relate it something that we already know (Ausubel, Novack, & Hanesian, 1978; Dole, Duffy, Roehler, & Pearson, 1991; Shapiro, 2004). For example, if students already have knowledge about spiders, it is much easier for them to remember related terms introduced during instruction. Students have considerable difficulty, however, when they can't relate new learning to their own experiences. When students do not have adequate background knowledge, it can be helpful to provide them with guidance on what things are most important to learn and how the information can be organized to make clear important relationships (McCrudden, Schraw, & Hartley, 2006; Wade, 1992). In Word Trees, students create a graphic that organizes information in ways that clarify the relationships among words and promotes the development of more sophisticated understandings of content area vocabulary.

## PURPOSE

Word Trees can be used for different purposes depending on the type of vocabulary that is being targeted and the ways in which the words are related. The most common use of Word Trees is to develop a graphic of families of words that are derived from the same root word. For example, students developing a Word Tree for the root word *geo* might include the words *geography*, *geologist*, and *geometry* in developing their tree. Word Trees can also be used to show the whole-to-part relationships that exist among some words. In this use of Word Trees, students might draw a flower (the whole) and label the parts (*stem, leaf, petals, stigma*). All forms of Word Trees have potential benefits. First, they provide a graphic that can facilitate students' understanding of how terms are related and the ways in which information can be organized. Second, Word Trees can be used to develop Morphemic Analysis (p. 106), an important strategy for supporting students' understanding of the semantic relationships among words. Finally, Word Trees can encourage students to take an interest in words and to develop the word consciousness necessary for independent word learning (Blachowicz & Fisher, 2004; Graves, 2000; Scott & Nagy, 2004).

## PROCEDURES

### Getting Ready

1. Choose the form of Word Trees that meets your purpose. Figure 17.1 provides the directions and an example for creating a Word Tree for root words. Figure 17.2 provides directions and an example for whole-to-part word relationships.
2. List the steps and post the requirements for students to use to complete their Word Trees. For example, you may want to provide students with a rubric for completing their

**Figure 17.1** Student directions and example for a Word Tree using root words

1. Draw a tree trunk.
2. Write the target root word and a definition on the trunk.
3. Add a branch to the tree for every word you can think of that contains the root word.
4. Write each word on a separate branch along with a definition.
5. Add a sentence using the word.
6. Add twigs to the branch for people you might hear using the word (optional).

Below is a Word Tree using root words that was created by a student studying *transportation*.

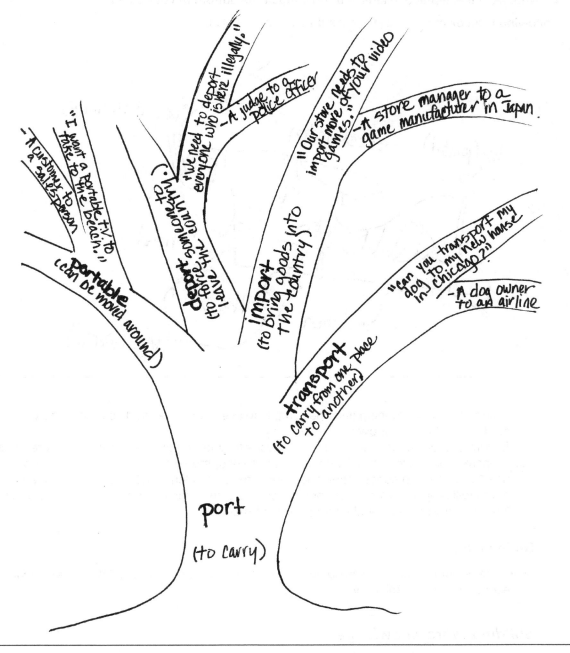

Word Trees that contains criteria such as the minimum number of words they must generate or the number of the details they must provide.

3. Create a sample Word Tree that meets your requirements.
4. Decide on group size. Although students may work individually, using partners or small groups increases opportunities for students to use the words in a variety of formats,

**Figure 17.2** Student directions and a sample drawing for a Word Tree using whole-to-part relationships

Use information from class discussions and other sources to complete the following steps:

1. On your paper, draw an outline of a(n) _____.
2. Identify the major parts or characteristics you will need to complete your drawing.
3. Add to your drawing the major parts or characteristics that you have identified and label them.
4. Write a sentence that explains your drawing at the bottom of your paper.

Following is an example of a student's drawing of a cricket.

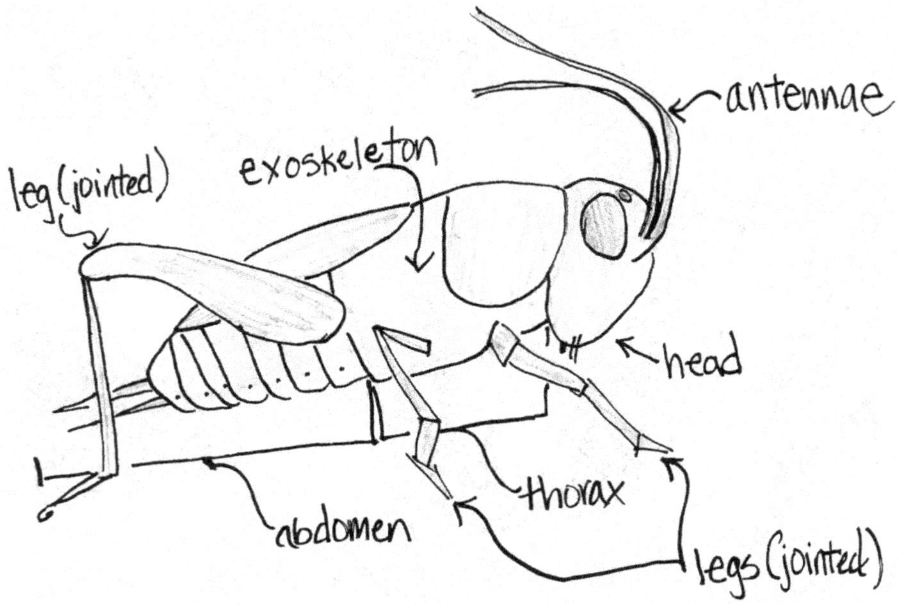

including in their listening and speaking. However, individual work is best if you want students to have their own copies.

5. Ensure that dictionaries and content sources (online or print) are available for reference.
6. Prepare Word Tree materials. If you intend to post students' Word Trees in the room, use 12- by 18-inch construction paper and provide students with markers. If the students will prepare Word Trees for individual use, they can use notebook paper or 8- by 11-inch drawing paper and either pencils or markers.

## During Class

Word Trees help students in *Building Word Knowledge* and *Applying Word Knowledge* by representing words graphically.

### *Building Word Knowledge*

1. Share your sample Word Tree. Lead a discussion of the features of the Word Tree. Ask students to assess your example using the posted list of requirements or rubric.
2. Provide students with target terms. If you are using a Word Tree with root words, you can assign a target root to either the whole class, small groups, or individuals. You may also want to consider letting individuals or groups choose a target root from several you have preselected. If using the whole-to-part form of Word Trees, the usual procedure is

**Figure 17.3** A whole-to-part graphic organizer for *estuary*

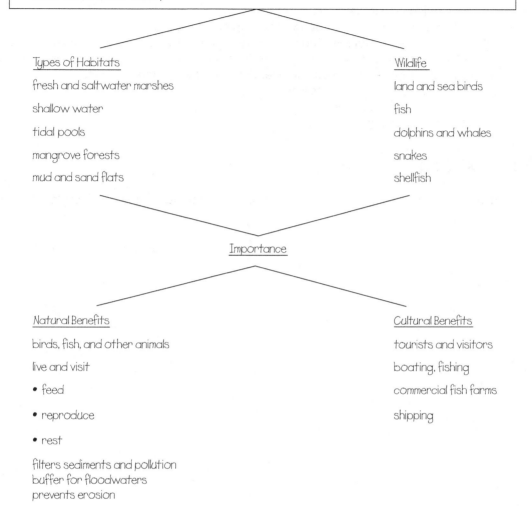

Estuary

Definition: A semienclosed body of water where freshwater from rivers and streams and salt-water mix (brackish water)

Types of Habitats
fresh and saltwater marshes
shallow water
tidal pools
mangrove forests
mud and sand flats

Wildlife
land and sea birds
fish
dolphins and whales
snakes
shellfish

Importance

Natural Benefits
birds, fish, and other animals
live and visit
• feed
• reproduce
• rest
filters sediments and pollution
buffer for floodwaters
prevents erosion

Cultural Benefits
tourists and visitors
boating, fishing
commercial fish farms
shipping

to have the whole class working on the same target term. However, if you were teaching a unit on insects, you could allow students to choose a specific insect to use in developing their Word Trees. In this version, after students have completed their Word Trees, they compare and contrast the features they included for individual insects to look for similarities and differences across all the insect drawings.

## Applying Word Knowledge

1. Ask students to refer to individual or posted Word Trees frequently.
2. Encourage students to apply their knowledge from Word Trees as they study for exams, write, or talk about the content.

## MODIFICATION

Sometimes a drawing is not adequate to capture all the categories of information in whole-to-part relationships. Consider having students construct a Word Tree graphic organizer instead of creating a drawing. Figure 17.3 shows a Word Tree graphic organizer that a student is creating for the term *estuary*.

## TROUBLESHOOTING

1. If students work in groups, address accountability concerns. Some ideas to ensure that all students participate include the following:
   a. Assign jobs
   b. Give individual tests on the terms
   c. Require peer and self-ratings of group performance
2. Although we encourage students to create their own drawings because it promotes active engagement, some may be reluctant to draw. There are Web resources that provide templates that you can use. For example, try the following:
   http://www.allaboutdrawings.com
   http://www.geology.com/nsta
   http://www.biology-resources.com

## NEXT STEPS

If you are using Word Trees for root words, see also Morphemic Analysis (p. 106).

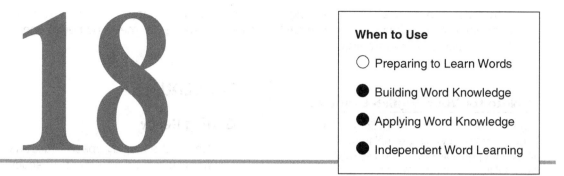

# Word Walls

Word Walls are large displays of carefully selected target terms. New words are added over time, so collections are cumulative and familiar words remain in view. Teacher and students use the words repeatedly through a variety of guided activities that help students understand and use the words well. Students also refer to Word Wall terms in their speaking and independent reading and writing activities.

Frequently used in the teaching of phonics in early literacy classrooms (e.g., Cunningham, 2005), Word Walls are increasingly used by content area teachers who wish to capitalize on their simplicity, versatility, and power for helping students enrich, reinforce, and apply their vocabulary through spoken and written language. Figure 18.1 presents a Word Wall used in a junior high school cooking class during a unit on kitchen equipment and food preparation techniques.

## PURPOSE

"Word walls offer great potential for transferring responsibility and control for reading and writing from teacher to students" (Brabham & Villaume, 2001, p. 700). They do so by serving as scaffolds in two ways. First, Word Walls provide visual reminders of target terms. Second, activities using Word Wall terms serve as conversational supports that help students comprehend

**Figure 18.1** A portion of a Word Wall from a junior high cooking class unit on kitchen equipment and food preparation techniques

| A–G | H–M | N–R | S–Z |
|-----|-----|-----|-----|
| baster | ladle | pastry blender | sauté |
| colander | marinate | peeler | sieve |
| cream | mince | pressure cooker | slotted spoon |
| cut in | scald | rubber scraper | spatula |
| double boiler | | | strainer |
| fold in | | | turner |
| | | | whip |

terms, develop nuanced understandings of them, build links among them, and apply them independently. Word Walls are highly versatile and can be adapted to meet the needs and interests found in particular classrooms.

 **PROCEDURES**

### Getting Ready

1. Select the display space. Bulletin boards are often used, but any free space can work. Other choices are magnetic whiteboards (which allow for annotations made in dry-erase markers) and carpeted walls. Vallejo (2006) uses two display spaces: one for words that are under active study (e.g., from the current unit) and one for inactive words. These are words that were previously introduced but are no longer the focus of instruction.

2. Select the terms. Include key terms from the upcoming unit and consider allowing student input as well.

3. By hand or computer, print the terms on card stock large enough so that they can be seen from everywhere in the room. Attach magnets to the back if you will be using them on a magnetic board; use Velcro if the display wall is carpeted.

4. Decide how words will be organized on the board. Often they are arranged in alphabetical categories, but other categories, such as semantic groupings, may work equally well.

### During Class

#### Building Word Knowledge

Use the cards to build understanding of the terms, perhaps by using activities such as the following:

1. Introduce terms using Word Wall cards. You might write definitions on the backs of terms, act out the definitions, talk about the terms' histories (see Word Histories, p. 115), or analyze the terms' parts (see Morphemic Analysis, p. 106).

2. Encourage students to compare and contrast terms. Ask, "How are my two terms alike? How are they different? Find your own contrasting words from the Word Wall."

3. Discuss multiple meanings. A glance at the terms in Figure 18.1 serves as a reminder that many content specific terms have multiple meanings. In fact, Bromley (2007) notes that 70% of the most commonly used English words have multiple meanings. Ask, "Who can find a word with more than one meaning?"

4. Build graphic organizers using a subset of cards. Have students move the terms around and add annotations such as arrows or other images to clarify meaning. For example, in a science class, students might create food webs with Word Wall cards to demonstrate energy flow through organisms (Stairs, 2007). Semantic Maps (p. 37) work well in many content areas.

5. Practice Word Wall terms during sponge times, such as during the last few minutes of class. For example, dismiss students at the end of class using the Word Wall: "Today guessing my Word Wall term is your ticket out. Here's your clue. Which Word Wall term [from Figure 18.1] is a close cousin to a *strainer*?" Allow students to present clues too.

**Figure 18.2** Sample form used by a junior high student during a peer teaching session about the class's Word Wall terms

| One word I know well: | Foggy word: |
|---|---|
| ladle | baster |
| One word I know well: | Foggy word: |
| colander | fold in |

## *Applying Word Knowledge*

Once students have learned basic meanings for the terms, provide opportunities to practice and apply Word Wall terms in a variety of contexts. Here are sample activities:

1. Help students link terms. "Who can come up and find two words related to my target term? Arrange them to demonstrate their connections." Next, invite another student to link yet another term. How many links can students find?
2. Encourage oral application of words. Say, "Turn to your partner and tell a brief story that uses at least four terms from our Word Wall. The funnier the better!"
3. Encourage students to use terms in their writing. For a simple activity, say, "Write a three-sentence summary of today's lesson using at least three words from the Word Wall."
4. Have students write Poetry (p. 149), such as haiku, using target terms.

## *Independent Word Learning*

Students can use Word Walls to continue their learning of terms during independent activities as well. For example, try these activities:

1. Encourage students to refer to the Word Wall for correct spelling of terms in their writing.
2. Invite students to create personal Word Walls to explore words of interest. Students' personal Word Walls can include mini versions of the class Word Wall and should include personally selected terms too.
3. Use peer teaching to foster comprehension of Word Wall terms, perhaps as follows: "Take a look at the Word Wall. Find two words you know best. Write them down and jot down some reminders or a sketch to accompany those words. Then find two about which you are foggy. Write them down. Now circulate, looking for a peer who can help with your foggy terms and helping peers with the words you know well." (Figure 18.2 gives a sample form used by a junior high student in cooking class.) Monitor and clarify as needed.

 ## MODIFICATIONS

1. Use color to provide clues about the words such as the units from which they were drawn or the larger semantic categories to which they belong. For instance, the Word Wall terms in Figure 18.1 could be printed in two colors: one for kitchen

equipment and one for food preparation techniques. Use colors to print the words themselves or print the words in black but use a different color of paper or a colored border.

2. Have students write the terms on cards. They may print them in a manner that hints at the terms' meanings (Vallejo, 2006).
3. Invite students to brainstorm words related to the content to be included on the Word Wall and then arrange them so that visual presentation supports the meaning of the terms (Buckelew, 2003).
4. Have students bring in actual items from home that can be used to represent terms on the Word Wall (Chanko, 2005). This can encourage home-school connections if family members help students select items.

 ## TROUBLESHOOTING

1. Be clear on the purpose of the Word Wall. Keep content area Word Walls separate from your general literacy Word Wall if you have one. They serve different purposes.
2. Words need to be appropriate for the students in your class. Select target terms carefully and develop each thoroughly.
3. Word Walls should be interactive or they will not provide effective scaffolding for students. Be sure to provide opportunities for students to interact with the displayed terms.
4. Introduce new words gradually to ensure that students can incorporate them into their memory and avoid becoming overwhelmed.

## NEXT STEPS

See Vocab Cards (p. 50) for a related strategy that gives additional uses of words on Word Walls.

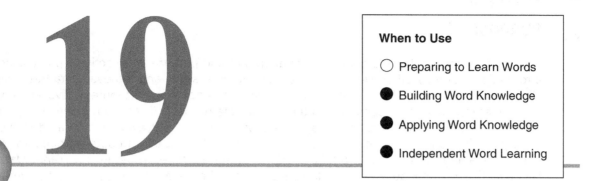

# Data Retrieval Charts

Data Retrieval Charts are graphic organizers that present information about selected characteristics of concepts that belong to the same family (Taba, Durkin, Fraenkel, & McNaughton, 1971). Like spreadsheets, the charts arrange specific information related to one topic in rows and columns. A single chart addresses one class of ideas, such as *biomes, whales, countries, coins,* or *planets.* Typically, the rows list examples, or exemplars, of the class (such as *Mercury* and *Mars* on a *planets* chart), and columns present characteristics (such as, for the *planet* chart, *structure* and *orbital period*). Data Retrieval Charts help students delve into the details of a concept and compare its attributes to those of another member of the class. To assist students in learning new content terms, then, Data Retrieval Charts provide deep information at different levels. Figure 19.1 presents a Data Retrieval Chart for planets in our solar system.

**Figure 19.1** A Data Retrieval Chart on planets

| Planet | Structure | Orbital period (in Earth years) | Myth and culture |
|---|---|---|---|
| Mercury | Rocky<br>Metallic core<br>Middle rocky layer<br>Brittle crust<br>Probably iron | 0.24 years | Mercury = Roman god of commerce and travel<br>Greek counterpart (Hermes) = The messenger of the gods<br>Probably named Mercury because it travels quickly across the sky |
| Mars | Rocky<br>By inference:<br>Dense core<br>Molten rocky mantle<br>Thin crust<br>Highly varied surface<br>Volcanoes<br>Canyons | 1.89 years | Mars = Roman mythology<br>God of war<br>Probably named for its red color<br>Hindu: associated with war god Karttikeya |
| Jupiter | Gaseous<br>Hydrogen<br>Helium<br>Probably<br>    rocky core | 11.86 years | Jupiter = Roman mythology<br>King of heaven, earth, and gods<br>Jupiter is largest planet in our solar system |

**PURPOSE**

Charts of all sorts help us organize information and find patterns in it, actively processing information that may otherwise be more difficult to sort, store, and retrieve. Data Retrieval Charts are most useful for helping students explore in detail the attributes of vocabulary terms that represent new concepts. In the *planet* Data Retrieval Chart from Figure 19.1, for example, students learn about the major concept, *planets*, about exemplars related to the topic given in the rows (*Mercury, Mars,* and *Jupiter*), and about the attributes suggested by column headings (*structure, orbital period, myth and culture*). Thus, in the *planet* Data Retrieval Chart from Figure 19.1, students learn about the major concept, *planets*, by examining how the exemplars (*Mercury, Mars,* and *Jupiter*) are the same and different across the characteristics given in the column headings (*structure, orbital period,* and *myth and culture*). Graphic Organizers that group and organize ideas help students see how ideas are related to an overarching concept (Galavan & Kottler, 2007). The charts also help students compare and contrast ideas, so they are also called Comparison Charts and Compare/Contrast Matrices.

Because they present information in such a logically organized way, Data Retrieval Charts can support the writing process. The charts provide an overall structure for the topic, and they allow students to make decisions about how to organize their writing. For instance, students can explore different characteristics of one exemplar, or they can compare and contrast one or more attributes for multiple conceptual exemplars. Finally, many students, including those with learning disabilities, find strategies that help them paraphrase and summarize to be helpful (Gajria, Jitendra, Sood, & Sacks, 2007). Data Retrieval Charts are one such organizer.

**PROCEDURES**

### Getting Ready

1. Determine the major class of ideas and possible exemplars of that topic. Figure 19.2 gives a variety of possible topics for Data Retrieval Charts across the curriculum.

**Figure 19.2** Possible concepts for Data Retrieval Charts from across the curriculum

| Curricular area | Concept | Exemplars | Characteristics |
|---|---|---|---|
| History and social science | Early civilizations | Mesopotamia<br>Egypt<br>Kush | Geography<br>Political structures<br>Economic structures<br>Social structures<br>Culture |
| Mathematics | Solid figures | Cube<br>Sphere<br>Cone<br>Cylinder | Surface area<br>Volume |
| Science | Vertebrates | Fish<br>Birds<br>Mammals<br>Amphibians<br>Reptiles | Body coverings<br>Physical structure<br>Reproduction<br>Habitat |
| Engineering | Engines | Internal combustion<br>Steam<br>Stirling | Power<br>Structure<br>Efficiency<br>Fuel<br>Emissions |

**Figure 19.3** Two sample Data Retrieval Charts

Topic _____

| Feature | X | Y | Z |
|---------|---|---|---|
| 1 | | | |
| 2 | | | |
| 3 | | | |

Major concept _____

| | Characteristic 1 | Characteristic 2 | Characteristic 3 |
|---|---|---|---|
| Exemplar 1 | | | |
| Exemplar 2 | | | |
| Exemplar 3 | | | |

2. Prepare a blank organizer. Use a blank paper/pencil chart or create a large space on a bulletin board to which students can add their information. You may also choose to use a spreadsheet or an interactive whiteboard to create the chart (Brabeck, Fisher, & Pitler, 2004; Painter, Whiting, & Wolters, 2005). Figure 19.3 presents two blank organizers.
3. Decide whether every student will complete an entire chart or whether partners or small groups will be responsible for completing a single cell, row, or column and contribute it to a class chart.

## During Class

Data Retrieval Charts are appropriate for use in many phases: *Building Word Knowledge, Applying Word Knowledge,* and *Independent Word Learning.*

### Building Word Knowledge

1. Share a sample completed Data Retrieval Chart (perhaps Figure 19.1), discussing its structure and benefits.
2. Discuss the students' responsibility in completing the chart, either during reading or other input activities or later.
3. Model completion of a row or column of the chart that pertains to your content.
4. Allow students to complete the chart in its entirety or their smaller piece of the chart.

*Applying Word Knowledge*

1. Leave the chart posted and refer to it in order to review and apply newer concepts. Discuss its benefits as a study tool.
2. Require students to work with information in the chart in order to use their knowledge of words. Students, alone or in partners or small groups, might be encouraged to prepare oral presentations or writings that require different uses of information on the chart, such as the following:
   - An overview of the characteristics that vary for the chosen topic (What are the major characteristics of this topic? How many exemplars are there?)
   - A detailed accounting of the information within just one cell of the chart
   - A report on one column of the chart, comparing several exemplars on one characteristic
   - A report on one row of the chart, addressing several characteristics of one exemplar

## *Independent Word Learning*

Teach students to use Data Retrieval Charts as an independent word learning strategy when appropriate, as in Vocabulary Self-Collection Strategy (p. 54) and I-Search a Word reports (p. 163).

 ## MODIFICATION

Allow students to include visual information (drawings), in addition to words, in their Data Retrieval Charts (Spencer & Guillaume, 2006).

## NEXT STEPS

1. Use Data Retrieval Charts to help organize Student-Made Books (p. 145), to inform Poetry (p. 149), or to assist with script development for Readers Theater presentations (p. 140). Students also may also choose to record terms from their charts in their Word Journals (p. 89).
2. See Semantic Feature Analysis (p. 24) for another graphic that can be used to compare and contrast exemplars across characteristics.

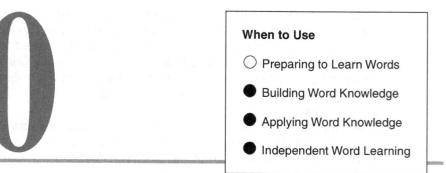

**When to Use**

○ Preparing to Learn Words

● Building Word Knowledge

● Applying Word Knowledge

● Independent Word Learning

# Word Journals

Word Journals are personal dictionaries that can help students expand their knowledge of vocabulary. Students can record unfamiliar words and phrases in their journal, or they can choose to write words they have learned but want to have access to over the long term. Word Journals are very versatile. For example, the terms selected for Word Journals can be placed in alphabetical order as in a traditional dictionary or they can be put into categories. In addition, students can include definitions, synonyms, antonyms, related words, pictures, or any other information that supports their learning. Words are added to Word Journals over time, so the collection is cumulative. Thus, Word Journals can be developed for a unit of study, for a semester, or for an entire year if desired. Students can refer to their Word Journals in speaking and independent reading and writing activities. Teachers can also use Word Journals as an assessment of students' vocabulary learning (Blachowicz & Fisher, 2002).

## PURPOSE

Word Journals have many potential benefits. First, because both students and teachers have input into the design of Word Journals, they are more likely to meet students' individual needs. Second, Word Journals can encourage students to take an interest in words and to develop the word consciousness necessary for independent word learning (Blachowicz & Fisher, 2004; Graves, 2000; Scott & Nagy, 2004). Third, Word Journals promote word study skills and support students in making connections with content vocabulary. Finally, Word Journals provide students with a resource they can use to review the meanings of target terms and to select words for use in speaking and writing.

## PROCEDURES

### Getting Ready

1. Decide the purpose and the time frame for using Word Journals. Some questions to consider follow:
   a. How long will students be collecting words in their journals? During the time it takes to complete a unit? Longer?
   b. Will you require students to include target terms that you provide to them? If so, how many? We suggest that you limit the list of terms to those that are essential. Fewer is better. Once students learn how to use the journals, the emphasis should be on student selection.
   c. What is the minimum number of new words, including any required terms, students should record during the time period you selected?
   d. How often will students make entries? Every day? Every 2 or 3 days? Once a week?

2. To teach students to use Word Journals, you will need a list of content terms from a text or other materials that students will read. The list should include both familiar and unfamiliar words. Limit the number of words that you choose to five or fewer.

3. Decide what students' Word Journal entries must include. Consider your students' age, background knowledge, and your goals in using Word Journals in making your choices. At a minimum, consider requiring the following:
   a. The word.
   b. A definition of the word. We recommend having students write the definition in their own words rather than simply copying it from a dictionary when possible.
   c. The original context in which the word was found.
   d. An original sentence using the word.

   Other word entry options include the following:
   a. An image from a magazine, clip art, or a drawing to support the term's meaning.
   b. Synonyms, antonyms, or related words.
   c. Word Histories (p. 115).
   d. Word parts (see Morphemic Analysis, p. 106).

4. List and post the requirements for students. Figure 20.1 gives a civics teacher's Word Journal assignment sheet for a unit of the U.S. federal government.

5. Create a sample Word Journal entry that meets your requirements. Figure 20.2 shows the civics teacher's Word Journal entry for the term *bicameral*. In addition to the required features, the teacher chose to include the optional feature: word parts.

6. Ensure that dictionaries and glossaries (online or print) are available for reference.

**Figure 20.1** A civics teacher's Word Journal assignment for a unit on the U.S. federal government

---

**U.S. Federal Government Word Journal**

Your Word Journal is a great way to help you remember the new vocabulary you are learning in our unit on the U.S. federal government. Each of the words or phrases you record in your journal will follow a similar pattern. For each entry you will provide the following information:

1. The word or phrase.
2. The sentence you read or heard that contained the word or phrase.
3. The dictionary or glossary definition that best matches the meaning in the sentence where you found the word. Don't just copy the definition! Try to write it using your own words.
4. A new sentence that you create for the word. Make sure that the word has the same meaning as it did in the original sentence.

*Important!* Your entry needs to include *one* more item. Choose *one* item from the list below that you think will provide you with the most help in remembering the word and its meaning. Words are different, so the same item will not work for every word. Make thoughtful choices.

- An image taken from clip art, a magazine, or other sources that explain the meaning of the word
- A drawing that explains the meaning
- A synonym or antonym of the word
- Words that are related to the word you are learning
- Word parts and their meanings
- The origins of the word

You will know that you are finished when your entry has five items.

*By the end of the unit, you should have between 15 and 20 entries in your Word Journal.*

**Figure 20.2** A Word Journal entry for the word *bicameral*

---

*bicameral*

*Original sentence:* The founding fathers of the United States favored a bicameral legislature.

*Definition:* A legislature that has two houses or chambers

*My sentence:* In the United States, we have a bicameral system that has a House of Representatives and a Senate.

*Word parts:* bi = two and camera = chamber.

---

7. Decide what materials you will use for the Word Journals. Many teachers use spiral-ringed notebooks, or they have students make their journals by creating a construction paper cover that is stapled over several pieces of notebook paper. If students create their own stapled journals, make sure that they contain enough paper to hold all the entries that are required plus extra for those students who want to collect more words than the minimum.

## During Class

Word Journals are useful vocabulary tools during three phases: *Building Word Knowledge, Applying Word Knowledge,* and *Independent Word Learning.*

### Building Word Knowledge

1. Discuss the purpose of Word Journals with students and the assignment requirements.
2. Share your sample Word Journal entry. Lead a discussion of elements of the entry. Ask students to assess it using the list of requirements on the assignment sheet.
3. Present students with the required words they will be using as their first entries in their Word Journals. After they have finished reading the text that contains the words, have them choose one of the words to enter into their journals. Having a choice in selecting the first word supports student motivation and engagement. The other required words can be entered during independent work or as homework.
4. Provide time and materials for students to complete their Word Journal entries.
5. Ask students to present their Word Journal entries to a partner. Invite a few students to share with the class. Invite discussion of the words by asking students questions about their entries: Why did you choose this word as your first entry? What does it mean? Why is it important to the lesson? Is there another context in which the word might be used? How is your word related to the other required words?
6. After students have made scheduled entries in their journals, invite some of them to share one or two of the words that they have chosen. Discuss the reasons for their choices and how the meanings of the words relate to the big ideas in the text.

### Applying Word Knowledge

1. Provide opportunities for students to refer to their journals frequently and to use journal words in discussions and in written work.
2. At an appropriate time during a unit of study have students create a Semantic Map (p. 37) in their journals that reflects the relationships among words they have collected. Make transparencies of some of their maps and use them for class discussion and review.
3. Having students place Word Journal words in categories is a worthy activity as well. Figure 20.3 shows some of the categories a fifth-grade student developed for

**Figure 20.3** Some of the negative mood categories created from Word Journal entries collected from *A Single Shard*

| Emotion words | How things sound |
|---|---|
| impatience | droning |
| scorn | squelching |
| placid | sharp |
| rejected | |
| **How things feel** | **How things appear** |
| throbbing | bulging |
| sluggardly | cumbersome |
| weary | incised |
| | shriveled |

"Words That Create a Negative Mood" using the Word Journal entries she collected from the novel *A Single Shard* (Park, 2001).

*Independent Word Learning*

1. As students become more proficient in choosing important terms for their journals, consider reducing the number of required words. This will support students in becoming independent, self-regulated learners.
2. Encourage students to keep special interest Word Journals in which students collect new or interesting words of their choice from a variety of written and oral sources. For example, a student who is learning English may want to collect words that are valuable in social interactions or words that are idioms. Students with a deep interest in a specific topic like technology or music may want to keep a Word Journal devoted to terms from these domains. Consider using words from special interests as word-of-the-day words. Students can also create special interest PowerPoint presentations or Student-Made Books (p. 145) that include important terms from their Word Journals.

## MODIFICATION

Have students record what they think a word means before they look it up in the dictionary. If the predicted definition is correct, have them put a check mark beside it and omit the requirement to write the dictionary definition.

## TROUBLESHOOTING

1. Check students' Word Journal entries to ensure that the terms are spelled correctly and that the definitions and other information are accurate.
2. If you use Word Journal entries as an assessment of vocabulary growth, you will want to take into consideration differences in student reading levels, English proficiency, and background knowledge. You may need to modify requirements for some students.

## NEXT STEPS

Word Journal entries can be used to create Word Posters (p. 159) or Vocabulary Graffiti (p. 155).

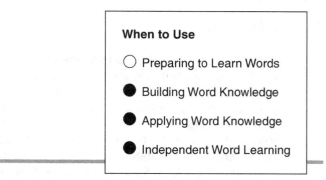

# Dictionaries

Did you know that when William Shakespeare was writing his sonnets and plays there were no English-language dictionaries? That means that he could not look up the meaning of a word, check to see if he had spelled it correctly, or search for a synonym that might help him express his ideas more precisely (Johnson, 2001). Although dictionaries have been around since about 2000 B.C., most of the early dictionaries were developed to help readers and writers of one language find words in a second language. It was not until 1755, when Samuel Johnson's *Dictionary of the English Language* was published, that dictionaries took on the role of providing meanings, spellings, and pronunciations. Today the components of an entry and the role of regular dictionaries remains largely the same as those reflected in Johnson's *Dictionary of the English Language*. However, in addition to regular dictionaries, today we also have a wide variety of special-purpose dictionaries that both you and your students may find useful. Many general-purpose dictionaries and special-purpose dictionaries have both print and electronic versions. Figure 21.1 lists some Internet sites that provide access to electronic versions of either general-purpose or special-purpose dictionaries or to both. Providing students with dictionary skills affords them a word learning tool that will be useful throughout their lives.

**Figure 21.1** Internet sites for different types of dictionaries

http://thesaurus.reference.com. Provides access to a thesaurus (synonyms), general-use dictionary, and an encyclopedia

http://www.bartleby.com. A database that includes dictionaries, a thesaurus, quotations, and works of fiction and nonfiction

http://www.clichesite.com. Provides definitions and explanations of clichés, euphemisms, and figures of speech

http://www.merriam-webster.com. Provides access to a general-use dictionary, thesaurus, translation dictionaries, subject matter dictionaries, and word games

http://www.onelook.com. A database with word definitions from multiple general dictionaries and specialized dictionaries such as a reverse dictionary (meaning to word), related word dictionary, slang dictionary, subject matter dictionary, and translation dictionaries.

http://www.rhymezone.com. Database with rhymes, synonyms, definitions, homophones, and more

http://www.synonym.com. Provides synonyms, antonyms, and definitions

http://www.yourdictionary.com. Provides access to general-use dictionaries and thesauri, synonym dictionaries, translation dictionaries, subject matter dictionaries, word games, and more

## PURPOSE

Reference books such as dictionaries can be a valuable resource to help students develop word meanings, but they are best used in conjunction with other vocabulary strategies, such as Context Clues (p. 124), Morphemic Analysis (p. 106), Concept of Definition Word Map (p. 9), or the Frayer Model (p. 18). This is true for several reasons. First, having students look up the meaning of words in a dictionary is often ineffective because many definitions are not precise. For example, the definition of *geologist* might be "a person who studies geology." This definition is accurate but provides no help to a student who does not already know the definition of *geology*. Second, many students have difficulty selecting the correct definition for a particular context from the several that are given. Third, students need to be shown how definitions are related to what they already know in order to apply them to subsequent learning. Finally, studies on vocabulary development indicate that having students look up definitions of words in a dictionary does not by itself increase comprehension (Nagy & Scott, 2000; Roe, Stoodt-Hill, & Burns, 2004).

However, when students are given supportive instruction in how to use a dictionary effectively, it can become an important word learning tool (Gardner, 2007). For example, with instruction and guidance, most students can learn how to choose the most appropriate meaning for a particular context and to look up the meanings of key words in definitions if they are unknown. Scholfield (1982) suggests that students need to develop the skills in Figure 21.2 in order to use a dictionary effectively.

## PROCEDURES

### Getting Ready

1. Decide the purpose for having students use either a general- or a special-purpose dictionary. Will you be teaching students how to use a dictionary or a thesaurus? Will they use the dictionary to check the meaning of unknown words in context? Or will they develop a definition of a term as they create a Concept of Definition Word Map (p. 9)?
2. Select the content to be addressed and which and how many vocabulary terms students will learn. Remember to limit the number of terms to a small set.
3. Decide what format you will use to teach students. If your purpose is to teach students to use a dictionary or other word resource, consider using direct instruction or a strategy that has a game-like structure. Students often find games motivating, and this may help them engage more actively. If you intend to integrate instruction in dictionary skills into another word learning strategy, choose the strategy you will be using. For instance, you might choose KIM Charts (p. 121), Word Chains (p. 67), or Word Decisions (p. 63).
4. Prepare any materials that are necessary for instruction. Students will need to have access to print or online dictionaries. Decide whether you want all students to use the same dictionary source or whether they can choose from a variety.

**Figure 21.2** Scholfield's (1982) suggestions of the understandings students need to use a dictionary effectively

1. Know when you need to use a dictionary (knowing that you don't know the meaning of the word)
2. Know how to locate the word in the dictionary
3. Know the parts of a dictionary entry
4. Choose among multiple meanings
5. Apply the meaning in new contexts

### During Class: Examples of Dictionary Instruction and Games

The following instructional strategies and games can help students with many phases of vocabulary learning: *Building Word Knowledge*, *Applying Word Knowledge*, and *Independent Word Knowledge*.

1.  If your students are new to dictionaries, talk about their layout and structure. You might, for instance, project a dictionary page or provide each student with a page. Then ask students to observe and share what they notice. Sample questions include the following:
    a.  What does every page have in common?
    b.  How are the words ordered?
    c.  What happens when two words start with the same letter?
    d.  Look at two entries. How are they the same?
    e.  Where in the dictionary can I find what various symbols (such as those in the pronunciations) mean?
    Use students' findings as the basis for direct instruction.

2.  Strategies in this book often require students to write a definition of a word, to predict the meaning of an unknown term, or to provide a synonym or antonym. Examples of such strategies follow:
    a.  Semantic Maps (p. 37)
    b.  Possible Sentences (p. 14)
    c.  Analogies (p. 111)
    d.  Word Histories (p. 115)
    e.  Context Clues (p. 124)
    These vocabulary strategies can easily be modified to include instruction on using dictionaries. For example, if students are predicting the meaning of unknown words from the context, you can guide them in how to use the dictionary to check the accuracy of their predictions. This type of instruction can help students gain insights into how the context can help them choose the correct dictionary definition for an unknown word when several are given.

3.  There are a number of game-like activities that help students to develop effective dictionary skills. Figure 21.3 provides one example. See Vocabulary Games (p. 73) for others.

**Figure 21.3** Sample game-like activity for developing dictionary skills.

---

**Steps for Dictionary Entry Search (Smith, 1983)**

1.  Students form groups of four.
2.  One person is chosen to record the group's responses.
3.  Each student is provided with the same page of the dictionary.
4.  Students are asked to focus on the entry of only one word, such as the word *corpulent*.
5.  The teacher tells the students the number of pieces of information that she or he found about the word—how to pronounce it, several definitions, the etymology, and so on. The teacher challenges the students to match or beat the number of pieces of information that the teacher found.
6.  In 10 minutes or less, students list all the information that they collected about the word from the dictionary entry and about the order in which the information was given.
7.  The teacher invites students to share the information they found and to compare it with that found by the teacher.

---

## ⦿ MODIFICATION

To encourage word consciousness and an interest in words, make dictionaries available in your class library. Model their use yourself. Allow students to read a dictionary—either a general one or one that is specific to your content—during silent reading time and talk about their interesting finds. Offer to post new word treasures on your Word Wall (p. 81).

## ⦿ TROUBLESHOOTING

1. Higher-achieving students often develop effective dictionary skills more quickly than average and struggling learners (Gardner, 2007). Plan on providing extra support for students who are not high achievers.
2. Students who struggle with spelling sometimes ask, "But how can I look it up if I don't know how to spell it?" Introduce phonetic dictionaries, organized by how words sound and not how they are spelled, as a classroom tool available to all. Be sure to quietly encourage their use for students who particularly need spelling support.
3. With the prevalence of wireless technology, many students have access to online dictionaries instantaneously via cell phone, personal digtal assistant, or laptop computer. Decide when students are allowed to use online dictionaries and when they are to use those in print. We recommend ensuring that students have skills with print-based dictionaries—and keeping those skills alive with occasional practice—but we also encourage use of the most efficient tool as well. Discuss with students the strengths and drawbacks of each type of dictionary and when it might be most appropriate to use each one.
4. Remember to keep dictionary work sessions brief and lively. Gone are the days of students copying lengthy, obscure definitions of long lists of unfamiliar terms into their notes.

## ⦿ NEXT STEPS

1. Have students produce their own dictionaries. Picture dictionaries can be developed in specific subject areas, such as art, mechanics, and various aspects of biology. Language learners can benefit from creating personal picture dictionaries that include both pictures and definitions in both their native language and the new language they are learning. You can have students view online picture dictionaries to get ideas for developing their own. Internet sites that provide resources and ideas for developing picture dictionaries follow:
   http://www.pdictionary.com. A free online picture dictionary
   http://www.adobe.com/education/digkids/lessons/index.html. Lesson plans and ideas for using digital photography to enhance learning
   http://www.getty.edu/education/for_teachers/curricula. Ideas for using works of art to teach vocabulary
2. Whitfield (1993) had English learners create slang dictionaries for other students acquiring English. The steps she used in creating the dictionaries are in Figure 21.4. Idiom dictionaries would also be particularly helpful for English learners.
3. Related to dictionaries by their organization, alphabet books exist for a myriad of topics. Find some related to your content and use them as Content Area Read Alouds (p. 135) or have students create them as Student-Made Books (p. 145).
4. See Word Journals (p. 89) for another example of student-made reference guides.

**Figure 21.4** Steps for developing a slang dictionary (Whitfield, 1993)

1. Consult a general-use dictionary to determine the format and the type of entry that will be used. Whitfield's students decided that English learners needed more than the word and the definition. They included the pronunciation and a sample sentence. Origins of the words were optional.
2. Each student is expected to submit at least two words. In order to be considered for the dictionary, an entry must include the student's name.
3. Once all entries are submitted, they are arranged alphabetically by the students and given to the teacher.
4. The teacher projects on a screen all the words that have been submitted. If a word received multiple entries, those are counted. Students decide how to handle multiple entries. For example, if entries reflect two different meanings of the same word, both are kept. If two or more entries give identical information, students vote for the entry that will be included in the dictionary.
5. Students choose a title, design the cover page, and pick which font will be used to type the entries. All students participate in typing the entries.
6. Once the typing is complete, copies are made, and students put together the books.

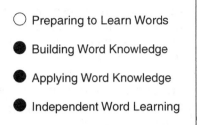

**When to Use**

○ Preparing to Learn Words

● Building Word Knowledge

● Applying Word Knowledge

● Independent Word Learning

# Home Connections

Parents and other family members exert a powerful influence on students' literacy development. All families, though, need support in continuing to foster their children's language development and content learning, particularly as students progress through the grades and gain the independence of adolescence. Through Home Connections, you can implement engaging activities that extend vocabulary learning beyond the classroom walls and into the nonschool contexts where students spend the majority of their day. In building family participation in content area literacy, choose several options from a variety of types of Home Connections:

1. Providing information
2. Encouraging rich home literacy environments
3. Interactive homework
4. Parents as experts
5. Families at school

## PURPOSE

Family contributions to students' early literacy are very well documented. Research suggests that parents' influence on students' literacy development begins no later than infancy, and the effects of early literacy efforts last for years. Figure 22.1 shares some of those positive effects.

There is less research on parents' continuing influence in older students' literacy development outside the school context. However, we do know that when schools reach out through family participation efforts, families do get involved and that the effects on student outcomes are quite positive. For instance, research reviewed by Henderson and Mapp (2002) and by Epstein (2005) indicates that, through high school, family participation contributes to higher student achievement and to several other indicators of school success. Studies in literacy support family involvement programs' effects on outcomes like vocabulary development (e.g., Fantuzzo, McWayne, & Perry, 2004). Notably, family participation can cancel out negative effects of factors such as poverty and low parental education (e.g., Dearing, Kreider, Simpkins, & Weiss, 2006). For all these reasons, researchers conclude that family involvement efforts offer an important tool to narrow the literacy gap.

## PROCEDURES

### Getting Ready

1. Select the type of Home Connection that supports your instructional goals for vocabulary and content area literacy.

**Figure 22.1** Positive, lasting parent effects on students' early vocabulary and literacy development

Many family practices encourage students' early literacy development. Each of the following has been found to support children's vocabulary development and other literacy components, such as comprehension:

- Providing a rich home literacy environment (van Steensel, 2006)
- Providing a stimulating, responsive home environment (Roberts, Burchinal, & Durham, 1999)
- Having positive and frequent interactions with children (Dodici, Draper, & Peterson, 2003)
- Encouraging mealtime talk that includes extended discourse and uses rare words used in informative ways (Snow & Beals, 2006)
- Providing early exposure to books (Sénéchal, 2006; Sénéchal & LeFevre, 2002)
- Reading aloud daily (Raikes et al., 2006)
- Actively engaging children in talk about words in the books they read together (Walsh & Blewitt, 2006)

2. If appropriate, talk with students, family members, and school personnel about your choices to ensure that they also meet families' needs and school policies. Revise your plan on the basis of this input.

3. Prepare materials required by your choices of Home Connections. In general, you might do the following:

   a. Collect texts for a lending library (such as topical dictionaries, historical fiction, biographies, maps, and other nonfiction works) that can be used by students and their families at home. Used book stores, yard sales, library book sales, and community donations can build your collection at no or little cost.

   b. Visit your local libraries for information on obtaining library cards and using library computers with Internet access.

   c. Collect articles and Web sites related to your content area and home literacy efforts.

   d. Collect or create vocabulary games to send home for family play. (See Vocabulary Games, p. 73.)

   e. Develop interactive homework assignments or projects that focus on supporting vocabulary development.

   f. Find a translator for each of the languages spoken by your students' families. Start with formal contacts, like the principal or school district, and look for informal support, like community volunteers, as well. Check for high levels of literacy for potential translators. Be suspicious of online translation programs.

   g. Set up a mechanism for two-way communication between school and home. Examples include course Web sites, journals, and home notes.

## A VARIETY OF VOCABULARY HOME CONNECTIONS

Home Connections encourage students' growth during many phases of vocabulary learning: *Building Word Knowledge*, *Applying Word Knowledge*, and *Independent Word Knowledge*. The following ideas are organized according to the categories of Providing Information, Encouraging Rich Home Literacy Environments, Interactive Homework, Parents as Experts, and Families at School.

### Providing Information

Parents are experts in many regards. For instance, they know their children from a deeper and longer-term perspective, and many have expertise in particular school-based topics. However, it's highly unlikely that very many family members have your evolving professional knowledge related both to the content and to methods of supporting effective learning of it for students at your particular grade level. Plan to share information with families regularly.

1. *Brief presentations.* (5 minutes or less) during regularly scheduled face-to-face meetings such as back-to-school night, parent conferences, and open house.
2. *Family literacy nights.* Plan age-appropriate vocabulary activities in stations attended by adults and students. Examples of stations include games such as Apples to Apples (see Vocabulary Games, p. 73), Internet treasure hunts, and bookmaking activities. Keep the tone light and include snacks.
3. *Class Web site.* Go through your district's site if possible to build yours or use a shell available online. Some are free, such as http://www.teacherwebsite.com and http://www.classnotesonline.com, and some have a fee, such as http://classWebs.net.
4. *Other Web sites.* Place links to them on your Web site or include them in a handout. Some examples that families might find helpful include the following:
   http://www.ed.gov/parents/academic/help/hyc.html. The U.S. Department of Education's series of booklets for parents, in English and Spanish.
   http://www.ala.org/gwstemplate.cfm?section=greatwebsites&template=/cfapps/gws/displaysection.cfm&sec=24. Sites for parents, caregivers, teachers, & others; a section of the American Library Association's Great Websites for Kids.
   http://www.gamequarium.com/evocabulary.html. Vocabulary games at Gamequarium. For other sites to share with families, see Vocabulary Games (p. 73).
5. *Professional articles.* Make sure they are accessible to lay readers. *Instructor* magazine is one source that has easy-to-read suggestions for families on supporting student literacy. Sample articles can be found online at www.scholastic.com.
6. *Newsletters and teacher-designed handouts.* Share information and tips in brief handouts. Figure 22.2 gives a sample handout a teacher used to encourage family involvement in vocabulary learning. He provides an information bite sheet once every 2 or 3 months, always soliciting feedback.

## Encouraging Rich Home Literacy Environments

Encourage families to provide home environments that support continued language and content learning and that encourage students to use the specialized vocabularies they are learning at school.

1. Create a classroom lending library of texts that can go home. Include a variety of materials, such as magazines (e.g., *Smithsonian*, *Nature*, and *National Geographic*), as well as traditional texts (both fiction and nonfiction). Have multiple copies so that a student and his parent can both read the work and compare, as in book clubs.
2. Teach family members how to obtain library cards. Families who do not have Internet-connected computers at home can use them free of charge at the public library.
3. Send home lists of words that students are learning at school and encourage families to talk about a few of them, perhaps those they have used recently or those with which they are unfamiliar. Make this a safe activity by reminding students and families that many words at school are uncommon in daily usage. Learning new and interesting words expands horizons.
4. Send home vocabulary games, either those commercially available or ones you have created specifically for your content (see Vocabulary Games, p. 73).

### A Note for Your English Learners

Although this book—and most schools today—focuses as on academic achievement in English, the power of biliteracy is great and should not be ignored. First-language literacy is a strong predictor of English achievement (August et al., 2006). Encourage parents to foster students' literacy in the home language. If the family members also know English, encourage them to draw connections between the home language and English.

**Figure 22.2** Information bite for family members

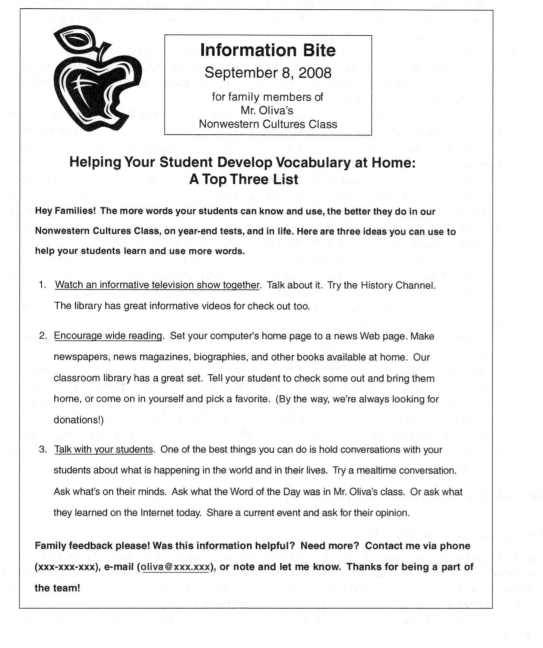

**Information Bite**

September 8, 2008

for family members of
Mr. Oliva's
Nonwestern Cultures Class

**Helping Your Student Develop Vocabulary at Home:
A Top Three List**

Hey Families! The more words your students can know and use, the better they do in our
Nonwestern Cultures Class, on year-end tests, and in life. Here are three ideas you can use to
help your students learn and use more words.

1. <u>Watch an informative television show together</u>. Talk about it. Try the History Channel.
   The library has great informative videos for check out too.

2. <u>Encourage wide reading</u>. Set your computer's home page to a news Web page. Make
   newspapers, news magazines, biographies, and other books available at home. Our
   classroom library has a great set. Tell your student to check some out and bring them
   home, or come on in yourself and pick a favorite. (By the way, we're always looking for
   donations!)

3. <u>Talk with your students</u>. One of the best things you can do is hold conversations with your
   students about what is happening in the world and in their lives. Try a mealtime conversation.
   Ask what's on their minds. Ask what the Word of the Day was in Mr. Oliva's class. Or ask what
   they learned on the Internet today. Share a current event and ask for their opinion.

**Family feedback please! Was this information helpful? Need more? Contact me via phone
(xxx-xxx-xxx), e-mail (<u>oliva@xxx.xxx</u>), or note and let me know. Thanks for being a part of
the team!**

## Interactive Homework

Most families appreciate and benefit from structured opportunities for involvement in students'
school experience, particularly as students become older and more independent. Assigning family
activities may increase the likelihood of completion and decrease resistance of students who may
find their families uncool.

1. *Read alouds.* Require students to read aloud to an adult family member or a child an interesting piece, either assigned or of their choosing. Other options include allowing the adult family
   member to read aloud or having the adult and student do a shared reading.
2. *Word jars (Barger, 2006).* If you teach elementary school, give each student a plastic jar or
   other container with 30 strips of paper. Place instructions in the jar informing family members
   that students are to find interesting and unusual words in nontraditional texts (such as soup
   labels). List sources that are likely to yield words relevant to your class. Students collect one
   word per day, discussing its meaning with a family member. At the end of a month, they

bring their jars back to class for additional word learning activities, such as sorts and partner shares. You can modify this activity for older students by distributing cards or small booklets instead of jars. See Vocabulary Self-Collection (p. 154) and Word Journals (p. 89) for related ideas.

3. *Journals.* Assign dialogue journals that include a family member and the student. Suggest a topic (e.g., "The most interesting idea or word I heard in school today is . . . ") but be flexible if writers select appropriate topics on their own. Include yourself as a writer in the journals if desired.

4. *Sign-off conversation cards.* Once per week, require an adult family member to talk with the student about the major concepts in your class. Have the family member (not the student) record the ideas and sign off. Figure 22.3 gives a biology teacher's form for conversation sign-offs.

5. *Word talks.* Require students to talk with a parent, grandparent, or other adult family member about a word-related topic. For example, you might send home a list of five major terms with which family members are likely to have at least some experience. The student and family member each independently pick one word on the list as their top choice and then defend their choices. They can include brief comments on the sheet listing the terms. Or a student might be instructed to interview a family member about a major term from an upcoming unit of study. An example from a government class might be *tolerance.* Where has the family member heard this word? Why might it be important? What words are related to it? Does it have any special meaning for the family member or family?

6. *Viewing vocabulary.* List suitable movies related to your content and ask students to view them with a family member. Include titles that are likely to be in families' home collections or that can be obtained at no cost from the library, rented, or borrowed from your own collection. Direct viewers to look and listen for a list of important terms. For example, one middle school teacher whose students were studying the Middle East invited students to view with their families Disney's *Aladdin.* Viewers were to listen for content terms and check them off a list and to watch for possible misconceptions about the Middle East. Family members can also be invited to suggest relevant movies that were popular when they were younger.

## Figure 22.3 Conversation sign-off slip

**Biology Conversation Sign Off**

**Family Members:** One way to help students practice what they learn is to talk about it at home. Please listen as your student tells you three main concepts we studied in biology this week. They should give you complete sentences. Students are allowed to check through their notes as they talk to you. Please record their ideas below. You should do the writing, not your student. Ask a couple questions of your student. Thank you!

Mrs. Knopff

**Date:**

**Student Name:**

**Three important concepts from Biology this week:**

1.

2.

3.

**Family Member signature:**

**Family Member comment:** _____

_____

7. *Interactive homework sheets.* Teachers Involving Parents in Schoolwork (TIPS; Epstein et al., 1992) uses interactive homework projects that allow students to talk with a family member about their learning. Students collect information and reactions from their family members using a structured sheet. Inspired by the structure of TIPS assignments, Figure 22.4 gives an interactive homework sheet for a U.S. history class.

### Parents as Experts

Utilize family members' expertise on their students and relevant content to enrich learning in your classroom.

**Figure 22.4** An interactive homework sheet from a U.S. history class

---

Name: _____ Class: _____ Date: _____

A COLONIAL PERIOD COLLAGE

Dear Family Member,
We are studying the colonial period of United States history. This activity will help me think about one of the important concepts related to the colonial period. I hope you enjoy this activity with me. This activity is due _____.

Sincerely,

_____

OBJECTIVE: To visually record the meaning of an important concept related to colonial U.S. history.

PROCEDURE:

1. Select one important concept from this list:

   | Free Market | Principle |
   | Hardship | Representation |
   | Liberty | Respect |

2. Talk together about the term's meaning. Use the textbook as a support if you like. See Chapter 3 in particular.
3. Together cut out pictures from magazines and newspapers that illustrate the term you choose. Talk about how each picture represents the term. Each student has three magazines, distributed in class. Use others from home too if you like. If the site gives you permission, you may also download images from websites like www.history.org. Check "permissions" on each site to be sure.
4. Cut out the pictures, arrange them in different directions on the construction paper, and glue them down.
5. Optional: Write a few related words, like specific examples, and glue those on the collage as well.

HOME-TO-SCHOOL COMMUNICATION:

Dear Family Member,
Please give your reactions to your student's work on this activity. Write yes or no for each statement.

_____ 1. My student understood the homework and was able to discuss it.

_____ 2. My student and I enjoyed the activity.

_____ 3. This assignment helped me to know what my student is learning in U.S. History.

Any other comments:

Family Member's Signature:

---

1. Distribute parent surveys (perhaps on your Web site, at back-to-school night, or as a homework assignment) to gather new perspectives on how best to help your students succeed. Rycik (1998) suggests questions such as the following:
   a. How does your child's performance so far compare with previous years?
   b. What subject (if any) does your child talk about at home?
   c. What does your child like to do during "free time" at home?
   d. What methods have previous teachers used successfully?
2. Invite parents to share their content expertise with your students. They can share through a visit, a digital recording, or a written response. For instance, when a science class recently wondered about the term *geoengineering*, student Erika asked her father, a volcanologist, for insights. He responded with a helpful e-mail to the class along with a Web site recommendation. The students not only had their question about a word answered but also interacted with a practicing scientist, learned of the power of inquiry and the written word, and saw a real-world context for their current studies.

## Families at School

Families can also encourage word learning by coming to school.

1. *Individual or small-group tutors.* Family members can work with individual students who need word learning support through activities such as Vocab Cards (p. 50), Semantic Feature Analysis (p. 24), Semantic Gradients (p. 59), or Concept Guides (p. 46).
2. *Read alouds.* Some schools hold them weekly; others use them to celebrate Read Across America Day. Invite family members (interpreted loosely to include babysitters and friends) into your class to serve as guest readers. Allow them to bring their own material (that you screen first) or provide them with material in advance (to allow for practice).
3. *Festivals.* Invite family members to join in celebrations such as read-ins, poetry festivals, bookmaking events, or dramatic reenactments of your content.
4. *Performance audiences.* Rather than having family members participate in special events, have them serve as audience members. They might attend Readers Theater performances (p. 140) or showings of students' Vocabulary Graffiti (p. 155) or Word Posters (p. 159). They can serve as virtual audience members if you send home written works (such as I-Search a Word reports, p. 163) and ask for comments or if you post them to the Web and invite audience reactions.

## TROUBLESHOOTING

1. As you build home-school connections to support vocabulary development, ensure that your efforts do the following:
   a. Focus on building collaborative relationships.
   b. Respect and address families' needs, including class and cultural differences
   c. Share power and responsibility for the partnership.
2. Families bring different strengths and challenges to the schooling endeavor. Encourage success for all by providing multiple avenues for participation:
   a. Define "parents" and "family" broadly, as appropriate for your students' living situations.
   b. Ensure that students can get necessary materials. Don't assume access to material resources such as money or computers. Until you have accurate information from your families, it may be safest to assume that some but not all students have access to computers, texts, and other materials and then plan a number of ways for families to be involved.
   c. Plan home-school connections that allow for success from a broad range of English and home-language literacy levels. You may need to translate materials or provide

audio or video recordings for families. Allow parents to serve primarily as sounding boards for their students' learning if their educational levels are low.

  d. Provide a "family member" at school if there isn't one at home.

3. Start small. It's probably better to do a couple little things successfully than to attempt a large-scale project of limited success. Using a family survey, including a couple of interactive homework assignments, and inviting family members as audience members for one literacy activity such as a Readers Theater performance may constitute a great first year's attempt.

# 23

# Morphemic Analysis

Morphemic Analysis refers to the process of analyzing words into morphemes. A morpheme is the smallest unit of meaning in a word, and when we analyze a word by morphemes, we examine word roots, prefixes, and suffixes to determine meaning (Edwards, Font, Baumann, & Boland, 2004). Morphology is one of the main sources of information that we have when we encounter new words. Almost 60% of the words that we meet have a morphology that can be used to help determine meaning (Nagy & Anderson, 1984).

## PURPOSE

The ability to break down words is related to reading comprehension (Kieffer & Lesaux, 2007). When students are taught to analyze the morphological structure of words, we give them a valuable tool for independent word learning. We teach them how to use their knowledge of root words, prefixes, and suffixes to figure out the meaning of words. Take the word *microscope,* for example. If I know that the root word *micro* in *microscope* means "small," I can use that understanding to make inferences about the meaning of other words that contain the same root, such as *microbiology, microbe,* and *microcosm.* Knowing the meaning of a root, prefix, or suffix of just *one* word can provide students with clues that can help in figuring out the meaning of dozens of other words (Stoller & Grabe, 1955). It is likely that many of the vocabulary gains that can occur through wide reading are related to the reader's ability to use the morphological structure to figure out the meaning of unknown words (Wysocki & Jenkins, 1987).

## PROCEDURES

### Getting Ready

1. Here are some general guidelines for choosing prefixes, suffixes, and root words:
   a. Teach the most frequently used prefixes and suffixes. White, Sowell, and Yanigihara (1989) identified 11 prefixes that account for 80% of all prefixed words and six suffixes that account for 80% of all suffixed words. These are listed in Figure 23.1.
   b. Knowledge of these affixes allows students access to the change in meaning that occurs when one or more of the affixes is combined with any known root word and, therefore, is an important tool for understanding how words are structured. As students move through the grades, it becomes more likely that the meanings of many of these affixes have been internalized; however, if you are in doubt, taking the time to assess students' understanding and selectively teaching those affixes that are not known makes sense given their high utility.
   c. Choose root words that are important to your content area or to a unit of instruction you are planning. If you were studying the physiology of humans, roots such as *endo*

**Figure 23.1** The most commonly used prefixes and suffixes (White, Sowell, & Yanigihara, 1989)

| Prefixes | Suffixes |
|---|---|
| *un-* (not) | *-s, -es* (plural) |
| *re-* (again) | *-ed* (past) |
| *in-* (not) | *-ing* (action or process) |
| *dis-* (the opposite of) | *-ly* (in a specified manner) |
| *en-, em-* (in, within) | *-er, -or* (one who) |
| *non-* (not) | *-ion, -tion* (state or condition) |
| *in-, im-* (in, within) | |
| *over-* (exceed, be above) | |
| *mis-* (bad, wrong) | |
| *sub-* (under) | |
| *pre-* (before) | |

("within") and *neuro* ("nerve") would be good choices since words with these roots (e.g., *endocrine, endoskeleton, neuromotor, neural*, and *neuroglia*) are likely to represent important concepts. Almost all subject areas have root words that play an important role in their domain. You can quickly find these by scanning through the resources that students will use during instruction. There are helpful online lists of common roots as well. Try http://www.factmonster.com to get you started.

   d. Bring to students' attention the morphological and meaning relationships among words. For example, examining words such as *autocrat, autocracy, autocratic, autocratical*, and *autocratically* builds generative knowledge about how words are related by spelling and meaning that can be used to analyze other words.

2. Choose the student grouping strategy that best meets your purposes.
   Will you have students work individually, in partners, or in small groups, or will you present a whole-group lesson? The number of words you choose and the strategy you want the students to learn often determine the grouping option you will want to use.

## During Class

Morphemic Analysis is a powerful strategy for *Building Word Knowledge* and *Independent Word Learning*.

### Building Word Knowledge

1. Present students with a prefix (or suffix) and explain its meaning. For example, you might explain that the prefix un- means "not." Place the prefix in a word they already know, such as *undo*. Discuss how *un-* changes the meaning of the root word *do*. Have students work in small groups or pairs to generate families of words that start with the prefix: *unliked, unmerciful, untimely, unwritten*, and so on. These words can be collected in a class vocabulary book or a Word Journal (p. 89). Entries for a prefix might have a cover page with the prefix and a definition followed by a list of the words. You might want to have students illustrate the words.

2. Figure 23.2 shares how a geometry teacher taught students to analyze the attributes of new geometry terms and to create connections. The teacher's lesson is based on a

**Figure 23.2** An example of students studying the morphology of words in geometry

1. As part of a unit on angles, the teacher writes the following four words on the board. He chose them because they were related in meaning and spelling and were important terms in the unit.

   | | |
   |---|---|
   | pentagon | tetrahedron |
   | hexagon | octahedron |

2. He pronounces the words slowly and has students repeat the pronunciation.
3. Then he writes the words again. This time he divides them into morphemes or word parts and writes them like this:

   pentagon = penta + gon        tetrahedron = tetra + hedron
   hexagon  = hexa + gon         octahedron = octa + hedron

4. He then asks students to make predictions about the words. Many students predict that they have something to do with geometry. Other students note that some of the words have endings that are spelled the same.
5. The teacher builds on what students noticed by sharing that the terms are indeed related to geometry and are the names of different geometric shapes. He adds that the ending -gon means "angle" and -hedron means "face" or "plane." After students explore the different angles and planes he brought in as examples, he explains that the first part of the word provides information about the number of angles or planes there are in each shape. He challenges students to figure out the number of planes or angles each shape has and to see what other information they can find.
6. The teacher divides the class into four groups and assigns each a word to investigate. Groups create posters that have the word, the word parts, an illustration, and information about the properties of their word.
7. As the students listen to each of the presentations, they begin to compare and contrast the features of the words and to make generalizations about how they are related.

lesson format adapted from Tompkins (2004). This lesson format can be used across the content areas to teach Morphemic Analysis.

### Independent Word Learning

1. Have a root word, prefix, or suffix of the week. Encourage students to find new words that use the root word or affix you are targeting. You can display the words on a bulletin board. At the end of the week, review the words with students and have them vote for the most unusual word, the most interesting word, or other categories that would be appropriate.
2. Make a list of five to seven root words and their meanings that students will meet during a unit of study. Encourage students to use the meanings of the roots to figure out any unknown terms. Have students make a list of the words they found that contained the roots along with a possible definition. Be sure to discuss these with students to ensure that they are making good inferences about the meanings of the words.

### ● MODIFICATIONS

1. Incorporate into your study of word parts "word stories" (Stahl, 2005). Word stories are accounts of word origins and derivations. They can create interest in words and help students understand the relationship between spelling and meaning. For example, the word pace comes from the Latin passus, "to step." It became associated with a unit of measurement and then with a person who sets the pace for others. Today we have words like

## A Note for Your English Learners

1. Just as understanding word origins can provide links between students' home language and English (see Word Histories, p. 115), so can knowledge of root words, prefixes, and suffixes. There are thousands of words that have similar pronunciations, spellings, and meanings across languages. Words that have similar pronunciations and spellings across languages are called cognates. Many cognates have prefixes, suffixes, and root words derived from Greek and Latin. For example, in science a teacher could support students who have Spanish as their first language by encouraging them to recognize English/Spanish cognates for words such as *circulation* (*circulacion*), *atmosphere* (*atmosphere*), *insect* (*insecto*), *lunar* (*luna*), and *biology* (*biologia*).

2. One way to make students aware of important cognates is to give them sets of cards that have an English word on one card and its cognate in the students' first language on another card. Figure 23.3 presents a word sort activity that can be used with the cards.

*pace horse*, *pacemaker*, and *pacesetter* that have their origins in the Latin root. See Word Histories (p. 115) for more ideas for incorporating word origins into your instruction.

2. Encourage students to use the context (words that come just before and after an unknown word) as a strategy for determining the meaning of unknown words. Baumann et al. (2003) found that giving students instruction that combined identification of words parts and using the context was effective in helping students infer the meaning of unknown words and enhanced their ability to transfer learning to new contexts.

3. The Internet is a good source for lists of English cognates. Here are some sites for you to explore:

Spanish Cognates Dictionary
http://www.latinamericalinks.com/spanish_cognates.htm.
Espangles
http://www.geocities.com/Athens/Thebes/6177/ws-cognates.html.
French/English Cognates
http://french.about.com/library/vocab/bl-vraisamis.htm.
English/German Cognates
http://german.about.com/library/blcognates_A.htm.

 ## TROUBLESHOOTING

1. Be selective. Teach only those root words and affixes that are the most important in the unit of study you are planning or that are most frequently used in your content area. Giving students multiple pages of roots, prefixes, and suffixes to learn is unnecessary and often boring.

2. Although cognates can be used to great advantage with English learners to increase English vocabulary knowledge, students need to be aware that they cannot assume that all words that are spelled alike across languages have the same meaning. For example, in Spanish, *tuna* is a type of cactus, *largo* means "long," and *pretender* means

**Figure 23.3** Sorting activity that can be used with cognates

1. Based on the subject area and the unit of study, choose a set of English words that have cognates in the students' first language.
2. Create sets of the words by writing each English word on a card and each cognate on a card. The number of sets you will need depends on how you decide to group your students. This activity works best in groups of two to four students.
3. Give each group a set of cards with the English and first-language cognates mixed together.
4. Have students sort the words into pairs and identify what the words have in common. They can also circle how the words differ.

"to try." The context can often help students determine if the words are true cognates. Also keep in mind that cognates are useful only if students already know the cognate of the English word that you want them to learn. It is unlikely that pointing out that the English word *germination* has a Spanish cognate, *germinacion,* will be helpful if the student doesn't already have knowledge of the Spanish form of the word. For immigrants, knowing students' education level when they immigrated can be useful in determining which cognates will be beneficial.

## NEXT STEPS

1. Games and puzzles are motivating ways to reinforce the meaning of word parts. Figure 23.4 shows an idea for a puzzle using the root word *cred* ("believe").
2. Have students create new word using words parts they have learned. You might have them create a new word for a new invention, creature, or plant or a novel word for a familiar item. For example, a *phonovideographer* would be a person who uses a phone to take videos. These can be illustrated and collected into a class book (see Student-Made Books, p. 145).
3. Are your students Harry Potter fans? See Nilson and Nilson (2006) for activities related to the morphemic analysis of words like *lumos* and *expelliarmus.*

**Figure 23.4** A puzzle for middle school students studying the root word *cred*

---

**Be a Word Detective**

**Root Out the Answer**

Directions: The root is *cred*, which means "believe." To solve the puzzle, use the word clue beneath the dashes to figure out the mystery word. The root word *cred* has already been entered for each word to get you started.

cred _ _ _ _
noun, 8 letters
Person or business to whom you owe money

_ _ cred _ _ _ _
adj., 10 letters
Hard to believe

_ _ _ cred _ _
verb, 9 letters
To cause a loss of belief in someone or some thing

cred _ _ _ _ _ _
noun, 10 letters
A certificate or other document that is the basis for the belief in a person's stated position or power

---

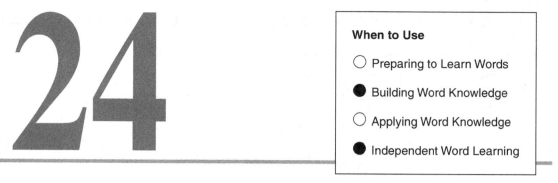

## When to Use

○ Preparing to Learn Words

● Building Word Knowledge

○ Applying Word Knowledge

● Independent Word Learning

# Analogies

*Using an Analogy in vocabulary learning is like building a bridge from a familiar place to a new place.* As the previous sentence illustrates, an Analogy compares ideas; it helps us connect the known to the unknown. The core of Analogies is, then, the mapping of a source (a familiar idea) to an unfamiliar one (the target) (Gentner, 1983) in order to make the unfamiliar familiar (Tabor, 2001). People of virtually all ages spontaneously, and through instruction, use Analogies when they hope to understand new, abstract ideas in terms of familiar, concrete ones (see Greenwood, 1987).

All Analogies focus on relationships between and among ideas, but they can vary in format. For developing concept knowledge through vocabulary instruction, Analogies often present comparisons of just two sets of ideas, such as in the simile "An atom is like our solar system." This Analogy helps students explore the unfamiliar concept *atom* by linking it with a familiar one, *solar system*. In contrast, the formal Analogies you may recall from standardized tests compare two or more pairs of ideas. One example is "cold is to hot as thick is to thin" (or, in shorthand, cold:hot::thick:thin). This example explores a relationship of opposition; words in the pairs are antonyms. Analogies can also represent synonymous relationships or others, such as time sequence, categorical, or definitional ones.

## PURPOSE

Research reviewed by Marzano (2004) suggests that analogical reasoning is complex and requires in-depth analysis of content. Using Analogies as instructional tools is effective for helping students develop such reasoning. Analogies are used widely in support of general problem solving and in science education to help students build conceptual understanding of new terms (Baumann & Duffy, 1997; Glynn, 1996; Tabor, 2001; Tobin & Tippins, 1996). They are also effective in helping students build word relatedness (Blachowicz & Fischer, 2004a) and can help students think divergently (Cardellicio & Field, 1997). Finally, Analogies serve the important purpose of providing students with multiple exposures to terms over time so that students build deep and shaded meanings for vocabulary terms (Marzano, 2004).

## PROCEDURES

### Getting Ready

1. Select the terms to be developed through Analogy. You may select a number of potentially unrelated terms to be developed through Analogies as stand-alone exercises. You may instead select several terms related to a single larger common Analogy, or you may elect to develop just one major term through an extended Analogy. Figure 24.1 gives examples of all three possibilities considered by a ninth-grade speech (oral communication) teacher.

**111**

**Figure 24.1** Three kinds of Analogies considered by a ninth-grade speech teacher

| Several terms explored through stand-alone Analogies | Reviewing important ideas for effective speeches:<br>_____ :first::conclusion: _____<br>chronological: _____ ::topical:subjects<br>Lincoln:Gettysburg Address::Martin Luther King Jr.: _____<br>_____ :type of proof::credibility:test for evidence<br>voice:verbal technique:: _____ :nonverbal technique |
|---|---|
| Terms related to a common Analogy topic | Parts of an effective speech:<br>The introduction is like _____.<br>Transitions are like _____.<br>The body is like _____.<br>The conclusion is like _____. |
| One term for an extended Analogy | Parts of an effective speech:<br>An effective speech has parts just as a _____ has parts. [explain] |

2. Decide who will generate the Analogy(-ies): you or the students.
3. Develop the Analogies and materials you will need to present them. For instance, you may need texts, concrete materials, or words on cards.

### During Class

Analogies help in *Building Word Knowledge* and *Independent Word Learning*.

### *Building Word Knowledge*

1. If you are using an extended Analogy to develop a concept, present it directly. For instance, in a technology lesson on a computer component, the central processing unit, a teacher may begin, "If we think of a computer as an organism, the central processing unit (CPU) is like the brain." The teacher might show a diagram making such a comparison and list the critical features of the CPU, further drawing explicit connections to the brain.
2. You might instead choose to use Analogies to solidify understandings near the end of a lesson or later for practice. Either you or the students can complete stems such as the following: Brain is to organism as _____ is to computer.
3. To practice and further refine terms near the end of a unit, construct formal Analogies for completion. Here are examples in social studies:
   • Capitalism is to United States as _____ is to China.
   • Sally Ride:Astronaut::George Washington Carver: _____.
   • Emancipation Proclamation: _____:: _____ : _____.
4. To encourage new perspectives and connections, ask students to develop their own Analogies for concepts under study, as in Figure 24.2. This figure shares a high school theater arts teacher's directions for students to analyze the attributes of new theater terms and create connections.

### *Independent Word Learning*

1. Encourage students to develop their own extended Analogies as they learn new concepts. Figure 24.3 is a seventh grader's extended Analogy for a cell: The Cell Café. He presents it as a brochure.

**Figure 24.2** A high school theater arts teacher's directions for students to analyze the attributes of new theater terms and create connections

Your group has a bag of objects:

- Each item can be seen as an Analogy for the terms we have been studying in class.
- Together, decide which item represents which term. Each group member must speak. To make your selection of items, listen to the number of connections your group members make in favor of the item. Also listen to the quality of the rationale they offer for each connection.
- Note: There are many "correct" responses to this task. All rests in your rationale!

Terms:

Acting method

American theater

Dramatic text

Heritage

Unified production concept

*(The bags contain an assortment of 10 household items such as a scrap of cloth, a rubber band, a small bar of soap, a paper clip, a piece of plastic wrap, a photograph, and a coin.)*

2. In solving formal Analogies, teach students to focus on the relationship between the terms in the first comparison and then select or determine a term for the second pair that will parallel that relationship.

 **MODIFICATIONS**

If students have created Vocab Cards (p. 50), pull them out occasionally and practice developing Analogies that include them.

 **TROUBLESHOOTING**

In order for extended Analogies to support student learning, they must be carefully selected and presented. Tabor (2004) gives three tips:

1. Ensure that the source (familiar idea) truly is familiar to the students. For instance, using the *solar system* as a source in studying the target term *atom* will not be effective if students are unfamiliar with or have misunderstandings of the solar system.
2. Ensure that the source and the target share a number of features.
3. No comparison is perfect. In addition to exploring with students the positive aspects of the Analogy, be sure to explore the negative ones.

 **TECH CONNECT**

The World Wide Web has a myriad of Analogy games for students of all ages. Use "analogy games" as the search term.

 **NEXT STEPS**

Because Analogies encourage exploration of relationships among words and ideas—often in deep ways—they can feed directly into poetry. See Poetry (p. 149) for poetry ideas that can be used to add a new dimension to students' Analogies.

**Figure 24.3** A seventh-grade student's Analogy for a cell:
The Cell Café

# The Cell Café

Great food!
Internet connections!
Dancing!
Great company!

If you are looking for a good time, Cell Café is the place to be.
Don't let the name fool you. Cell Café is really a hip and happenin' place.

Take a Peek at Cell Café's Many Interesting Features!

## Manager Nucleus

The manager is like a nucleus because it has the basic information to keep the cell running.

## Cashier Mitochondria

The mitochondria are like cashiers because they take in the money from
customers and break it down into energy for the café to run.

## Sliding Door Cell Membrane

The sliding doors in our café allow things
in and out of the restaurant, just like a cell membrane.

## Cell Café Cytoplasm Carpet

Just as the cell's cytoplasm houses the organelles outside of the nucleus,
our lush shag carpet provides a soft walkway throughout the café.

## Ribosomes

Ribosomes put amino acids together to make proteins, but our Ribosome chefs mix our
ingredients to make great meals—fun for everyone!

## Vacuole Pump Room

In unicellular organisms, a vacuole works as a pump to remove extra water from within
the cell. To prevent flooding, Cell Café has a room to pump out water, much like a
unicellular animal's vacuole.

## Endoplasmic Reticulum: ER Waiters

ER is the internal cell delivery system. Our ER waiters are similar because they deliver
food to hungry customers.

## Lysosome Security Guards

Our lysosome security guards can get rid of any unwanted trouble within Cell Café.
They can also shut down Cell Café in case of an emergency, much like how the lysosomes
in cells can cause the cell to commit suicide.

## Chromosome Menus

Much like the chromosome is the blueprint for life, our chromosome menus contain the
instructions for a good meal—something you can count on at the cell café!

## Nucleolus: The Manager's Organizer

Cell Café's Nucleus Manager carries an organizer we call the nucleolus. It holds the
information about who is on the waiting list to be hired as a Ribosome Waiter.

# 25

**When to Use**

○ Preparing to Learn Words

● Building Word Knowledge

○ Applying Word Knowledge

● Independent Word Learning

# Word Histories

Every word we meet hints at a tiny piece of history. By stepping up to the counter and saying, "One *café mocha* with *sugar* please," you use three words that found their way into English from Arabic as a result of trade centuries ago (Smolik, 2006). When students study Word Histories, they learn that words have intriguing stories that have traveled down to us through time and from many places. Word Histories provide vibrant proof that our language continues to grow and change with the people and societies who speak it.

Students can study Word Histories in many ways, including research into dictionaries in print and online and readings of more extended reports about word origins, or *etymologies*, from a variety of sources. As students explore Word Histories, teachers fuel a sense of discovery and intrigue.

## PURPOSE

Study of Word Histories serves a number of valuable purposes. Exploring Word Histories encourages students to find predictability in a language that includes many apparent inconsistencies. Such predictability can give students a sense of control over their language, its vocabulary, and some of its spelling patterns. Knowing Word Histories can help students predict and develop meanings for new words by connecting them with previously studied words or common English words (Thompson & Rubenstein, 2000).

Studying word origins is especially important in the content areas, as many subject areas present large numbers of words to be learned, and many content areas have their roots in particular languages that can assist students in learning the discipline's important words. One example is the influence of Arabic, Greek, and Latin on mathematics and science (think about *zero, polyhedron*, and *percent*). Study of Word History in the content areas can also deepen students' content knowledge and appreciation for language and history (Milligan & Ruff, 1990; Rubenstein & Schwartz, 2000). In every content area, Word History explorations can capture the interests of students who are fascinated by people, their stories, and the words they create.

### A Note for Your English Learners

Understanding word origins can provide links between students' home language and English. For instance, speakers of Romance languages such as Spanish and French will be assisted by the fact that a solid half of all English words are borrowed from Latin, either directly or through other languages. All English learners can be encouraged to find links between their primary language and English. Even though English includes few words of Chinese origin, your speakers of Chinese may be glad to hear that English borrowed some words like *tea, ketchup*, and *gung ho* from China.

**115**

## ● PROCEDURES

### Getting Ready

1. From the larger set of words you determined before a unit of instruction, select a sub-set of words that have interesting histories. You can quickly find these histories by look-ing up your selections in an online or print-based dictionary that includes etymological information, or word origins. (See step 3 for sources.) Alternatively, students can inves-tigate many words for themselves and select those with appealing histories.

2. Choose your student grouping strategy: will you have students work individually, in partners, or in small groups? The number of words you selected in step 1 determines the number of student groups you need.

3. Secure sources for your students' research. Sources can include electronic resources and print-based materials such as the following:
   a. Online dictionaries:
      - Online Etymology Dictionary (http://www.etymonline.com)
      - One Look Dictionary Search (http://www.onelook.com)
      - Dictionary.com (http://www.dictionary.com)
      - The American Heritage Dictionary of the English Language (online version at http://bartleby.com)
   b. Dictionaries that include information on origins. Careful! Many dictionaries for chil-dren do not include information on word origins. Examples of those with etymologi-cal information include the *Oxford English Dictionary* and *Merriam-Webster's Collegiate Dictionary*.
   c. Specialized etymological dictionaries. Barnhart (1995) is a good example, and it avoids use of abbreviations.
   d. Books on word origins such as Lieberman's (2005) *Word Origins . . . and How We Know Them: Etymology for Everyone* and American Heritage Dictionaries' (2004) *Word Histories and Mysteries: From Abracadabra to Zeus.*

### During Class

Word Histories help students with *Building Word Knowledge* and *Independent Word Learning.*

### *Building Word Knowledge*

1. *The Hook*
   Introduce an interesting word and its history:
   a. Present one target word to the class (perhaps using a Vocab Card, p. 50).
   b. Present the history of the word, using vivid language, maps, graphic images, or other techniques that bring the history to life. Alternatively, you may ask students to pre-dict the word's history first. Or, you may present two histories—one true and one false—and ask students to determine the correct one.
   c. Provide background information on etymology as appropriate for students' age and interest. See Figure 25.1 for some information to get you started.

2. *Present the Task*
   Students are to select words, study their histories, and report to the class:
   a. Match students with words for exploration. You can allow students to form interest groups to pursue certain words. The seventh-grade teacher in the mathematics example found in Figure 25.2 distributed the words randomly on cards. Because exploration of word origins should fan students' interest in inquiry, we recommend that you allow more than one group to study the same word if they strongly desire to do so.
   b. Tell the students what their finished product or report should look and sound like: Will it be a page in a printed or electronic class dictionary (see Dictionaries, p. 93)?

**Figure 25.1** Some facts about English word origins

- *The English language is a language of people on the move.* English is a Germanic language. Early speakers traveled from the Netherlands and what is now Germany to Britain, conquering the Celtic people there. Roman troops and trade brought a heavy Latin influence. People from Scandinavia and the French-speaking Normans also provided a heavy influence on English.
- *The English language has a huge number of words.* Although it is difficult to count, many believe that English has more words than any other language. This is because of the history of English and because English borrows so readily from other languages. Some estimates put the lexicon of English at twice that of the Spanish language and three times larger than that of French (Bromley, 2007).
- *Class differences can be found through study of the English language.* For example, the people who spoke French early on were of the upper class and thus were more likely to eat meat, which was expensive. Those who tended the farm animals were English speakers too poor to eat much meat. Thus, names for meats tend to derive most immediately from French, whereas the names for the animals who bear the meat tend to come from earlier versions of English. *Beef* comes from the French *boef*, whereas *cow* was used by the Anglo-Saxon peasants who served the French-speaking noblemen.
- *English relies heavily on borrowing.* A small number of our words come from earlier versions of English; most come from other sources, primarily Latin either directly or through another Romance language, such as French.
- *English is constantly changing.* Its speakers adapt to the world around them and absorb elements of the cultures and other languages with whom they have contact.
- *Words come from a variety of sources.* Fresch and Wheaton (2002) suggest six sources for most words in the English language:
  1. Words reflect historical conquests.
  2. Words are mistakes.
  3. Words are misinterpretations.
  4. Words come from people's names.
  5. Words are invented by combining words.
  6. Words evolve from other words.

A Word Poster (see p. 159)? A slide in a PowerPoint show? A brief oral retelling? We encourage you to choose a format that makes the information available later and to all. In the example in Figure 25.2, students present skits. In the Figure 25.3 example, students recorded and displayed information on a large U.S. map.

3. *Conduct Word History Explorations*
   a. Teach students to use sources to investigate their words. Likely important information for you to share includes the following:
      - The structure of a dictionary entry and where to locate etymological information within it
      - Meanings of abbreviations related to word origins (such as the names of countries and languages)
      - Key terms, such as *Old English* and *Indo-European*, that students are likely to encounter in studying word origins (You may wish to build and display a chart with this information.)
      - The necessity of checking more than one source to triangulate findings (It is not unusual to unearth conflicting findings.)
   b. Monitor as students conduct their research.
   c. Support students in recording their findings and preparing to report.
   d. Later, encourage students to draw connections across their discoveries related to word patterns, geography, chronology, and important ideas from history. For instance, study of word origins often overlaps with an understanding of word parts, such as affixes and roots (see Morphemic Analysis, p. 106). A historical generalization that students might draw is that words are often the product of cultural contact,

**Figure 25.2** A seventh-grade example of students studying word origins in mathematics

1. To introduce a unit on geometry, the teacher distributes words on cards, one to each small group:

| | | |
|---|---|---|
| angle | parallel | point |
| area | perpendicular | radius |
| circumference | perimeter | slope |
| line | pi | volume |

2. Students use the three classroom computers and a variety of dictionaries to conduct 10 minutes of research on their word's origin.
3. Each group contributes to a Data Retrieval Chart (p. 85):

| Word | Origin | Meaning | Example |
|---|---|---|---|
| Angle | Latin: *Angulum* | Corner | Those two paths meet to form an *angle*. |
| Line | Latin: *Linea* | Linea thread | The *line* is straight. |

4. In quick skits (less than 30 seconds), each group acts out the origin of its word, using makeshift props:
   - The group with the word *perpendicular* hung a weight from a string and noted the word's connection to *pendere*, which means "to hang" in Latin. Classmates noted the connection to the familiar *pendant*.
   - The favorite of the day: The group with *pi* ($\pi$) noted the word's connection to Hebrew for "little mouth." All group members fashioned their "little mouths" into circles and pointed to them. In Greek, $\pi$ is the abbreviation for *peripheria*, or *circumference*. Later, in their geometry unit, students vividly recalled the fact that $\pi$ represents the ratio of a circumference of a circle to its diameter ($\pi = c/d$).

such as trade or invasion. A linguistic one is that English is a flexible language with many borrowings and a huge vocabulary.

4. *Independent Word Learning*
   a. Encourage students to pursue their own research into Word Histories. Students might keep small loose-leaf booklets akin to personal dictionaries to track their explorations, adding pages as they go. (See Word Journals, p.89.)
   b. Display a world map and invite students to add words on pins to the places of their origin.
   c. Create a permanent bulletin board to fuel students' independent research. Encourage students to post illustrated accounts of Word Histories found in their travels. Be sure to share the board periodically with the class or in some way ensure that they interact with the information.
   d. Play games with words and their histories. For instance, you might develop a list of 15 words students have not yet met but whose histories connect somehow to those of words they previously studied. Place each word on a card and place its brief history on another. Distribute the cards, one per student, and then ask them to find their match by moving throughout the classroom and reading their cards to each other. Students can play with Word Histories online at sites such as Etymologic!, deemed "the toughest word game on the Web." Find it at http://www.etymologic.com.

## MODIFICATIONS

1. Invite students to research words that are connected to their own cultural histories or immigration stories. For example, my great grandparents came to the United States from Germany. What are the influences of German on English?

**Figure 25.3** A fifth-grade example of students studying Word Histories in U.S. geography

Based on their state content standards, fifth graders are memorizing the state names, capitals, and locations. When the teacher notices students struggling to spell state names correctly, he interjects with a lesson on origin of state names.

1. The teacher starts with a hook. He says, "See if you can figure out my group." He presents state names, one at a time, and has students guess *yes* or *no* about the state's membership in his group. In the *yes* group are *Connecticut, Kentucky*, and *Utah*. In the *no* group are *California, New Jersey*, and *Washington*. Students are stumped—and intrigued—so the teacher moves on: "It has something to do with the origins of the state's names." Students excitedly share their conjectures. The teacher smiles and responds, "Let's find out!"
2. Each partner group receives one or two state names circled on a photocopied U.S. map.
3. Students investigate the origin of their states' names. They don't find a pocket dictionary helpful and turn instead to the almanac and to the Internet using the search terms "state name origins."
4. On an enlarged U.S. class map, traced on butcher paper, partner groups color their states according to a key that gives the origin of their states' names (e.g., French = green). Early on, they discover their teacher's group: states with names of American Indian origin.
5. Afterward, they discuss the implications for remembering the spellings of state names.
6. Teachable moment: The class discusses their surprises (half of our states' names originate from American Indian words!) and collect more information to test an emergent hypothesis that the date of a state's entry to the Union is reflected in the origin of the state's name. They add dates to their colored class map. Some interesting conversations about the formation of the United States ensue.
7. A few highly motivated students continue their studies of word origins with the names of state capitals. They add them to the class map.

2. Each year, new words—*neologisms*—enter our language. Recent examples include additions to *Merriam-Webster's Collegiate Dictionary*, 11th edition (2006), such as *aquascape, mouse potato, ringtone*, and *unibrow* (http://www.m-w.com/info/new_words.htm). Students can explore the origins of new words, compare their places of use, and perhaps nominate their own.

 **TROUBLESHOOTING**

1. Be sure to check the abbreviations used by each source to avoid drawing inaccurate conclusions. For instance, in some sources, *fr.* means "from" whereas *FR.* means "French."
2. Some words sound like they are related to others but actually have no connection. Be on the lookout for these *false cognates*. In addition, try Wilton's (2004) *Word Myths: Debunking Linguistic Urban Legends* to help students steer clear of inaccurate word stories.
3. Keep study of Word Histories light; a heavy-handed approach can turn students away from etymology.

**TECH CONNECT**

1. The Internet provides a highly efficient means of searching many dictionaries at once. It is also invaluable for providing information on history quickly and from a number of sources. See Dictionaries, p. 93, for many online sources.

2. Students can publish their works electronically. Posting word origins to a class Web site can allow families to join in the discoveries.

 ## NEXT STEPS

Keep words, studied through Word Histories, alive by applying them at other times and in other contexts. Students might enjoy creating Readers Theater presentations (p. 140) to share Word Histories. Word Chains (p. 67) show connections among words.

# 26

**When to Use**

○ Preparing to Learn Words

● Building Word Knowledge

○ Applying Word Knowledge

● Independent Word Learning

# KIM (Key Term, Information Memory) Charts

Key term, Information Memory (KIM) Charts are a handy tool for students to study and internalize word meanings (Allen, 1999). In KIM Charts, students list key vocabulary terms, provide brief definitions, and compose a memory clue that will help them recall the term in the future. Figure 26.1 provides a sample KIM Chart for an economics class.

## PURPOSE

Charts help us record information briefly, organize it, and see patterns. Further, drawing images for memory clues requires students to think more deeply about terms as they decide how to represent them (Bromley, 2007; Edens & Potter, 2001) and choose images that are personally meaningful (Hopkins & Bean, 1998–1999; Standerfer, 2006). Both of these factors make it more likely that students will be able to recall the terms later. Their brevity makes KIM Charts useful study tools. Finally, the simplicity of KIM Charts also raises the chances that students will use them as part of their independent word learning efforts.

**Figure 26.1** A sample KIM Chart for economics class

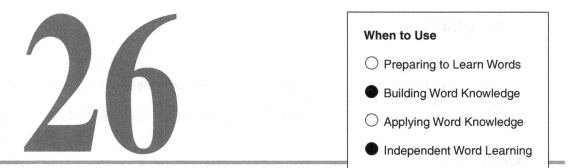

| Key term | Information | Memory clue |
|---|---|---|
| consumption | Buying and using products | "I'll take two!" |
| demand | How much of a good or service that buyers will purchase at all prices | Gotta have those shoes! |
| free market system | Individuals (not the government) own and run the businesses | Lemonade $1? / I'm the boss of me! |

**PROCEDURES**

### Getting Ready

1. Choose key terms and decide whether students will compose KIM Charts while they are learning the terms or later as a review.
2. If you wish, supply students with a blank KIM Chart or give them paper to fold their own.

### During Class

KIM Charts are useful for *Building Word Knowledge* and *Independent Word Learning*.

### *Building Word Knowledge and Independent Word Learning*

1. Share a sample KIM Chart and discuss its usefulness as a tool for learning and remembering new terms.
2. Ask students to fold a paper into three columns. (The number of rows depends on the number of terms you choose.) Have them label the columns "Key term," "Information," and "Memory clue."
3. Compose a chart's first row together as a class.
4. Allow students to work as individuals, with partners, or in small groups to complete their charts.
5. Show the students how to use the completed chart as a study tool by folding the paper to expose only the desired information:
   a. Fold the rows back so that only the term of interest is showing.
   b. Fold the columns back so that only one kind of information is showing: the term, the definition, or the memory clue. Have students quiz themselves or each other as they look at their folded charts: Can they give the term when viewing only the memory clue? Can they define it when looking only at the term?

## MODIFICATION

Try other types of charts to support vocabulary learning as well. A popular choice is the Vocabulary Four Square (Johns, Lenski, & Bergland, 2003). In the Four Square, each term requires one piece of paper. The paper is folded into quarters. In a common version, each quadrant is devoted to one of the following: the term, a student-friendly definition, a personal connection, and a drawing. Teachers in both the primary grades (Schippert, 2005) and high school grades (Hopkins & Bean, 1998–1999) have appreciated the power of the Four Square because it combines verbal and visual information about target terms. Figure 26.2 gives a sample Vocabulary Four Square for the term *demand* from an economics class.

## TROUBLESHOOTING

Any strategy can be overused, which is likely to cause resentment from students and decrease meaningful learning. Be sure to limit the number of terms included in KIM Charts and vary its usage with other word building strategies.

## NEXT STEPS

To ensure that students can *use* terms, not just *recall* them, follow up with a strategy that requires application. Two *Applying Word Knowledge* examples are Word Chains (p. 67) and Word Decisions (p. 63).

**Figure 26.2** A Vocabulary Four Square for the
economics term *demand*

| | |
|---|---|
| demand | Demand is how much of a good or service that buyers will purchase at all prices. |
| In my town, the demand for Pokémon cards has gone way down since I was a little kid. | 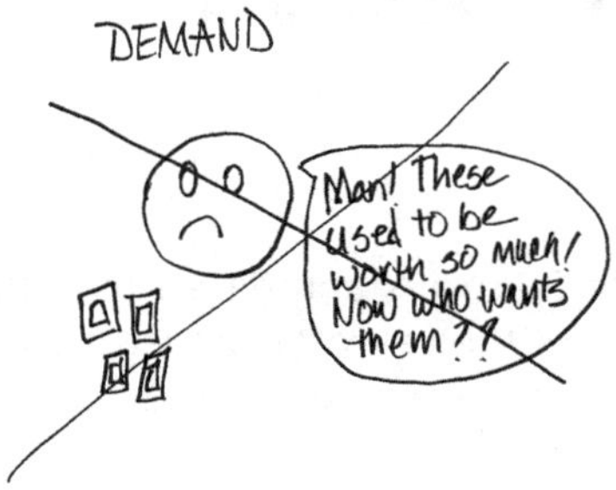 |

# 27

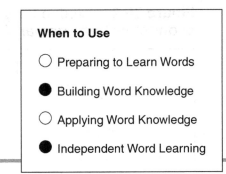

**When to Use**

○ Preparing to Learn Words

● Building Word Knowledge

○ Applying Word Knowledge

● Independent Word Learning

# Context Clues

School-aged students learn an estimated average of 3,000 words every year (Nagy & Anderson, 1984). Most of these words are learned not through direct instruction but through repeated exposure to words in books, magazines, and other print materials, in conversations, and by watching television and movies. As students encounter words over time in meaningful contexts, they build their understanding of an impressive number of words. Thus, the ability to figure out the meaning of a word using the context is one of the most powerful of all vocabulary learning strategies.

However, students are much more likely to be able to successfully use the context to figure out words in narratives than in informational materials (Anderson & Nagy, 1992). The level of difficulty of content area materials, and the number and complexity of many of the concepts that they contain, make it much more difficult for students to figure out the meaning of the unknown words they encounter. However, instruction in using context clues can improve the students' ability to predict the meaning of words from context. Therefore, it is important that we sensitize students to the large variety of context clues that are available.

## PURPOSE

Context Clues is a flexible strategy that can help students learn to contend with unknown vocabulary in a wide variety of texts. The context of a word is generally defined as the words, phrases, and sentences that surround the target word. The surrounding words often contain clues that help the reader figure out the meaning of an unknown word. In the content areas, charts, graphs, and illustrations are examples of other types of context that can help illuminate the meaning of a word. The overall goal of teaching students to use context clues is to improve their ability to independently learn the meaning of words as they encounter them in text (Kuhn & Stahl, 1998).

## PROCEDURES

### Getting Ready

1. Figure 27.1 provides a list and examples of the most common types of context clues. From the list, determine the types of clues that are used most often by the authors of materials that your students will be using. Depending on the background and reading level of your students, you can select to focus on one type of context clue during instruction, or you can choose to address all those that apply. It is often beneficial to share with students a list of the context clues they are likely to encounter in your subject area.

**Figure 27.1** Five types of context clues with examples

1. **Definition/explanation**

   The word or phrase's meaning is included in the sentence. Science example: A *planet* is a large body in space that orbits a star.

2. **Restatement/synonym**

   A word with a similar meaning or an example is included. Art studies example: *Classical Greek sculpture* had as its main focus figures and statues of the human body.

3. **Contrast/antonym**

   A word or phrase is clarified by giving the opposite meaning. Geography example: Quartz is a *mineral*, but granite is a rock made up of many compounds.

4. **Inference/general context clues**

   In some cases, the meaning of the word is not explicitly stated but is implied. The reader has to look for clues before, within, and after the sentence in which the word is used.

   Social studies example: In the early 18th century, farmers raised most of the nation's food on small strips of land, a method that was not very productive. The *Agricultural Revolution* occurred because of growth in the demand for food. Farmers were forced to change the way they raised their crops and to invent new machines to increase productivity.

5. **Graphs, tables, pictures, figures, and other illustrations**

   Some content area materials use graphs and other illustrations to clarify words.

   Mathematics example:

   Right triangle

2. Identify passages from materials that your students use that have example words to be defined. There are many commercial programs and materials available to teach context clues, but it is best to use authentic materials whenever possible. In choosing your materials, keep the following criteria in mind. First, choose passages that have the types of context clues you want to target during instruction. Second, start with passages that contain concepts that students are familiar with. You want your students to be able to use their background knowledge to help them reason through the clues in the context to find the meaning. As students become more proficient at using context clues, you can use more challenging passages. Third, choose passages that have various levels of context explicitness (Greenwood & Flanigan, 2007). Sometimes the context does not provide enough information to construct the meaning of a word, or the context is misleading. Eventually, students will need to be able to determine for themselves if the context is supportive. They will require teacher modeling and guided practice to be able to do this. Consider starting with examples in which the context is less supportive and building up to richer contexts. Finally, limit the number of words you introduce during a single lesson to 10 or fewer.

3. Prepare the passages so that you can display the words in their context one at a time. Two examples include overhead transparencies that are slowly uncovered as the lesson progresses and presentation software that adds text to the screen on mouse clicks. Make copies for your students to use in pairs or individually. If you wish students to have the passages in their hands while you instruct, make copies of the passages for students to use individually or in pairs.

### During Class

Context Clues are most powerful when they are used across many instructional phases with different materials. Students will need frequent teacher modeling and guided practice before they are able to use the strategy independently.

### *Building Word Knowledge*

1. Introduce the Context Clues strategy to students by telling them that sometimes when they come across a word they don't know, they can get an idea about the meaning of the word by looking at the context, or the words around the unknown word, for clues. Explain that they will need to look for clues both before and after the word.
2. Display an unknown word that has limited context. Read the word and the passage in which it appears orally. Model for students your reasoning as you try to figure out (unsuccessfully) the meaning of that word. Continue modeling, using words in progressively richer contexts and demonstrating for students how to use the clues to construct meaning. Figure 27.2 shows the beginning of a ninth-grade teacher's lesson in which he models for students the Context Clue strategy with words related to a unit on medieval Europe.
3. After modeling, guide students in analyzing the context to construct meaning. Present a passage with an unknown word, drawing from students their reasoning in predicting the meaning and then providing additional instruction in using Context Clues as needed. Consider using the following prompts to help guide students:
   • Where do you see clues to the word's meaning? Do we need to read the information before the word appears? After it appears? Both?
   • How can having the opposite meaning of a word help us define a word?

**Figure 27.2** The beginning of a ninth-grade teacher's lesson on Context Clues using passages on feudal society

---

*Getting ready*: The teacher chose passages that varied in the richness of the context and the types of Context Clues that were present.

*During class*:

1. To open the lesson, the teacher describes Context Clues and the importance of using them to figure out unknown words when reading. He explains that to find the clues, a reader needs to look before and after the unknown word.
2. The teacher presents the sentence "*Manors* were important in *feudal* society" and reads it orally.
3. He models his thinking as he tries to figure out the unknown words *manors* and *feudal*. He says, "Wow! There are two words in this sentence that I am not sure about: *manors* and *feudal*. The word *important* comes after *manors*, so I know that *manors* had some value or interest in feudal society. I also know something about the word *society*. Society usually refers to people and has to do with how they interact with one another. But I don't know what the word *feudal* means, and I don't see any clues that help me define it. Can anyone see anything I am missing?" A student suggests that the word *manor* may refer to a house. The teacher replies, "Good! You are using your background knowledge to try to figure it out. You may be right, but there are not enough clues for us to be sure. I think we need more information. We could look the word up in the dictionary, but let's read further to see if we find more clues."
4. The teacher presents the next sentence, "*Manors*, not villages, were the center of life in rural areas," and reads it orally.
5. He models his thinking as he uses the context clues to figure out the meaning of *manor*. He says, "Aha! The word *not* is very helpful here! It tells us that a *manor* is different from a *village,* and we know lots about villages. Also, the last part of the sentence shows us that both *manors* and *villages* were found not in what we might call cities but were instead in the country.

---

- Which words surrounding your word tell you its part of speech?
- Did you notice any words that helped you know that a clue to the meaning would follow?
- Are there any illustrations, figures, or other graphics that can help clarify the word's meaning?
- What words do you think are clues? Why?
- Do we have enough information to predict what the word means?
- What do you think the word means?

These questions are restated in Figure 27.3 as a bookmark that can be duplicated on card stock and shared with students for later use during *Independent Word Learning*. Ask students to confirm their predictions of the meaning of words by looking up the definition in a dictionary or glossary or by doing further reading. Teach students to check "chapter close" features as well, as key terms are often restated or embedded in practice items.

**Figure 27.3** Bookmark with Context Clues reminders

**Using Context Clues
for New Words**

✓ Check the words before and after the new word. Which give clues about the new word's meaning?

✓ Look for clues that point to the opposite of the new word. Do you see the word <u>not</u>?

✓ Look for clues about the word's part of speech. Is it a noun, a verb, or maybe an adjective?

✓ Check for illustrations, figures, and other graphics that clarify the word's meaning.

✓ Predict the new word's meaning.

✓ Confirm your prediction.

4. Have students work in pairs or small groups to use Context Clues. Ask them to write down what they think a word means and the clues that they used to make the prediction. Invite students to share some of their predictions and evidence to the class. Guide students in resolving any differences in meaning that may arise.

### Independent Word Learning

1. Students will benefit if you post the steps of the Context Clues strategy for them to use. You may wish to make a poster-size version of the information found in Figure 27.3 for this purpose.
2. Create a bulletin board that displays the types of Context Clues that are used most often in your subject area. Invite students to find examples of each type in their reading and display them on the bulletin board.
3. As words arise in the context of a lesson, have students predict the meaning before you provide instruction.
4. Ask students to identify two words from a chapter or other reading that they are able to define using the context. Have them write down their words, the definitions, and the page numbers where the words appeared. In class, invite students to share their words and the context with a partner or in a small group. Have students provide the reasoning they used to predict meaning. Invite a few students to share with the class. You may want to post the words and their predicted meanings in the classroom and revisit them during the lesson or unit.

## MODIFICATIONS

1. You can also use a cloze procedure to help students learn to use the context. In a cloze procedure, selected words are omitted from the text. The words that are omitted can be replaced by a line or a space or can be covered by a piece of opaque tape. As you read the passage, students are asked to suggest words for the omitted words that create a meaningful passage. The number of words that are omitted is up to you, although every fifth or seventh word is often suggested. Whatever method you use to delete words, make sure that you provide enough context that students are able to suggest appropriate words for those that are deleted. In general, the more background knowledge your students have about a topic, the more words you can omit.

   Figure 27.4 provides an example of a cloze passage used by the ninth-grade teacher teaching Context Clues to his students in a unit on medieval Europe. The teacher provided a list of possible words to use in the blanks of the cloze. This list can be omitted if you wish, although it will make filling in the blanks more difficult.
2. Cloze procedures can also be used for assessment. If you are using the procedure for assessment, structure the cloze so that you omit key words but provide clues in the sentence that will make it likely that students will fill in the blank. Usually, a list of possible words is not provided when a cloze passage is used as an assessment.

**Figure 27.4** Part of a cloze procedure used by a ninth-grade teacher in a unit on medieval Europe

Serfs were not slaves but were bound to their _____ for life. They could not own _____ . Serfs could not leave the land or _____ without their lord's permission. Serfs not only worked on the _____ of their lords, but they also worked in other areas such as forestry and _____ . However, they did have some rights. They were _____ by their lords and could not be _____ off of the land, even if the land changed hands.

Choose the word that makes sense in each of the blanks: *property, protected, lords, marry, village, forced, mining*

## TROUBLESHOOTING

1. To ensure student success and motivation, select a reasonable number of words and provide enough practice so that students can be successful.
2. Students will have a wide range of prior knowledge about the concepts you will use as examples. A class discussion of students' collective knowledge will help motivate students and facilitate learning the Context Clues strategies. Students must have some background knowledge to be able to use reasoning to predict the meaning of words.

## TECH CONNECT

Free or trial version software can be used to construct cloze passages. See http://www.schoolhousetech.com, http://bestsoftware4download.com, and http://edhelper.com/cloze.htm.

## NEXT STEPS

Context Clues strategies work very well with Morphemic Analysis (see p. 106). The morphology of a word and its context provide two important sources of information about a word's meaning that can be combined to enhance the likelihood that the predicted meaning of the word will be correct.

# 28

# Keyword Method

The Keyword Method uses a mnemonic or memory strategy for learning the meaning of vocabulary terms. Extensive research has been conducted on the effectiveness of this strategy (Lawson & Hogben 1998; Mastropieri, Scruggs & Fulk, 1990; Pressley, Levin, & Delany, 1982; Terrell, Scruggs, & Mastropieri, 2004; Uberti, Scruggs & Mastropieri, 2003; Wyra & Hungi, 2007). The research indicates that under most conditions, the Keyword Method improves vocabulary knowledge for students at all academic levels, including English learners, students with learning disabilities, and students working at grade level. However, because the focus of the strategy is on remembering the definition of words, it does not result in an elaborated understanding of the meaning of a word. Although this limits its application, the Keyword Method is a useful strategy for building a basic understanding of vocabulary that can be elaborated through further instruction and reading (Blachowicz & Fisher, 2006).

## PURPOSE

The Keyword Method is a strategy that uses personalized auditory and visual mnemonic devices to build a link between an unknown word and its definition. It is useful in circumstances where students need to memorize and recall the definitions of words.

There are many occasions when students must learn the definitions of words. First, students with low vocabulary, content knowledge, or learning disabilities may find that they are overwhelmed with the number of unknown words they meet. These students can benefit from the Keyword Method because it helps develop a basic understanding of the meaning of words. Once the method is taught to students, it can also be used independently to enhance word learning. Second, students who are learning a new language find the strategy to be beneficial because they must be able to remember the meaning of many words in a relatively short period of time. Finally, vocabulary knowledge is often evaluated on important standardized tests such as state and national assessments of academic achievement. The Keyword Method can be helpful as a study tool for students in studying for those tests.

## PROCEDURES

### Getting Ready

1. Figure 28.1 provides the steps for using the Keyword Method that are based on those suggested by Levin (1988). Study these for an overview of the method and consider reproducing these steps for students.
2. Identify words that you will use to teach the Keyword Method to your students. Keep the number of words to five or fewer. Make sure to choose words that can be easily

**Figure 28.1** Steps in the Keyword Method

1. Select a target term.
2. Record the definition of the word.
3. Recode the new word by thinking of a familiar word (keyword) that sounds like the new word. For example, the word *insidious* means "seeking to trap." A good keyword for *insidious* would be *inside*.
4. Form a visual image of the keyword and the definition interacting by writing a description or drawing a picture. To form an association between "seeking to trap" and *inside,* you could draw a picture of a man trapped inside a box.
5. When asked for the definition of the word, think of the image of the keyword interacting with the definition and retrieve the definition.

**Figure 28.2** Spanish 1 adjectives with English cognates

| Spanish term | English translation |
| --- | --- |
| *artístico(a)* | *artistic* |
| *atlético(a)* | *athletic* |
| *cómico(a)* | *funny* |
| *desorganizado(a)* | *disorganized* |
| *inteligente* | *intelligent* |
| *serio(a)* | *serious* |

visualized. For students studying a new language, consider words with English cognates, or related words, as intuitive starting points for the Keyword Method. Figure 28.2 shows a few adjectives a Spanish 1 teacher presented to her students as she taught them to use the Keyword Method.

3. Select keywords for each of the terms and describe or draw images that could be used to connect the keywords to the definitions. A political science teacher used the Keyword Method to teach students important terms at the beginning of a unit on propaganda in politics. Figure 28.3 shows a partial list of the keywords and images that she developed for her lesson.
4. Decide what method you will use for students to record the words, definitions, and mnemonics. Index cards or teacher-prepared cards are good choices because students can place the new word on one side of the card and the definition, keyword, and image on the other side. This arrangement allows students to learn the words and definitions by testing their memory both forward and backward.

## During Class

The Keyword Method is effective during the *Building Word Knowledge* and *Independent Word Learning* phases.

### Building Word Knowledge

1. Present the target words one at a time. As you introduce each word, ask students to record the word and the definition. You can have students look up the definition, or, if you prefer, you can provide it to students. If you have students look up the definition,

**Figure 28.3** Vocabulary terms chosen to introduce a unit on political propaganda in politics

| Word | Definition | Key word | Image |
|------|-----------|----------|-------|
| slander | To say something untrue that damages a person's reputation | word slayer | Predator with the word *lies* hurling out of his mouth with enough force to injure someone |
| boycott | To show disapproval by refusing to buy a product or take part in an activity | boy stop | Boy with a stop sign in front of a store |
| stereotype | To describe or think about all members of a group in the same way | typecast | A group of people drawn to look exactly alike |

consider presenting the new word in a sentence or a phrase so that you can use the context to help them choose the correct definition.

2. Model for students how to think of a familiar word or words that will help them remember the definition. Explain to students that the key word or words should sound like the new word and be easily pictured. For example, for the word *slander*, you might say, "First, I looked up the meaning of *slander* and wrote it down, 'speak untruths that cause harm to someone.' Next, I thought of some keywords that would help me remember the word *slander* and its definition. I needed to think of a word that sounded like *slander*. *Slayer* sounds like *slander*, so I chose *slayer*. I also thought about the definition. The definition says that slander occurs when someone says something untruthful that harms another person. That made me think that *word slayer* would be good keyword to help me remember *slander* and its definition. Finally, I needed an image that shows the keywords interacting with the definition. My idea was to draw a picture of a predator attacking a man by hurling the word *lie* out of his mouth. So whenever I am asked the definition for slander, first I will think of the keywords *word slayer*, and then I will think of the image I drew. That should help me remember the definition."

3. Once students understand the steps of the Keyword Method, invite them to join you in the process. For example, after you have introduced a new word, definition, and keyword, have the students work in pairs or small groups to create an appropriate image. Encourage them to evaluate their word by checking back to see if it clearly shows the keyword interacting with the definition. Finally, provide guided practice by having students work in pairs or small groups to complete all the steps of the Keyword Method.

4. Ask students to independently complete the steps of the Keyword Method with three or four words from instruction or readings as homework. In class, invite them to share their work with a partner and explain their reasoning in choosing their keywords and images. Discuss the choices of a few students with the whole group. Remind students that the terms are ones they will be expected to learn and to practice using their keywords and images to recall the definitions.

**Figure 28.4** A sample of a student's keyword cards used to learn Spanish 1 vocabulary

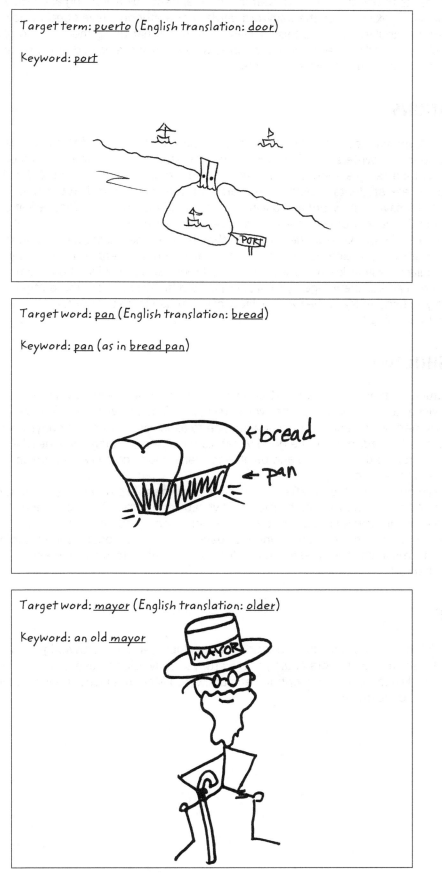

Target term: <u>puerto</u> (English translation: <u>door</u>)

Keyword: <u>port</u>

Target word: <u>pan</u> (English translation: <u>bread</u>)

Keyword: <u>pan</u> (as in <u>bread pan</u>)

Target word: <u>mayor</u> (English translation: <u>older</u>)

Keyword: an old <u>mayor</u>

*Independent Word Learning*

Encourage students to use the Keyword Method independently as a learning and study tool. Figure 28.4 gives an example of the keyword cards that a student developed to help him remember new vocabulary in his Spanish 1 class. He found that using the cards to review terms before class helped him remember the terms when they were used during instruction. He also used them as a study tool before tests.

## MODIFICATIONS

1. Provide students with opportunities to practice. Distribute two sets of Vocab Cards (p. 50). On one set, write each of the words that the students are learning. On the other set, write a sample sentence and the definition for each word. Give the definition of a word and ask students to hold up the card with the correct word. You can reverse the process by saying the word and asking students to hold up the correct definition. Continue in this manner until all the words have been reviewed.
2. Assess students' word knowledge on words they have learned using the Keyword Method. After the assessment, ask students to reflect on their learning. Which terms were particularly easy to learn? Which ones need more attention? Did the keywords that you chose and/or the images you drew make a difference? Were there other strategies you used to learn the words? How can you use this strategy for independent learning?

## TROUBLESHOOTING

1. Remind students that the Keyword Method does not work well with words that cannot be easily visualized. For example, the word *quality* is difficult to visualize. A more appropriate method for learning quality would be to associate it with a synonym such as *characteristic* or *attribute*. To be good vocabulary learners, students will need a variety of strategies they can use and be able to make good choices about which one is most appropriate.
2. For the Keyword Method to be effective as an *Independent Word Learning* strategy, students need to be able to identify important vocabulary terms. Provide students with strategies for locating important terms, including jotting down terms that are emphasized during instruction and using the readers' aids in textbooks such as bolded terms, key terms in chapter questions, and lists of vocabulary terms at the end of textbook chapters or units.

## NEXT STEPS

The Keyword Method does not result in students developing a deep knowledge of words. Once students have a basic understanding of a word, you may want to use other strategies, such as Semantic Maps (p. 37), Concept of Definition Word Map (p. 9), and the Frayer Model (p. 18), to enrich their learning.

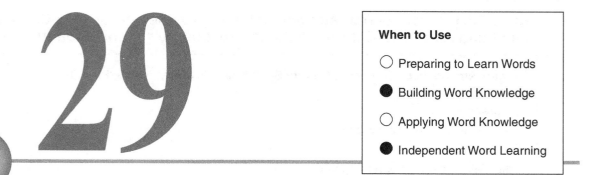

**When to Use**

○ Preparing to Learn Words

● Building Word Knowledge

○ Applying Word Knowledge

● Independent Word Learning

# Content Area Read Alouds

In Content Area Read Alouds, students listen as their teachers orally read appealing selections related to the content at hand. Content Area Read Alouds are usually brief, often lasting 10 to 15 minutes or less. Teachers typically mediate the read alouds by talking about new vocabulary terms (e.g., Hickman, Pollard-Durodola, & Vaughn, 2004), asking comprehension questions (Whitehurst et al., 1999), fostering discussions that involve critical thinking, or asking students to make personal connections to the text (e.g., Albright, 2002; Albright & Ariail, 2005). Often teachers select Content Area Read Aloud materials that fall beyond students' independent reading level but that are within their listening comprehension levels. Read aloud materials include narratives but should extend far beyond storybooks to represent a variety of genres. Figure 29.1 suggests some materials that may be appropriate for read alouds in your content areas.

## PURPOSE

Decades of research and teacher experience support read alouds across the grade levels, including the secondary school years. Here is a Top Ten list of purposes served by read alouds, with the purposes most directly related to vocabulary presented last.

1. Read alouds provide fluent, enthusiastic modeling of reading (Richardson, 1994).
2. Read alouds can provide access to information and experiences otherwise unavailable to students given their current reading levels.
3. Read alouds can enhance motivation and interest, fostering a love for reading (Bigelow & Vokoun, 2005).
4. Teachers enjoy read alouds (e.g., Bigelow & Vokoun, 2005; Kelly, 2006).
5. Students, including middle and high school students, enjoy Read Alouds and report benefiting from them (Goldfinch, 2002; Kelly, 2006; Meehan, 2006; Pflaum & Bishop, 2004).
6. Read alouds provide a means to reach reluctant readers (Erickson, 1996).
7. Teachers report that Read Alouds support student understanding of the content (Albright & Ariail, 2005; Ivey, 2003).
8. By immersing students in content-rich language, read alouds can help students, particularly those who are not voracious readers, master the 3,000 or so words that K–12 students should learn each year. Recall that most vocabulary knowledge develops not through direct instruction but through wide reading and oral language (Nagy, Herman, & Anderson, 1985; Stahl, 1999) and that daily conversations usually do not contain the content-based terms that school-aged children need to enhance their vocabularies (Cunningham & Stanovich, 1998). Content Area Read Alouds can thus provide vital access to key vocabulary.
9. Research with primary students does indeed link read alouds to achievement, comprehension, and vocabulary development (Apthorp, 2006; Beck & McKeown, 2007; Blachowicz & Obrochta, 2005; Santaro, Chard, Howard, & Baker, 2008).

**Figure 29.1** A variety of materials that may provide appropriate Content Area Read Alouds for intermediate and secondary school students

Award winners (e.g., Caldecott, Coretta Scott King, Newbery, Nobel, Pura Belpré, and Pulitzer Prize)

Biographies

Comic books (see Ranker, 2007)

Diary entries

Editorials, including opposing viewpoints

Graphic novels

Historical documents

Informational texts

Joke and riddle books

Letters

Magazine articles and features

Newspaper stories and columns

Nonfiction chapter books

Novels

Picture books (fiction and nonfiction)

Plays

Poetry

Primary sources

Short stories

Song lyrics

Textbook passages

Web-based materials

10. Finally, read alouds offer a mechanism to narrow the vocabulary gap between middle- and lower-income students (Beck & McKeown, 2007).

In sum, students of all ages can enjoy and profit from Content Area Read Alouds, with vocabulary development being one of many important benefits.

## PROCEDURES

### Getting Ready

1. Create a file of promising Content Area Read Aloud selections. In your own reading, choose materials from Figure 29.1 and store them with your unit materials. As you read the newspaper or a newsmagazine, clip articles that place your content in contexts your students are likely to appreciate. For instance, scientific discoveries and science-related social issues abound in the popular press ("Giant Sea Creatures Found in Antarctic Search," reported at CNN.com on March 21, 2008. These creatures included sea stars measuring 2 feet across!).

For leads on good read aloud books, ask your students, fellow teachers, and the librarian for sources that students will find interesting. You can also follow the Web for good leads. Try these sites:

http://www.ala.org/ala/awards/books_media/index.cfm. The Book and Media Awards page of the American Library Association's site

http://www.bookspot.com/awards. Book Spot awards

http://www.ala.org/ala/yalsa/booklistsawards/quickpicks/quickpicksreluctant.cfm. Young
Adult Library Services Association's Quick Picks for Reluctant Readers
http://www.guysread.com. Guys Read, by Jon Scieszka
http://www.trelease-on-reading.com. Home page of Jim Trelease, author of the Read
Aloud Handbook and others (see his weekly Read Aloud pick)

2. As you build your Content Area Read Aloud stories, consider picture books. Don't worry
that older students will consider books with pictures babyish; the term *picture book*
refers to the format for telling the story and not to the reading or interest level of the
story (Giourgis, 1999). Many picture books are sophisticated enough even for adult
readers, and there are good picture books for most every content area (for older but
good social studies leads, see ERIC Development Team, 1997). Many subject area
organizations, such as National Science Teachers Association and National Council of
Social Studies, also publish annual lists of exemplary trade books.

Picture books offer a number of benefits as Content Area Read Alouds. They are relatively short, have supportive illustrations, can encourage an aesthetic response to the
content, encourage discussion (Albright, 2002), and can support visual literacy (Johnson,
2002). As you make your picture book selections, consider the following criteria
(Albright, 2002; Giorgis, 1999):
a. Overall quality
b. Relevance
c. Interest for students

3. Choose three vocabulary terms. Criteria for selecting terms for primary-grade read
alouds appear to fit for older students as well. Choose terms that are the following:
a. Functional and meaningful
b. Rich, varied, and interesting
c. Important for understanding the passage (Santaro et al., 2008).

4. Plan a few starter questions to prompt discussion before the reading session. Albright
(2002) suggests questions such as "What can you tell us about (topic)? What do you
think this book might be about? Why might I read it to you?" If appropriate, plan a few
questions to raise during the session as well.

As an example, in the state where she works, a fourth-grade teacher's students
must learn to work with whole numbers in the millions, and when they reach sixth
grade, these students will be expected to calculate interest. So, for her Content Area
Read Aloud, she chooses David M. Schwartz's (1989) picture book *If You Made a
Million*. Figure 29.2 shares the vocabulary terms and prompts that this fourth-grade
math teacher uses in support of her read aloud session.

## During Class

Content Area Read Alouds are effective during both the *Building Word Knowledge* and
*Independent Word Learning* phases.

### Building Word Knowledge

1. Introduce the text, asking students just a few questions to build personal connections
and to pique their interest in the content and the selection. Examples include, "Who
here has ever . . ." and "Why do you think the woman on the cover is holding an . . .?"
2. Introduce a limited set of vocabulary terms. Write them on the board or on Vocab Cards
(p. 50) and post them for continued reference. The depth of your treatment of the terms
will depend on such factors as how well the text treats the terms and how well the
terms will be addressed in later lessons. Be careful not to overdo your preteaching of
the terms. Less is probably better.
3. Read. Pause as appropriate to encourage personal connections and critical thinking
(Albright & Ariail, 2005).
4. Close. Even brief read aloud sessions and ones that extend over time should be closed.
Ask students to summarize, to share a surprise, or to connect what they heard to
another part of life.

**Figure 29.2** A fourth-grade teacher's preparation and introduction of the *If You Made a Million* Content Area Read Aloud

---

***Vocabulary Terms***

Mathematics terms:        *interest*

                              *value*

                              *down payment*

And one for fun:        *obstreperous*

**The Content Area Read Aloud**

***Vocabulary Talk***

- [The book is out of students' view.] "Before we start our read aloud today, I'm going to show you a few words, one at a time. Let's talk about each one. Talk with your partner about what you think that word means, and then we'll talk as a class. It may help to use it in a sentence. Here goes." [Teacher presents and leads discussion of math terms, one at a time.]

    *interest*

    *value*

    *down payment*

- "From your discussion, you make it clear that at least two of these words can mean different things in different settings. Let me show you the book we'll read aloud today. You can refine your predictions if you like."
- [Teacher makes a show of pulling out *If You Made a Million*. Some students accurately define the target terms, given the mathematical context. Teacher encourages the class to check as they listen to the book. She leaves the Vocab Cards on the board.]
- "I'd like to show you one more word that you'll meet in this book. It isn't a mathematics term, but I love the sound of it."

    *obstreperous*

    "Say it with me: *obstreperous*. Impressive, isn't it? Any guesses on its meaning or what it's doing in our mathematics read aloud?"

***Starter Questions***

- [Teacher reads the author, illustrator, and title.] "Have you been alive for a million seconds?" [Teacher supports students' estimation process as they discuss the question for a few minutes.]
- "Do you know of anyone, maybe someone in the news, who makes a million dollars? Tell us about that." [Students discuss media reports of the salaries of sports figures and actors. Some note with indignation the differences in income associated with different U.S. professions.]
- "Let's see what it would be like if *you* made a million."

***During the Reading***

- [As they come across the terms in the text, the class talks about how close they came in their definitions, and they add to the terms' meanings. Students write meanings on the backs of the Vocab Cards and move them to the Word Wall (see p. 81). They discuss situations where people might be considered *obstreperous*.]

***After the Reading***

- Students discuss their own responses to the final question in the text, "So what would you do if you made a million?"
- "What would be some reasons I'd choose this book for our read aloud today?"

**A Note for Your English Learners**

Hickman et al. (2004) suggest a storybook read aloud structure that can be useful in Content Area Read Alouds to support vocabulary development and comprehension for your English learners:

1. Preview the selection and the three terms.
2. Read the selection, focusing on literal and inferential comprehension.
3. Reread the selection, extending comprehension of the target terms.
4. Summarize the selection and the content students learned through the read aloud.

## Independent Word Learning

Transfer the power of Content Area Read Alouds into your students' hands through a special reading event. Ross, Hunter, and Chazanow (2006) describe an all-day Read Aloud festival of *Moby Dick* organized and run by students.

Read alouds can encourage strong family relationships (as in Schnur, 1999), home-based discussions of the content, and a shared love of literacy. Send home materials for students and families to appreciate together, perhaps providing a structure for sharing and responding to the selection. You might, for example, ask students to reread materials from class to their families and ask family members to write a brief response, sharing their reactions to the piece. See Home Connections (p. 98) for other ideas for including families in literacy learning.

## TROUBLESHOOTING

1. If you are new to read alouds, start with brief selections and practice reading the selection aloud (Albright & Ariail, 2004).
2. Not all students hold still as they listen. Goldfinch (2002) finds it effective to allow students to doodle as she reads. You might devote a bulletin board or Vocabulary Graffiti (p. 155) board to share students' Content Area Read Aloud drawings.
3. Not every Content Area Read Aloud selection works with every group of students. If the selection doesn't match your students' needs or interests, strongly consider abandoning it in favor of a more promising selection.
4. Be wary of one Content Area Read Aloud practice: oral reading of the textbook, either by teacher or students. Although a teacher's oral reading of the textbook can support students' comprehension of the content, teacher read alouds of the textbook should be used judiciously.

   Similarly, student read alouds should be carefully planned. We urge you to consider alternatives to student Read Aloud practices such as public, unrehearsed, round-robin reading or popcorn reading of the textbook. These practices offer questionable support of student engagement and the complex demands of literacy today (Blanton, Wood, & Taylor, 2007).

## NEXT STEPS

1. April is National Poetry Month. Use poetry as an occasion to spread your Content Area Read Alouds to the broader community (Higashi, 1998). Include local poets, librarians, teachers, and your student poets in read aloud sessions at public libraries and other inviting locales. Students can read famous works or their own (Wilkinson & Minter, 2004). See Poetry (p. 149) for ideas to get students started in composing content vocabulary–rich poems.

# 30

**When to Use**

○ Preparing to Learn Words

○ Building Word Knowledge

● Applying Word Knowledge

○ Independent Word Learning

# Readers Theater

Popular for decades with teachers and students alike, Readers Theater allows two or more performers to read a script aloud for their audience. The emphasis is on effective oral reading and communication and not on memorization, elaborate costumes, staging, props, or movements. No attempt is made to hide the scripts, and all performers stay on stage during the entire performance. Given its power to support many positive learning outcomes—including vocabulary development—Readers Theater is working its way into content area classrooms with increasing frequency.

## PURPOSE

With its emphasis on purposeful rereading, expressive communication, and performance, Readers Theater has a number of documented benefits. Research clearly indicates that Readers Theater supports fluency (Corcoran & Davis, 2005; Keehn, 2003; Rinehart, 2001; Worthy & Prater, 2002). It also supports comprehension (Kornfeld & Leyden, 2005), writing skills (Liu, 2000), and student motivation (Block, 2003; Wolf, 1998).

In the content areas, Readers Theater provides a motivating context for students to practice and apply important concepts and terms from recently studied subject matter. When students write and perform scripts to capture important ideas and terms, they must meet the dual challenges of informing and entertaining, and by doing so, students use the many facets of language (Flynn, 2004). Readers Theater also allows students to engage in the thought processes required by particular disciplines, such as science (El-Hindi, 2003). Content-based Readers Theater, with its purposeful rehearsal and presentation, is likely to support students' content and vocabulary retention and improve academic performance.

### A Note for Your English Learners

Readers Theater holds special promise for students acquiring English (Liu, 2000) because it can help students build confidence and enthusiasm as they practice content vocabulary and English pronunciation. Readers Theater can enhance students' appreciation of expository text, support their writing skills, enhance their oral skills, and boost their confidence in handling spoken dialogue (Boucher & Leong, 2002). Finally, Readers Theater can support cross-cultural understanding when scripts are selected or developed to help students learn about different cultures, including those represented in the classroom.

## PROCEDURES

### Getting Ready

1. Select the key terms that must be addressed in the Readers Theater script(s). Figure 30.1 gives the sixth-grade content standard a teacher used

**Figure 30.1** Content standard and related key terms for a sixth-grade science Readers Theater lesson

Content standard: Students know populations of organisms can be categorized by the functions they serve in the ecosystem (California Department of Education, 2004).

Selected key terms:

| | |
|---|---|
| *organism* | *producer* |
| *function* | *consumer* |
| *ecosystem* | *predator* |
| *food web* | *scavenger* |
| *energy pyramid* | *decomposer* |

to guide a series of science lessons. It also gives the teacher's selection of related key terms developed through those lessons.

2. Decide whether you will provide a prepared script or whether students will write their own scripts:
   a. If you choose to provide a script, you can search for scripts written by others (see *Tech Connect*), or you can write your own.
   b. If you choose to have students compose their own scripts, develop the criteria that must be addressed in students' scripts and presentations.
   c. If students are to compose scripts, collect content-based materials that will support script development. Examples of source materials include fact sheets, a page from a textbook, and graphic organizers or other materials students created during *Building Word Knowledge* activities. Semantic Maps (p. 37), Concept of Definition Word Maps (p. 9), Frayer Model organizers (p. 18), and Sketch to Stretch drawings (p. 28) are examples.
3. If you or your students will develop the scripts, share and follow the criteria found in Figure 30.2 for script development.

**Figure 30.2** Tips for developing content-based Readers Theater scripts (influenced by Flynn, 2004)

**Keep in Mind**

- The performance needs to do at least two things: teach people things *and* entertain them. It needs to be informative *and* interesting. Should the performance also *influence* people to think or act in a certain way?
- The content needs a context. Provide a setting. Are the performers at a party? At the store? Solving a problem at home?

**Steps**

1. Check the requirements:
   - Which information must you include? Which key terms?
   - How long must the performance be? (Five to 10 minutes is a good guideline. The script will probably be no more than two pages in length.)
   - Anything else?
2. Brainstorm and organize the information you must include. Try a Semantic Map (p. 37), for example, or a Frayer Model graphic organizer (p. 18).
3. Decide on how many speakers you will use during the performance. Include parts for people who like to read aloud and for those who don't yet. Use narrators in addition to other speakers.
4. Edit the script. One draft is *never* enough.

## During Class

Readers Theater provides a motivating opportunity for *Applying Word Knowledge*.

### *Applying Word Knowledge*

1. If students are to develop scripts, provide sufficient modeling, support, and time for students to develop them. Engage in prewriting activities such as developing graphic organizers. Also refer to the products of *Building Word Knowledge* (such as those listed previously). For example, Figure 30.3 gives the graphic organizer used by the sixth-grade class to summarize major terms given previously in Figure 30.2. Provide opportunities—perhaps based on rough readings—for students to edit their scripts.
2. Duplicate and distribute the scripts.
3. Assign parts. Note that more than one student may be assigned to a part. Figure 30.4 gives the opening snippet of the script created by sixth graders in their science class. Note that the script divides performers into two groups and has the capacity to expand the number of performers from four to an entire class.
4. Highlight lines. Provide students with highlighter pens to mark their lines.
5. Rehearse. As appropriate for the age, reading level, and English proficiency of your students, follow this general sequence:
   a. Model reading (read the script for the students).
   b. Echo reading (read a line for the students and have the students repeat it).
   c. Choral reading (allow students assigned to given parts to rehearse those parts aloud by reading them in unison).
   d. Partner reading (have individual students read their lines to a partner).
   e. Allow for independent practice, such as homework, as well.
6. Perform. Ensure a realistic audience for each performance. This may be half of your own class, the class next door, students in a different grade level or subject area, family members, or community members.
7. Reflect. While students are still excited about their performance, invite them to review their work. Offer prompts such as the following:
   a. "How well did we *inform*? How do we know they learned something new?"

### Figure 30.3 Prewriting graphic organizer for sixth-grade science terms

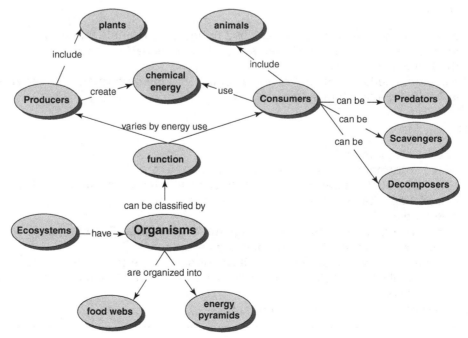

**Figure 30.4** Opening snippet of the script created by a sixth-grade science class

Performers are arranged into two groups: right side and left side. The left side is pitted against the right in a challenge, like the home team and visitors' side at a sporting event.

**Performers**

| Left | Right |
|------|-------|
| 1 | 2 |
| 3 | 4 |
| All (left) | All (right) |

| | |
|---|---|
| 1: | Hey now. |
| All (right): | What? |
| All (left): | We said, "Hey now." |
| All (right): | *(louder)* What? |
| 1: | Are you an *organism*? |
| All (right): | *(Gesture to communicate "We don't know" or "We don't care.")* |
| 1: | I said, Are you an *organism*? |
| 2: | Organism. What's that? |
| 1: | Anything alive. |
| All (right) | Anything alive? |
| 2: | Oh yeah. I'm an organism. |
| 3: | Well then, what's your *function?* |
| 4: | What's my function? |
| All (left): | What do you do? |
| 2: | Oh! Yeah. My function! What I do! |
| 3: | Every organism has a function. It *does* something! |
| 2: | Like what? Text message? |
| 4: | Throw a pass? Download? |
| 1: | No way! Do you *produce* chemical energy . . . |
| 3: | . . . Or do you *consume* it? |

b. "How well did we *entertain*? How do we know they enjoyed it?"
c. "What did we do especially well? How can we include that strength in our next performance?"
d. "What didn't go quite as well? How can we improve next time?"

## MODIFICATIONS

1. Consider adding visual effects. For instance, you may allow students to improvise costumes or other props. Some teachers allow students to create character tags that performers hang around their necks on yarn. As another visual effect, you may choose to project related images on a screen behind the performers using a computer-based system or an overhead projector.

2. Use different kinds of theater to practice new words in engaging ways. Shadow puppetry (Peck & Virkler, 2006), tableaux vivants (Tortello, 2004), and movie script performances (Hoffner, 2003) can all provide highly engaging mechanisms for applying new content vocabulary knowledge through performance.

## TROUBLESHOOTING

1. When students are new script writers, they may tend to write boring scripts that provide merely a recitation of facts. Review students' scripts with them to ensure that they use popular appeal, intrigue, humor, or other mechanisms to build and sustain audience interest.
2. Rest assured that Readers Theater can be used with students at all reading and skill levels, including emergent readers (Moran, 2006). Support emergent readers in script development by writing at least one script together and model through think-aloud processes the development of effective scripts and presentations.
3. Most classes contain struggling readers, many of whom are uncomfortable with their literacy performance, particularly in oral reading. Although Readers Theater is documented as an effective practice in building both skills and confidence, Rinehart (2001) offers specific suggestions to ensure the success of struggling readers in Readers Theater:
   a. Use known books. Source materials that are familiar to students transfer most easily to Readers Theater scripts. Additionally, supports such as graphic organizers and other knowledge resources can aid struggling readers.
   b. Use texts and scripts at students' instructional levels.
   c. Provide an incentive for performance (provide a real audience).
   d. Help students come to see "good" reading as "expressive" reading.
   e. Provide plentiful practice to ensure student success.

## TECH CONNECT

1. Many scripts are available online. Carrick (2001), available online, has plentiful examples, all just a click away. In addition, search for *content-based Readers Theater scripts* for other leads.
2. Post your students' scripts as documents or performances as podcasts to the Web to share with even broader audiences.

# 31

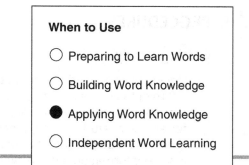

**When to Use**

○ Preparing to Learn Words

○ Building Word Knowledge

● Applying Word Knowledge

○ Independent Word Learning

# Student-Made Books

We recently asked Jack, a ninth-grade student, whether he ever makes books at school: "Yeah. My biology teacher just had us make a little book to study terms for the body systems test. It didn't get lost like my other papers, and I had everything I needed to know right there." Jack's response suggests that bookmaking, popular with younger students, can continue to support students' learning through the secondary grades. Student-Made Books can range from the very simple fold-and-staple variety to hardback editions with stitched bindings. They can pop up, fold out, flip over, or fit into our pockets. No matter their form, Student-Made Books help students like Jack summarize, organize, and use their content vocabulary in meaningful contexts.

## PURPOSE

Student-Made Books support major goals of effective vocabulary development. First, students need to be immersed in words (Alvermann, Swafford, & Montero, 2004). Book writing experiences are rich, and Student-Made Books often become valued fixtures in the classroom. In addition, students need multiple exposures and meaningful opportunities to use new words (Nagy, 1988; Pearson, Hiebert, & Kamil, 2007), and Student-Made Books can help. Further, like others, Curtis and Longo (2001) note that writing is a crucial method for students to actively process word meanings and apply them in a generative way. Finally, Student-Made Books can extend and express students' understandings of concepts, enhance meaning through combined use of text and images, support motivation for reluctant writers, encourage rereading, and deepen students' understanding of art (Guzzetti & Wooten, 2002).

> ### A Note for Your English Learners
>
> It's especially important that students who are mastering English have plentiful opportunities to produce output in English, the target language. Writing experiences, particularly collaborative ones, allow them to use new vocabulary and interact with their peers (Anthony, 2008). English learners should be encouraged to talk about the writing process and to reread what they have written both in their first language and in English. Bookmaking activities provide engaging writing and oral opportunities for English learners and their peers.

## ● PROCEDURES

### Getting Ready

1. Decide the scope of the project. Student-Made Books can be completed quickly (10 minutes or less) to be used as study guides, or they can be long-term projects that serve to culminate extensive studies. For a simple study guide with eight pages, for example, students might stack two half sheets of paper, fold the stack down the middle, and staple near the fold. On each page, they can write an assigned term and include information such as its definition, its origins, a sentence including it, and a picture. (See Dictionaries, p. 93.)

   As a more ambitious, culminating project, students might construct elaborate pop-up books that organize and explore terms (concepts, people, or places) they consider most important to the topic. One of our favorites was an eighth grader's work titled "The Middle Ages: Famous People and How They Died." Although a work of dark comedy, the book successfully traced the accomplishments and demise of many people she studied in history class, complete with memorable swinging ropes and dancing flames.

2. Select the content to be addressed in students' books. Decide which and how many vocabulary terms students must use in their books. Will students select the topic and terms, or will you? Will the books explore a single topic in great detail? Will they survey a large variety of terms? Two sources of vocabulary terms include Word Walls (p. 81) and Vocab Cards (p. 50).

3. Choose one or more techniques that meet your purposes. Figure 31.1 lists some of the many bookmaking techniques that can be used effectively in the classroom.

   A treasure trove of free illustrated examples, instructional videos, and downloadable templates for bookmaking can be found on the Web. Two rich sites include the following:
   http://www.vickiblackwell.com/makingbooks/index.htm. Let's Book It with
      Tech'Knowledge'y
   http://www.homeschoolshare.com/lapbooking_resources.php. Homeschool Share:
      Lapbooking Resources

**Figure 31.1** Some ideas for book formats

- ABC books (see a content vocabulary lesson with ABC books at http://www.readwritethink. org/lessons/lesson_view.asp?id=276)
- Accordion books (Paper is folded back and forth, back and forth.)
- Artists books (see Guzzetti & Wooten, 2002)
- Plastic baggie books (Tape several resealable plastic bags together at the spine—the edge opposite the opening. Fill the baggies with paper and objects. Use dry erase pens to write on the baggies, making the books interactive if you like.)
- Counting books
- Dial books (Two circles are connected with a brad. The top circle has a section cut away to reveal information below.)
- Fan books (A deck of pages is connected with a brad or ring.)
- Lift the flap books*
- Match books*
- Paper bag books
- Petal books*
- Photo album books (Slip pages, cut to size, into album pockets.)
- Pop-up books
- Shape books
- Step books*

*An example is found in Figure 31.2.

The directions and resources for making the books can be found on these Web sites, and others. Use a search engine to find directions for your book of interest, entering a phrase such as "how to make pop-up books."

4. Make or gather samples of books to serve as models.
5. Gather materials. Card stock and recycled cardboard (such as that from cereal boxes) are helpful. So is masking tape or painter's tape.

**Figure 31.2** Sample Student-Made Books from across the fifth-grade curriculum

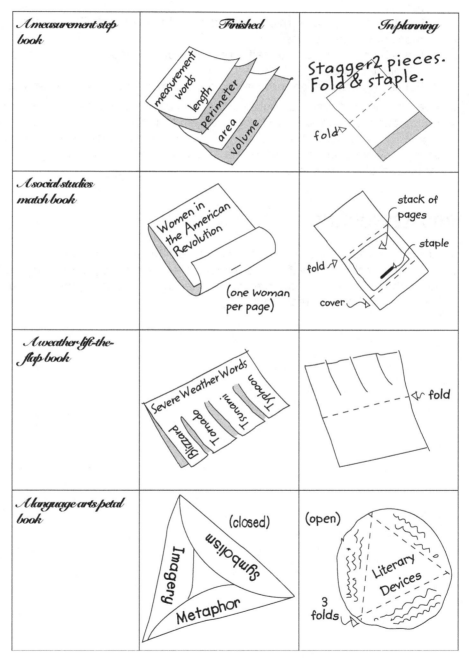

| A measurement step book | Finished | In planning |
|---|---|---|
| | measurement words length perimeter area volume | Stagger 2 pieces. Fold & staple. fold▷ |
| A social studies match book | Women in the American Revolution — (one woman per page) | stack of pages staple fold cover |
| A weather lift-the-flap book | Severe Weather Words Typhoon Tsunami Tornado Blizzard | ◁ fold |
| A language arts petal book | (closed) Imagery Symbolism Metaphor | (open) Literary Devices 3 folds |

**During Class**

Student-Made Books are an appealing strategy for *Applying Word Knowledge*.

### *Applying Word Knowledge*

1. Introduce the bookmaking project. Show published or homemade samples. Set the criteria for content and format.
2. For informal projects such as study guides, have students compose just one draft. For more formal projects, engage students in the writing process:
   a. Prewriting: Discuss chosen vocabulary terms. Brainstorm content and book formats.
   b. Drafting: Write one or more rough drafts of the content. Create storyboards (or mock-ups) of the pages.
   c. Revising and editing: Use self-feedback, peer feedback, and teacher feedback to polish the books.
   d. Publishing: Use varied materials to transform drafts to the finished product.
3. Read the books to real audiences and encourage students to reread them often.
4. Encourage students to make books frequently and in different subject areas. Figure 31.2 depicts sample Student-Made Books from mathematics, social studies, science, and the language arts. Each of these books can be constructed in fewer than 20 minutes.

## TROUBLESHOOTING

1. Emphasize meaning over form to encourage reluctant writers.
2. If the bookmaking project is an ambitious one, be sure to provide plentiful support along the way. Save students from procrastinating by setting deadlines and helping them check their progress frequently.

# 32

**When to Use**

○ Preparing to Learn Words

○ Building Word Knowledge

● Applying Word Knowledge

○ Independent Word Learning

# Poetry

A highly concentrated form of writing, poetry evokes emotional responses to phenomena by using carefully selected words (and often beautiful language), images, rhythm, and sound to suggest meaning. Relaxed in its syntax, poetry frequently employs vivid description and symbolism to convey experiences and ideas imaginatively and often with great depth of meaning.

## PURPOSE

Researchers note that many U.S. students engage in a limited range of literary experiences at school (Delpit, 2003, 2006; Franzak, 2006; Rosenblatt, 2003). As a result, some students become marginalized and approach text submissively rather than vigorously engaging in text transactions (Franzak, 2006). Students need authentic school-based literacy experiences that provide opportunities to use complex, domain-specific language in creative and critical ways (Delpit, 2006), and poetry can help meet this need. Poetry holds great promise for encouraging students to attach personal meaning to the content, transforming it and distilling it to reveal their experiences and aesthetic responses to what they learn (see Rosenblatt, 2005).

Poetry in the content area classroom serves a number of important purposes. First, when students transfer concepts from one form to another, they understand them better and are more likely to remember them (Pearson & Fielding, 1991). Second, because precise language is so important, poetry encourages students to think carefully about word choice and thus can draw attention to finer gradations of meaning in recently mastered terms. Also, in addition to boosting comprehension and vocabulary development, performing poetry can link oral and written language and build oral reading fluency (Krehel, 2003).

Reading and writing poetry also offer new ways for students to see the world. According to Gill (2007), poems help us see things using fresh eyes; thus, poetry can help students reenvision content. Writing poetry also helps students understand the poet's way of knowing—a way that includes paying attention, listening, and sifting experiences (Kucan, 2007).

For these reasons, many educators find that reading and writing poetry helps students understand content more deeply and more appreciatively (Karwoski, 2003), take multiple perspectives, develop social conscience (Jocson, 2006), and cultivate a range of responses to their world (Finney, 2003; Kucan, 2007; Pappas, 2003; Young, 2003). As an example, Figure 32.1 shares a Spanish 4 student's poem that was composed to apply Spanish vocabulary from a chapter on human rights. The work demonstrates how a poem can encourage practice of new domain-specific terminology while simultaneously fostering exploration of deeply held personal perspectives.

**Figure 32.1** A Spanish 4 student's poem, composed after studying Spanish vocabulary related to human rights

---

**La Paz**

*Veo que las mujeres están llorando por sus hijos muertes*

*Leo en el periódico que no existe una solución fácil de la guerra*

*Oigo de los problemas que occurren cuando no apoyamos la paz*

*Es muy importante que todas las personas del mundo se lleven bien*

*No quiero más matanza*

*No quiero madres sin hijos*

*No quiero que el delito de la guerra a continue*

*Me gustan las vidas de otras personas de la Tierra*

*Me importa la paz*

**Peace**

I see that women are crying over their dead children

I see in the newspaper that there is not an easy solution to the war

I hear of the problems that occur when we do not support peace

It is very important that all the people of the world get along

I do not want more killing

I do not want mothers without children

I do not want the crime of the war to continue

The lives of other people of the Earth please me

Peace is important to me

---

## PROCEDURES

### Getting Ready

1. Select the target terms that must be included in students' poems. Key terms from adopted student content standards and the textbook provide clues, as can Vocab Cards (p. 50) if you completed them. You will raise these required terms during a brainstorming session in class later. Figure 32.2 presents, for example, the bank of terms a science teacher selected related to a lesson on sand dollars.

2. Decide on the form(s) students may use for their poems. You may elect to allow free verse (which has no rhyme or set meter), or you might select from among the many poetry formats available. Figure 32.3 gives a sampling. We recommend that you give

**Figure 32.2** A science teacher's selection of vocabulary terms from a lesson on sand dollars. See Figure 32.4 for a poem that uses some of these terms

| | | |
|---|---|---|
| *bilateral* | *filter feeder* | *larvae* |
| *burrow* | *food chain* | *radial* |
| *convex* | *intertidal zone* | *symmetry* |
| | | *test* |

**Figure 32.3** A sampling of poetry formats

| | |
|---|---|
| Cinquain | • Five lines each have a given number of syllables: two, four, six, eight, two. In some forms, the number of words for each line rather than the number of syllables is specified: one, two, three, four, one.<br>• Each line has a distinct purpose: title, description of title, description of action, description of feeling, synonym for title. |
| Found poem (see Guillaume, Yopp, & Yopp, 2007) | • Existing sources of text (such as advertisements or newspaper articles) are cut up and rearranged to convey a new message.<br>• Physical placement of terms contributes to the meaning of the poem.<br>• Figure 32.5 gives an example, based on Poe's *The Tell-Tale Heart*. |
| Haiku | • Three lines each have a given number of syllables: five, seven, five.<br>• Themes often address nature and its fragility. |
| "I" poem (see Kucan, 2007) | • The defining feature is the poem's use of the first-person point of view.<br>• Narration is highly descriptive.<br>• The format can be open, ranging from free verse to a highly structured poem where the first words of each line are specified (e.g., "I am . . ." "I wonder . . ." "I fear . . ."). |
| Name poem (or acrostic) | • A target term is selected, and each letter of the term is recorded on one line.<br>• For each line, the given letter becomes the first letter of a word or phrase that describes the target term. |
| Poem for two voices (see Finney, 2003) | • Two narrators explore the topic with contrasting points of view.<br>• Stanzas are written in two columns.<br>• Read aloud, voices are sometimes heard in sequence and sometimes in tandem. |
| Shape poem | • Words or phrases related to the topic are arranged spatially to evoke an image.<br>• For example, a poem about a snail could be arranged in a spiral to emulate the snail's shell.<br>• Tiffany's sand dollar poem in Figure 32.4 is an example. |
| Windspark | • Five lines follow a given pattern:<br>1. I dreamed<br>2. I was . . .<br>3. where<br>4. an action<br>5. how |

students a choice of more than one format if possible. Gather or compose at least two contrasting samples to serve as models. Although models directly related to your content will be most powerful, the Internet is a gold mine for examples of a myriad of poetry formats if time is short. In a search engine, enter the name of the format (e.g., "haiku") as your search term.

3. Decide how students will publish and share their poems. Will they present them during a poetry slam? Pen them on greeting cards? Post them on the Web?

## During Class

Poetry is an engaging strategy for *Applying Word Knowledge.*

### *Applying Word Knowledge*

1. As general preparation, students need exposure to poetry in order to gain a sense of language, sound, and rhythm used to convey meaning. If your students have had limited exposure to a wide variety of great poems, provide broader exposure. See Gill (2007) for ideas for expanding your collection of poetry.

   As you share a poem, draw students' attention to the content and how it is conveyed. Discuss the layout of the poem as well, as the "white space" around the poem can contribute to its meaning (Cane, 2003). As an example of how layout affects meaning in poetry, see Figure 32.4, which shares Tiffany's shape poem about sand dollars. She composed it during the sand dollar science lesson mentioned in Figure 32.2.

2. Poems will be richest when students are well prepared to write and have access to many words that can spark their imagination or that they may use in their poems.

**Figure 32.4** Tiffany's shape poem on sand dollars. Note that Tiffany integrated five vocabulary terms from Figure 32.2 into her poem: *intertidal zone, food chain, symmetry, filter feeders*, and *test*

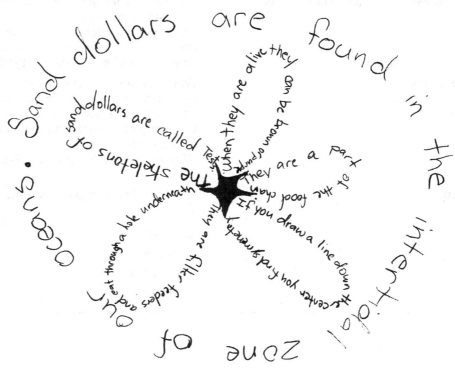

Generate a word bank together during a brainstorming session. During this session, draw students' attention to the subset of required terms selected earlier.

3. Teach the format(s) that students are required to use. To do so, share the model's critical attributes. Then share samples, including your own models.

4. Depending on students' age and expertise, write one poem together. Through think-aloud procedures, model how sound, rhythm, and words combine to communicate experience and evoke an image.

5. Monitor and support students as they write their own poems.

6. Share poems by reading them aloud or publishing them, as determined earlier.

## MODIFICATIONS

1. Young (2007) recommends using "poetry generating loops" (similar to literature circles) to foster students' poetry writing. Students form small groups and are assigned jobs: image weaver, language keeper, metaphor generator, and music maker.

2. Pappas (2003) recommends combining poetry with pictures to add a new dimension to students' understanding and communication.

## TROUBLESHOOTING

1. If students react unenthusiastically to a poetry assignment, ask about their past experiences with poetry. Experiences may have been negative, as when rhyme or meter are emphasized above the message of the poem. At least initially, select poetry formats that deemphasize rhyme and keep poems short.

   Found poems, which rearrange existing text, provide a powerful way for students to create meaning and explore words through poetry—without requiring them to compose original text. Figure 32.5 provides an example of a found poem based on Poe's short story *The Tell-Tale Heart* (Poe, 1843). The eighth-grade poet's intent was to crystallize the range of powerful emotions and the depth of insanity experienced by the narrator in Poe's original work.

2. Because poems explore and convey the poet's emotions, sharing them can be risky. Advise students in advance of the requirements for sharing them. Don't require

**Figure 32.5** An excerpt of an eighth grader's found poem based on *The Tell-Tale Heart* (Poe, 1843)

---

### Violent Gesticulations

True!—Nervous—very, very dreadfully nervous I had been and am.

I heard all things in hell. How, then, am I mad?

I think it was his eye! Yes, it was this!

I fairly chuckled at the idea; and perhaps he heard me.

It was the groan of mortal terror.

I placed my hand upon the heart and held it there for many minutes.

I dismembered the corpse.

His eye would trouble me no more.

I smiled—for *what* had I to fear?

My head ached, and I fancied a ringing in my ears.

Why would they not be gone?

students to read their work aloud. Instead, allow them to share it with a partner or small group and then ask for potential volunteers. Or publish the work without requiring students to read it aloud in a whole-class setting.

## TECH CONNECT

1. Read about the National Council of Teachers of English's Award for Poetry for Children and visit links to sites of recent winners at http://www.ncte.org/about/awards/sect/elem/106857.htm.
2. Check out http://www.e-poets.net to consider poetry shared via new media.

**When to Use**

○ Preparing to Learn Words

○ Building Word Knowledge

● Applying Word Knowledge

● Independent Word Learning

# Vocabulary Graffiti

For as long as we've been able to scrape stone, humans have been creating graffiti. The ancient Greeks, Romans, Vikings, and Mayans all left their marks by scratching images into the hard surfaces of public places. For instance, a humorous caricature of a politician smiles down through the ages from a wall of ancient Pompeii. Vocabulary Graffiti capitalizes on the appeal of art by the common person and the human desire to communicate with the world. In Vocabulary Graffiti, students compose quick line drawings of the target terms. They can also combine the use of symbols like letters and numbers with their visual images. The graffiti are usually displayed in public spaces, such as bulletin boards, although they may reside solely in students' notes.

## PURPOSE

Images are powerful learning tools. Viewing them alone can support vocabulary development. Viewing an image rather than reading text is often more efficient because images reduce the demands on working memory and thus allow us to gather information at a glance (Carlson, Chandler, & Sweller, 2003). Images also serve as a mnemonic, helping us to access information from memory more readily (Atkinson et al., 1999). Figure 33.1 gives math graffiti, for example, that make it easier to remember meanings for the terms *substitute* and *area*.

When students draw their own graphics, they reap added benefits. Drawing images can support meaningful learning by requiring students to select, organize, and represent ideas (Edens & Potter, 2001). Drawing requires students to translate information from one form to another, thus supporting memory (Bromley, 2007) and providing another opportunity to think about and practice new words. Further, creating images for vocabulary terms can fuel student interest and allow students to create personal associations with unfamiliar terms (Hopkins & Bean, 1998–1999; Standerfer, 2006). The public nature of graffiti is often appealing to

**Figure 33.1** Math graffiti that aid memory

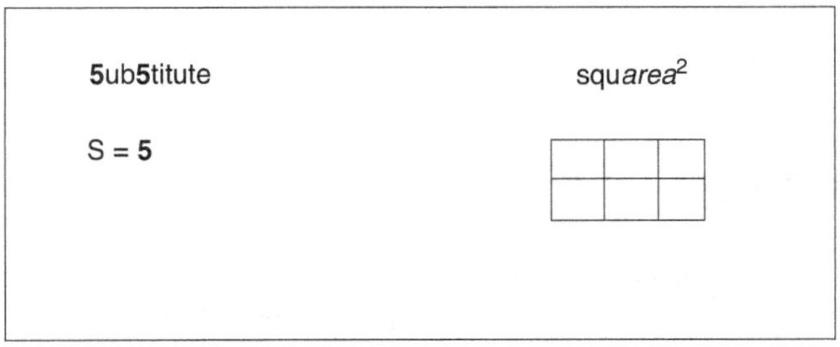

*Source:* http://www.mathgraffiti.net

students, feeding the desire to express themselves and communicate with others. Sharing images also increases the number of representations of terms with which students interact and fosters discussion of terms (Pederson, 2008), providing yet another opportunity to think about and use new vocabulary.

 ## PROCEDURES

### Getting Ready

1. If you have not yet used Vocabulary Graffiti with students, search the Web for some images of ancient graffiti to share with students during the lesson's introduction. An image search of the term *ancient graffiti* reveals hundreds of choices. Place a few on transparencies or plan to project them.
2. If you plan to provide the graffiti for students, locate or develop the images to support understanding of target terms.
3. If you plan to have students create their own graffiti, select the terms from which students can make their choices.
4. Prepare a place for students to display their graffiti, perhaps covering a board or wall with butcher paper for individual drawings. Or plan to distribute a large piece of paper to each group. Gather markers.

### During Class

Vocabularly Graffiti is useful during both the *Applying Word Knowledge* and *Independent Word Learning* phases.

### *Applying Word Knowledge*

1. Introduce the strategy by sharing the word *graffiti*. It's an Italian word that comes from *graffiare*, which means "to scratch or scribble." Display a few samples of ancient graffiti from around the world, showing that words, pictures, or combinations are often used as common folk convey messages to others.
2. If you provide the graffiti rather than having students create their own, display your image for each term and have students predict meanings based on your images. Throughout the lesson, check on students' predictions. Provide accurate information through reading, research, or direct explanation.
3. If students are to create their own graffiti, present the terms and allow students to choose from among them. Show students where their work will be displayed and provide materials such as markers and paper.
4. Model the process of creating a graffito. Share a few student samples if you have them. Figure 33.2 shows a fifth-grade student's graffiti for different classes of vertebrates.
5. Allow for work time and then post the Vocabulary Graffiti. Discuss differences and similarities among the images and encourage students to add to the board over time.

### *Independent Word Learning*

Encourage students to use Vocabulary Graffiti in their personal dictionaries or class notes.

## MODIFICATIONS

Use Vocabulary Graffiti as a review game. Divide students into teams and give each a different vocabulary list. Have each team draw graffiti of their terms for the other team, who guesses the words.

**Figure 33.2** A fifth grader's graffiti for different classes of vertebrates

## TECH CONNECT

1. Give students digital cameras and have them take photos to represent new terms. Students can post images on a class Web site or blog and allow their peers to comment (O'Hanlon, 2008).
2. Use presentation software such as PowerPoint or Key Note to animate Vocabulary Graffiti. For instance, one teacher illustrated the difference between *revolve* and *rotate* with words that moved on the screen according to their definitions: one traveling in a path around an image of the sun and one spinning on its axis.
3. Through virtual graffiti, people can use their computers, personal digital assistants, and mobile phones to decorate a designated public space. Some artists use "virtual paint cans" based on laser technology. Students, too, can become digital graffiti artists using electronic art tools. Word processing programs have drawing applications, and other specialized drawing programs, such as the popular Kids Pix and Photoshop, are powerful. Some programs are available free online. Two examples are Tux Paint for young students and Paint.NET for older ones. The free and popular social networking site Facebook also has a graffiti application. Or increase your skills by playing on online drawing game at http://www.isketch.net.

## TROUBLESHOOTING

1. Vocabulary Graffiti works best with concrete terms. It can be difficult to develop graffiti for terms that are both abstract and new to the learner. At least initially, use the strategy with words that are easy to visualize.
2. Because graffiti is meant to be public, set criteria for acceptable postings and set ground rules for whether and when students are allowed to add to existing works.

## NEXT STEPS

1. Some authors, such as MacGillivray and Curwen (2007), view tagging, or the act of painting names or brief images in public places, as a social literacy practice, allowing

often alienated youths to carve out an identity and group affiliation. Consider thinking about ways that youth culture can provide avenues for disaffected youth to expand their literacy practices and to foster their academic success.

2. For other strategies that capitalize on student-created images, try Sketch to Stretch (p. 28), Word Posters (p. 159) and the Keyword Method (p. 130).

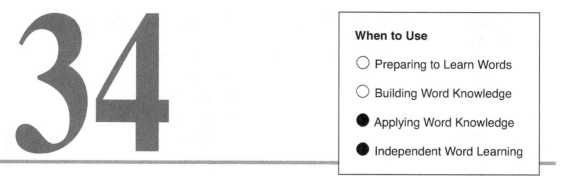

# Word Posters

Many students jump at the chance to draw, create, and talk with their peers. In Word Posters, students engage in these favored activities while they deepen and apply their knowledge of content vocabulary terms and sharpen their independent word learning skills. They create large visual displays that explore the meanings and uses of selected vocabulary terms through a combination of words and images. Although the type of information presented on the posters is a matter of teacher choice, required categories can support facets of word learning by including the word's definition, context, and a student-composed sentence (Graves, 2007). Word study findings such as an analysis of the term's parts (see Morphemic Analysis, p. 106), its etymology (see Word Histories, p. 115), or cognates shared by the students' home language also are effective poster components.

## PURPOSE

Word Posters have many potential benefits. First, because they are displayed throughout the classroom and spark discussion, Word Posters contribute to the language-rich environment recommended by researchers (e.g., Blachowicz, Fisher, Ogle, & Watts-Taffe, 2006). Second, according to Graves (2007), a vigorous interest in learning words is essential for middle grade students. Word Posters can fuel this interest and raise students' *word consciousness*, an important impetus for continued vocabulary learning (Fisher & Blachowicz, 2007; Graves, 2007). Additionally, word study—including morphemic analysis—takes on an increasingly important role as students move through the middle grades (Hennings, 2000), and Word Posters can support word study skills. Finally, some students are left nonplussed by literacy instruction that feels unrelated to their lives (Hunsberger, 2007). By encouraging students to actively engage with content terms and link them to their own experiences, Word Posters can provide an avenue for students to connect with content literacy.

## PROCEDURES

### Getting Ready

1. Prepare a bank of content terms from which students may select. Figure 34.1 gives the terms from which students in a strength-training class might choose.
2. Decide what the posters must include. Consider the age and readiness of your students in addition to your vocabulary goals. At minimum, consider requiring the following:
   a. The word, written in large letters (perhaps as Vocabulary Graffiti, p. 155)
   b. A definition of the word
   c. The context in which the word was found
   d. An image, such as a funny cartoon or drawing, to support the term's meaning
   e. An original sentence using the word

**Figure 34.1** Strength-training vocabulary terms for Word Poster selection

| | |
|---|---|
| *collar* | *isometric exercise* |
| *concentric contraction* | *isotonic exercise* |
| *eccentric contraction* | *plyometric exercise* |
| *exercise* | *recovery* |
| *fatigue* | *repetition* |
| *form* | *resistance* |
| *frequency* | *set* |
| *intensity* | |

Additionally, Graves (2007) and Henning (2000) recommend analysis of word parts. Clusters of words with related parts can be captured on the posters too.

3. List and post the requirements for students. Figure 34.2 gives the strength-training teacher's grading sheet.

**Figure 34.2** Grading sheet for strength-training Word Posters

| | Not yet | Getting there | Right on |
|---|---|---|---|
| **The term**<br>• Large<br>• Font is related to the term's meaning | | | |
| **Definition**<br>• Dictionary<br>• Your words | | | |
| **An image**<br>• Supports meaning<br>• Appropriate<br>• Uses clip art and graphic elements effectively<br>• Follows copyright laws in obtaining and importing images | | | |
| **A sentence**<br>• Shows that you understand the term<br>• Helps others remember the term | | | |
| **Word study (include one)**<br>• Word history<br>• Word parts<br>• Related words<br>• Cognates (similar words in another language) | | | |
| **Appeal and tech skills**<br>• Poster is clear and interesting to look at<br>• Uses tools in the software application to increase the quality of the poster | | | |

4. Create a sample Word Poster that meets your requirements. Figure 34.3 presents the strength-training teacher's Word Poster for the term *isometric exercise*. To sharpen their tech skills, her students will create their posters electronically, so the teacher created her poster electronically as a model.

5. Decide on group size. Although students may work individually, using partners or small groups increases opportunities for students to use the words in a variety of formats, including in their listening and speaking.

6. Ensure that dictionaries and content sources (online or print) are available for reference.

7. Prepare poster materials. Many teachers use 12- by 18-inch construction paper. That and markers may be all you need. Or consider supplying magazines for images that are cut out and added to the posters, perhaps in collage style. The Internet is a rich source of clip art and photographic images that can enrich students' posters. Photo-sharing sites, such as http:///www.flikr.com, can be a gold mine. Gather scissors and glue if students will be adding printed images to their posters.

## During Class

Word Posters support students in *Applying Word Knowledge* and *Independent Word Learning*.

**Figure 34.3** Sample Word Poster for *isometric exercise*

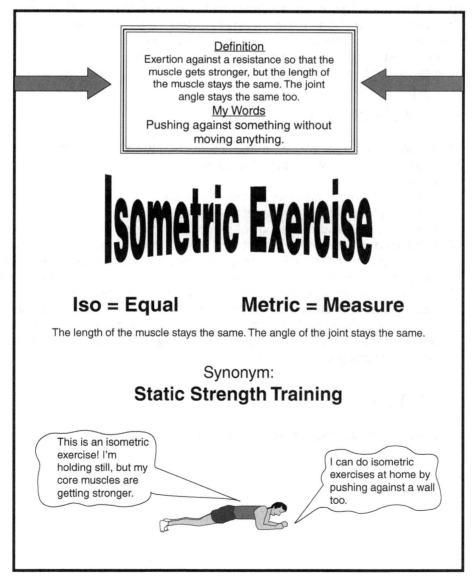

*Applying Word Knowledge and Independent Word Learning*

1. Share your sample Word Poster. Lead a discussion of elements of the poster that are more and less effective. Ask students to assess it using the posted list of requirements or a grading sheet.
2. Group students and have them choose their words. We recommend letting more than one group study a word, if reasonable, because self-selection supports student motivation.
3. Provide time and materials for students to complete their posters. Hurry them along.
4. Ask students to present their posters to the class. One idea is to have one group present their poster as a Word of the Day each day.
5. Display the posters and refer to them frequently. Invite students to do the same.

 ## MODIFICATIONS

1. Vary the product. For instance, students could create word T-shirts instead of posters.
2. Word boxes are an appealing alternative to posters as well. Students can glue information inside and outside a shoebox and then fill the box with items related to the word.

 ## TECH CONNECT

Rather than creating posters, students might use presentation software such as Keynote or PowerPoint and post their presentations to a class Web site. A drawback to this alternative is that presentations would need to be printed for posting around the room, but a benefit is that students and families could access the posters remotely. Additionally, electronic presentations can include video, animations, and sound.

## TROUBLESHOOTING

1. If students work in groups, address accountability concerns. Some ideas to ensure that all students participate include the following:
   a. Assign jobs
   b. Divide the materials among group members
   c. Give individual tests on the terms
   d. Require peer and self-ratings of group performance
2. Although most students enjoy art and design activities, many have limited experience with principles of design. Provide tips on effective use of color, images, font size and type, positive and negative space, and balance if your students are beginning designers.
3. Introducing a graphic aspect to students' work opens the door for some additional instructional considerations. For instance, check students' images to ensure that they are accurate. Also check that they are appropriate, avoiding stereotypes related to gender, ethnicity, age, and other factors. Finally, check that students followed legal guidelines in obtaining and using their images.

 ## NEXT STEPS

Word Posters might lead well to Student-Made Books (p. 145).

# 35

**When to Use**

○ Preparing to Learn Words

○ Building Word Knowledge

○ Applying Word Knowledge

● Independent Word Learning

# I-Search a Word

The narrowing of today's curriculum in service of standardized test scores fuels concerns for many educators who see a lack of connectedness in what students learn about literacy at school—and what they live (Hunsberger, 2007). Perhaps for this reason, interest in Macrorie's (1988) I-Search paper remains high (e.g., Tallman & Joyce, 2006). The I-Search process addresses the gap between students' lives and the school's agenda by supporting students in pursuing research questions of personal interest—those that create "a genuine itch" for students. Key to the I-Search process are curiosity, collaboration, the habits and skills of inquiry, and metacognition, or reflection on the transformations that research and writing can bring. These keys are revealed as students first conduct their research and then compose a narrative I-Search paper, typically with four components:

1. A summary of what the student knows about the topic prior to study
2. A statement of what the student wants to find out
3. A record of research activities
4. A statement of what the student learned through the process

Anderson (1990) borrows the power of the I-Search process and applies it to vocabulary instruction through I-Search a Word. In I-Search a Word, students select a single important term and investigate it thoroughly using a number of sources, including print-based, electronic, and other resources. They write a report on what they learned, emphasizing first-person narration and clear voice. They may instead share their process and findings in a different way, such as through multimedia projects (Smith & Throne, 2007–2008).

## PURPOSE

The I-Search process serves a number of purposes that support students' independent word learning skills. First, because students choose their topics and because they write in the first person rather than the third person, teachers report that motivation is high (Anderson, 1990; Bowen, 2001; Kaszyca & Krueger, 1994; Young, 1994). Second, the I-Search process supports the development of inquiry skills that are vital in the 21st century (Partnership for 21st Century Skills, 2002); information literacy skills include those such as accessing material from a variety of sources, judging the quality and veracity of what students read, synthesizing large amounts of information, and formulating a personal response based on solid evidence. Third, the I-Search process necessitates that students encounter words in a number of contexts. The use of a variety of sources provides repeated exposure to words and allows students to develop shades of meaning. Further, I-Search provides for meaningful practice of terms, another essential component of vocabulary learning (Nagy, 1988). In sum, I-Search a Word requires students to be *active word learners* who use a variety of sources to meet their

**163**

purposes, a prerequisite to successful vocabulary mastery (Alvermann, Swafford, & Montero, 2004) and a likely facilitator of future word sleuthing success.

 **PROCEDURES**

### Getting Ready

1. Develop a potential list of I-Search terms. This list can be used as a springboard for students' brainstorming of additional terms later. Anderson (1990) suggests the use of abstract nouns, given the important role they play in our lives. Abstract nouns, such as *principle, interdependence*, and *conflict*, also have wide applicability as integrative themes across the content areas; thus, they have high utility. Figure 35.1 presents a teacher's brainstormed list of terms for her U.S. history class.

2. Decide on the information sources you will require students to use and those that are available to students as options. Consider the balance between primary and secondary sources. Choose sources that are important for students learning both the *content* and the *research skills* of your discipline. For example, in her English class, Anderson (1990) requires the following sources:

   a. An unabridged dictionary
   b. A thesaurus
   c. A concordance to the Bible
   d. The *Concordance to Shakespeare*
   e. *Granger's Index to Poetry*

   f. A book of quotations
   g. The *Readers' Guide to Periodical Literature* (and a magazine cited in the guide)
   h. The *Oxford English Dictionary*

   Teachers in the natural or social sciences might well include a firsthand interview with an expert as a required source. Those in the visual and performing arts or in physical education may require the use of digital images or video sources.

   Given their prevalence today, electronic resources will probably figure in your list of required sources (Davis, 1995; Lyman, 2006). Select search engines, Web sites, and databases that are appropriate and productive for students' searches. For example, teachers at Whitmore Lake High School in Michigan have developed an impressive site with links for I-Search a Word. It is found at http://teachers.wlps.net/WLHSMedia/Assignments/Word%20Project/Word%20Project.htm.

3. Assemble your resources and provide any necessary preteaching so that students' research time is maximized. Some of these steps may be appropriate:
   a. If students will work in the library, schedule with your librarian several days in advance and provide for an orientation as necessary.
   b. Collect print sources and take them to your classroom if that's where students will work.
   c. Ensure that students have laptop or desktop computers with Internet access available to them. Check that your school's firewall allows access to your selected sites.

**Figure 35.1** A teacher's brainstormed list of terms related to U.S. history

| | | |
|---|---|---|
| *colony* | *institution* | *religion* |
| *conflict* | *interchange* | *republic* |
| *culture* | *liberty* | *respect* |
| *free market* | *nation* | *safeguard* |
| *hardship* | *politics* | *technology* |
| *immigration* | *principle* | *tolerance* |
| *incentive* | | |

In working with large numbers of English learners, many with new immigrant families, Werner (1993) discovered that the I-Search process requires special support for English learners. Her suggestions are as follows:

1. Check the home cultures' perspectives on library research and incorporate direct instruction on the attitudes and skills of library inquiry.

2. Make available source material in students' home language and make this material accessible through practices such as effective color coding and shelving techniques.

3. Build partnerships among teachers (across the disciplines and including the English-language specialists) and librarians to ensure that English learners have rich opportunities to build the important skills and knowledge embedded in the I-Search process.

d. Assess and provide instruction on students' Internet searching skills and their skills in judging the quality of what they find. Valuable online sources are available for these purposes. One is assistance in validating Web-based materials. Try the sources given at http://people.uis.edu/rschr1/valid.htm for this purpose.

4. Decide on the format that students' papers (or other products) are to take. You may adopt the earlier described model from Macrorie (1988). An outline of Anderson's I-Search a Word paper is found in Figure 35.2.

## During Class

I-Search a Word papers engage students in *Independent Word Learning*.

## Independent Word Learning

1. Present your list of important terms and hold a conversation where students feel free to share which words are familiar, unfamiliar, and particularly interesting to them. Invite them to add words to the list. Students may glance through the textbook or recall past experiences with the content to add their own terms.

2. Ask students to write about their experience with their selected word. What do they currently know? Figure 35.3 shows a student's selection from the U.S. history list presented earlier, and it gives his account of his prior experience with the term.

3. Share the assignment, including a rubric or scoring guide, for the final product. Share model products if they are available.

4. Guide students in their research, ensuring that research times are focused and relatively brief. Two to three periods of research may be enough.

5. Encourage students to support each other and to serve as audiences for the I-Search a Word projects as they unfold. For example, you might have students keep partner journals throughout the process (Kaszyca & Krueger, 1994). Kaszyca and Krueger include parents as members of the research community as well.

**Figure 35.2** Anderson's (1990) format for the I-Search a Word paper

| Introduction | What was the most interesting thing you discovered about your word? What is the story of your search for information about your word? |
| --- | --- |
| Body | Write at least one paragraph for each source. Summarize the information you learned, interpret it, and offer a comment. |
| Conclusion | Write your overall response to this project. What did you learn about research and about yourself? |
| Bibliography | |

**Figure 35.3** A student's selected U.S. history term for I-Search a Word and his prior experience with the term

> *My word is <u>immigration</u>. I chose this word because it captures so many important things about history—not just <u>U.S.</u> history but <u>world</u> history. As long as there have been humans, there has been immigration. And U.S. history is <u>immigration</u>. Almost everyone who lives in the United States is an immigrant in this generation or earlier.*
>
> *I feel like I know some important things about <u>immigration</u>. It's related to the word <u>migration</u>, which seems to have to do with movement. A related word is <u>emigration</u>, which happens when a person moves out of one country. So one thing I'm wondering is what other words are similar to <u>immigration</u> and where they come from.*
>
> *We have studied immigration before, so I know some things about what the word means. For example, humans as a species began in just a few places in the world and then spread all over. In U.S. history, I know that people move because of hardships and opportunities, or what Mr. F. called push/pull factors. I want to learn why people at the beginning of human history decided to stay in one spot or why they decided to move to others. I'm interested in how people spread all over the world. I'd also like to know more about people's individual stories in U.S. immigration. I also want to know if Americans have always had some negative connotations for the word <u>immigration</u>. It seems like many people consider immigration as a bad thing, and I wonder if the word is viewed negatively all over the world and in the past.*

6. Provide an avenue for sharing the final products. Students may present their findings as shared dialogues or create multimedia projects. The audience should extend beyond the teacher.

## MODIFICATION

For a related strategy that requires less time, consider the Vocabulary Self-Collection Strategy (p. 54).

## TROUBLESHOOTING

1. Much of the success of the I-Search a Word process lies in students' genuine interest in their selected terms. Ensure that students select a word rather than being assigned one.
2. Also be sure to build a sense of intrigue about the terms, perhaps by sharing your own sense of wonder about one or more of the words. For example, a teacher with an infant discussed with her students the heightened importance that the word *transition* had recently taken in her life as she went from being single to married and from pregnant to new mother and as she and her husband managed the transition between home and work (and day care) each day. She used her sense of wonder about the word to set the stage for further word study as students selected their own words.

# References

Albright, L. K. (2002). Bringing the Ice Maiden to life: Engaging adolescents in learning through picture book read-alouds in content areas. *Journal of Adolescent and Adult Literacy, 45*, 418–428.

Albright, L. K., & Ariail, M. (2005). Tapping the potential of teacher read-alouds in middle schools. *Journal of Adolescent and Adult Literacy, 48*, 582–591.

Allen, J. (1999). *Words, words, words: Teaching vocabulary in grades 4–12*. Portland, ME: Stenhouse.

Alvermann, D. E., Swafford, J., & Montero, M. K. (2004). *Content area literacy instruction for the elementary grades*. Boston: Pearson Education.

American Heritage Dictionaries. (2004). *Word Histories and mysteries: From abracadabra to Zeus*. Boston: Houghton Mifflin.

Anders, P. L., & Bos, C. S. (1986). Semantic feature analysis: An interactive strategy for vocabulary development and text comprehension. *Journal of Reading, 29*, 610–616.

Anderson, G. K. (1990). 'I-Search a Word': Reclaiming the library's reference section. *English Journal, 79*(1), 53–57.

Anderson, R. C., & Freebody, P. (1981). Vocabulary knowledge. In J. Guthrie (Ed.), *Comprehension and teaching: Research reviews* (pp. 77–117). Newark, DE: International Reading Association.

Anderson, R. C., & Nagy, W. (1992). The vocabulary conundrum. *American Educator, 16*, 14–18.

Anthony, A. R. B. (2008). Output strategies for English-language learners: Theory to practice. *The Reading Teacher, 61*, 472–482.

Apthorp, H. S. (2006). Effects of a supplemental vocabulary program in third-grade reading/language arts. *Journal of Educational Research, 100*(2), 67–79.

Atkinson, R. K., et al. (1999). Matrix and mnemonic text-processing adjuncts: Comparing and combining their components. *Journal of Educational Psychology, 91*, 342–357.

August, D., Snow, C., Carlo, M., Proctor, C. P., Francisco, A. R., Duursma, E., et al. (2006). Literacy development in elementary school second-language learners. *Topics in Language Disorders, 26*, 351–364.

Ausubel, D. P. (1963). *The psychology of meaningful verbal learning*. New York: Grune and Statton.

Ausubel, D. P., Novack, J. D., & Hanesian, H. (1978). *Educational psychology: A cognitive view* (2nd ed.). New York: Holt, Rinehart, and Winston.

Baker, L., & Brown, A. L. (1984). Metacognitive skills and reading. In P. D. Pearson (Ed.), *Handbook of reading research* (pp. 491–572). New York: Longman.

Baker, S. K., Simmons, D. C., & Kame'enui, E. J. (1995). *Vocabulary acquisition: Synthesis of the research* (Technical Report No.13). Eugene, OR: National Center to Improve the Tools of Educators.

Baker, S. K., Simmons, D. C., & Kame'enui, E. J. (1997). Vocabulary acquisition: Research bases. In D. C. Simmons & E. J. Kame'enui (Eds.), *What reading research tells us about children with diverse learning needs: Bases and basics.* (pp. 183–219). Mahwah, NJ: Lawrence Erlbaum Associates.

Barger, J. (2006). Building word consciousness. *The Reading Teacher, 60*, 279–281.

Barnhart, R. (1995). *Barnhart concise dictionary of etymology*. New York: Collins.

Barron, R. F. (1969). The use of vocabulary as an advance organizer. In H. L. Herber & P. L. Sanders (Eds.), *Research in reading in the content areas: First year report* (pp. 29–39). Syracuse, NY: Syracuse University, Reading and Language Arts Center.

Baumann, J. F., & Duffy, A. M. (1997). *Engaged reading for pleasure and learning: A report from the National Reading Research Center*. College Park, MD: National Reading Research Center.

Baumann, J. F., Edwards, E. C., Boland, E., Olejnik, S., & Kame'enui, E. J. (2003). Vocabulary tricks: Effects of instruction in morphology and content on fifth-grade students' ability to derive and infer word meanings. *American Educational Research Journal, 40*, 447–494.

Baumann, J. F., Kame'enui, E. J., & Ash, G. E. (2003). Research on vocabulary instruction: Voltaire redux. In J. Flood, D. Lapp, J. R. Squire, & J. M. Jensen (Eds.), *Handbook on research on teaching the English language arts* (2nd ed., pp. 752–785). Mahwah, NJ: Lawrence Erlbaum Associates.

Beck, I., & McKeown, M. (1991). Conditions of vocabulary acquisition. In R. Barr, M. Kamil, P. Mosenthal, & P. D. Pearson (Eds.), *Handbook of reading research* (Vol. 2, pp. 789–814). New York: Longman.

Beck, I. L., & McKeown, M. G. (2003). Taking delight in words: Using oral language to build young children's vocabularies. *American Educator, 27*, 36–39, 41, 45–46.

Beck, I. L., & McKeown, M. G. (2007). Increasing young low-income children's oral vocabulary repertoires through rich and focused instruction. *Elementary School Journal, 107*, 251–271.

Beck, I. L., McKeown, M. G., & Kucan, L. (2002). *Bringing words to life: Robust vocabulary instruction.* New York: Guilford.

Bigelow, T. P., & Vokoun, M. J. (2005). Stepping into the classroom. *English Journal, 95*(2), 113–117.

Blachowicz, C., & Fisher, P. J. (2000). Vocabulary instruction. In M. L. Kamil, P. D. Mosentahal, P. D. Pearson, & R. Barr (Eds.), *Handbook of reading research* (Vol. 3, pp. 503–524). Mahwah, NJ: Lawrence Erlbaum Associates.

Blachowicz, C. L. Z., & Fisher, P. J. L. (2002). *Teaching vocabulary in all classrooms* (2nd ed.). Upper Saddle River, NJ: Pearson.

Blachowicz, C. L. Z., & Fisher, P. (2004a). Building vocabulary in remedial settings: Focus on word relatedness. *Perspectives, 30*, 1. Retrieved June 25, 2008, from http://www.resourceroom.net/comprehension/idavocab2004.asp

Blachowicz, C., & Fisher, P. (2004b). Keep the "fun" in fundamental: Encouraging word awareness and incidental word learning in the classroom through word play. In J. F. Baumann & E. J. Kame'enui (Eds.), *Vocabulary instruction: Research to practice* (pp. 218–237). New York: Guilford.

Blachowicz, C., & Fisher, P. J. (2006). *Teaching vocabulary in all classrooms* (3rd ed.). Upper Saddle River, NJ: Pearson Merrill Prentice Hall.

Blachowicz, C. L. Z., & Fisher, P. J. (2007). Best practices in vocabulary instruction. In L. B. Gambrell & L. M. Morrow (Eds.), *Best practices in literacy instruction* (3rd ed., pp. 178–203). New York: Guilford.

Blachowicz, C. L. Z., Fisher, P. J. L., Ogle, D., & Watts-Taffe, S. (2006). Theory and research into practice: Vocabulary: Questions from the classroom. *Reading Research Quarterly, 41*, 524–539.

Blachowicz, C., & Obrochta, C. (2005). Vocabulary visits: Virtual field trips for content vocabulary development. *The Reading Teacher, 59*, 262–268.

Blanton, W. E., Wood, K. D., & Taylor, D. B. (2007). Rethinking middle school reading instruction: A basic literacy activity. *Reading Psychology, 28*, 75–95.

Block, L. A. (2003). Containing energy, sustaining agency—Drama in middle years. *English Quarterly, 35*(1), 21–24.

Borasi, R., Siegel, M., Fonzi, J., & Smith, C. F. (1998). Using transactional reading strategies to support sense-making and discussion in mathematics classrooms: An exploratory study. *Journal for Research in Mathematics Education, 29*, 275–305.

Bos, C. S., & Anders, P. L. (1990). Effects of interactive vocabulary instruction on the vocabulary learning and reading comprehension of junior-high learning disabled students. *Learning Disability Quarterly, 13*, 31–42.

Boucher, E. F., & Leong, P. N. C. (2002). "Theatre" in the classroom: Using readers theatre to improve EFL learners' oral skills. *English Teacher: An International Journal, 5*, 230–241.

Boulware-Gooden, R., Carreker, S., Thornhill, A., & Joshi, R. M. (2007). Instruction of metacognitive strategies enhances reading comprehension and vocabulary achievement of third-grade students. *The Reading Teacher, 61*, 70–77.

Bowen, C. (2001). A process approach: The I-Search with grade 5: They learn! *Teacher Librarian, 29*(2), 14–18.

Brabeck, K., Fisher, K., & Pitler, H. (2004). Building better instruction: How technology supports nine research-proven instructional strategies. *Learning and Leading with Technology, 31*(5), 7–11. Retrieved April 9, 2008, from http://www.mcrel.org/pdf/educationtechnology/9713IR_BuildingBetterInstruction.pdf

Brabham, E. G., & Villaume, S. K. (2001). Building walls of words. *The Reading Teacher, 54*, 700–702.

Bransford, J., Brown, A., & Corking, R. (1999). *How people learn: Brain, mind, experience, and school.* Washington, DC: National Research Council.

Bromley, K. (2007). Nine things every teacher should know about words and vocabulary instruction. *Journal of Adolescent and Adult Literacy, 50*, 528–537.

Brookbank, D., Grover, S., Kullberg, K., & Strawser, C. (1999). *Improving student achievement through organization of student learning.* Chicago: Master's Action Research Project, Saint Xavier University and IRI/Skylight. (ERIC Document Reproduction Service No. ED435094)

Buckelew, M. B. (2003). The value of art in the English classroom: Imagination, making the tacit visible. *The English Journal, 92*(5), 49–55.

Buckles, S. (2007). *A case study: The inflation rate.* Retrieved May 31, 2007, from http://www.econedling.org/lesson

Calhoun, E., Poirier, T., Simon, N., & Mueller, L. (2001, April). *Teacher (and district) research: Three inquiries into the Picture Word Inductive Model.* Paper presented at the annual meeting of the American Educational Research Association, Seattle, WA.

California Department of Education. (2004). *Science framework for California public schools kindergarten through grade twelve*. Sacramento: California Department of Education.

Cane, T. (2003). Meditations on white space. *Teachers and Writers, 34*(5), 23–25.

Cardellicio, T., & Field, W. (1997). Seven strategies that encourage neural branching. *Educational Leadership, 54*(6), 33–36.

Carlo, M. S., August, D., McLaughlin, B., Snow, C. E., Dressler, C., Lippman, D. N., et al. (2004). Closing the gap: Addressing the vocabulary needs of English-language learners in bilingual and mainstream classrooms. *Reading Research Quarterly, 39*, 188–215.

Carlson, R., Chandler, P., & Sweller, J. (2003). Learning and understanding science instructional material. *Journal of Educational Psychology, 95*, 629–640.

Carrick, L. (2001). Internet resources for conducting readers theatre. *Reading Online, 5*(1). Retrieved March 23, 2008, from http://www.readingonline.org/electronic/elec_index.asp?HREF=carrick/index.html

Chanko, P. (2005). Make a tasty word wall. *Instructor, 115*(2), 55–56.

Christen, W. L., & Murphy, T. J. (1991). *Increasing comprehension by activating prior knowledge*. (ERIC Document Reproduction Service No. ED328885). Retrieved June 26, 2008 from http://www.ericdigests.org/pre-9219/prior.htm

Corcoran, C. A., & Davis, A. D. (2005). A study of the effects of readers' theater on second and third grade special education students' fluency growth. *Reading Improvement, 42*(2), 105–111.

Cunningham, P. M. (2005). *Phonics they use* (4th ed.). Boston: Allyn & Bacon.

Cunningham, A. E., & Stanovich, K. E. (1998). What reading does for the mind. *American Educator, 22*(1–2), 8–15.

Curtis, M. C., & Longo, A. M. (2001). Teaching vocabulary to adolescents to improve comprehension. *Reading Online, 5*(4). Retrieved March 23, 2008, from http://www.readingonline.org/articles/curtis

Davis, C. (1995). The I-Search paper goes global: Using the Internet as a research tool. *English Journal, 84*(6), 27–33.

Dearing, E., Kreider, H., Simpkins, S., & Weiss, H. B. (2006). Family involvement in school and low-income children's literacy: Longitudinal associations between and within families. *Journal of Educational Psychology, 98*, 653–664.

Delpit, L. (2003). Educators as "seed people" growing a new future. *Educational Researcher, 7*(32), 14–21.

Delpit, L. (2006). Lessons from teachers. *Journal of Teacher Education, 57*, 220–231.

Dodici, B. J., Draper, D. C., & Peterson, C. A. (2003). Early parent–child interactions and early literacy development. *Topics in Early Childhood Special Education, 23*(3), 124–136.

Dole, J. A., Duffy, G. G., Roehler, L. R., & Pearson, P. D. (1991). Moving from old to new: Research on reading comprehension instruction. *Review of Educational Research, 61*, 239–264.

Douglas-Hall, A., & Chau, M. (2007). *Basic facts about low-income children birth to age 18*. National Center for Children in Poverty. Retrieved March 23, 2008, from http://www.nccp.org/publications/pdf/text_762.pdf

Edens, K. H., & Potter, E. F. (2001). Promoting conceptual understanding through pictorial representation. *Studies in Art Education, 42*, 214–233.

Edwards, E., Font, G., Baumann, J. F., & Boland, E. (2004). Unlocking word meaning: Strategies and guidelines for teaching morphemic and contextual analysis. In J. Baumann & E. Kame'enui (Eds.), *Vocabulary instruction: Research to practice* (pp. 159–176). New York: Guilford.

El-Hindi, A. E. (2003). Integrating literacy and science in the classroom: From ecomysteries to readers theatre. *Reading Teacher, 56*, 536–538.

Epstein, J. L. (2005). Developing and sustaining research-based programs of school, family, and community partnerships: Summary of five years of NNPS research. National Network of Partnership Schools. Retrieved April 5, 2008, from http://www.csos.jhu.edu/p2000/pdf/Research%20Summary.pdf

Epstein, J. L., et al. (1992). *TIPS: Teachers Involve Parents in Schoolwork. Language arts and science/health. Interactive homework in the middle grades. Manual for teachers*. Baltimore: Center on Families, Communities, Schools, and Children's Learning, Johns Hopkins University.

ERIC Development Team. (1997). *Picture books as a social studies resource in the elementary school classroom*. Retrieved March 28, 2007, from http://www.eric.ed.gov/ERICDocs/data/ericdocs2sql/content_storage_01/0000019b/80/14/fd/82.pdf

Erickson, B. (1996). Read-alouds reluctant readers relish. *Journal of Adolescent and Adult Literacy, 40*, 212–214.

Eyraud, K., Giles, G., Koenig, S., & Stoller, F. L. (2002). The word wall approach: Promoting L2 vocabulary learning. *Forum, 38*(3), 2–11.

Fantuzzo, J., McWayne, C., & Perry, M. A. (2004). Multiple dimensions of family involvement and their relations to behavioral and learning competencies for urban, low-income children. *School Psychology Review, 33*, 467–480.

Finney, M. J. (2003). A bumper sticker, Columbus, and a poem for two voices. *Reading Teacher, 5*, 74–78.

Fisher, P., & Blachowicz, C. (2007). Teaching how to think about words. *Voices from the Middle, 15*(1), 6–12.

Fisher, P. J. L., Blachowicz, C. L. Z., & Smith, J. C. (1991). Vocabulary learning in literature groups. In J. Zutell & S. McCormick (Eds.), *Learner factors/teacher factors: Issues in literacy research and instruction, 40th Yearbook of the National Reading Conference* (pp. 201–209). Chicago: National Reading Conference.

Flynn, R. M. (2004). Curriculum-based readers theatre: Setting the stage for reading and retention. *The Reading Teacher, 58*, 360–365.

Flynt, E. S., & Brozo, W. G. (2008). Developing academic language: Got words? *The Reading Teacher, 61*, 500–502.

Franzak, J. K. (2006). *Zoom*: A review of the literature on marginalized adolescent readers, literacy theory, and policy implications. *Review of Educational Research, 76*, 209–248.

Frayer, D. A., Fredrick, W. C., & Klausmeir, H. J. (1969). *A schema for testing the level of concept mastery* (Technical Report No. 16). Madison: University of Wisconsin.

Fresch, M. J., & Wheaton, A. (2002). *Teaching and assessing spelling*. New York: Scholastic.

Gajria, M., Jitendra, A. K., Sood, S., & Sacks, G. (2007). Improving comprehension of expository text in students with LD: A research synthesis. *Journal of Learning Disabilities, 40*(3), 210–225.

Gallavan, N. P., & Kottler, E. (2007). Eight types of graphic organizers for empowering social studies students and teachers. *The Social Studies, 98*(3), 117–128.

Gardner, D. (2007). Children's immediate understanding of vocabulary: Contexts and dictionary definitions. *Reading Psychology, 28*, 331–373.

Gentner, D. (1983). A theoretical framework for Analogy. *Cognitive Science, 7*, 155–170.

Gill, S. R. (2007). The forgotten genre of children's poetry. *The Reading Teacher, 60*, 622–625.

Giorgis, C. (1999). The power of reading picture books aloud to secondary students. *Clearing House, 73*(1), 51–54.

Glasser, W. (1986). *Control theory in the classroom*. New York: Harper and Row.

Glynn, S. (1996). Teaching with analogies: Building on the science textbook. *The Reading Teacher, 49*, 490–492.

Goldfinch, E. (2002). Reading aloud to high school students—What a pleasure! *Book Report, 21*(3), 16–17.

Graves, M. F. (2000). A vocabulary program to complement and bolster a middle-grade comprehension program. In B. M. Taylor, M. F. Graves, & P. van den Broek (Eds.), *Reading for meaning: Fostering comprehension in the middle grades* (pp. 116–135). Newark, DE: International Reading Association.

Graves, M. F. (2007). Vocabulary instruction in the middle grades. *Voices from the Middle, 15*(1), 13–19.

Greenwood, S. C. (1987). The use of analogy instruction to reinforce vocabulary in reading class. *Middle School Journal, 19*(2), 11–13.

Greenwood, S. C., & Flanigan, K. (2007). Overlapping vocabulary and comprehension: Context clues complement semantic gradients. *The Reading Teacher, 61*, 249–254.

Guillaume, A. M., Yopp R. H., & Yopp, H. K. (2007). *Active teaching: 50 strategies for engaging K–12 Learners*. Columbus, OH: Merrill Prentice Hall.

Guzzetti, B. J., & Wooten, C. M. (2002). Children creating artists' books: Integrating visual arts and language arts. *Reading Online, 5*(10). Retrieved March 23, 2008, from http://www.readingonline.org/newliteracies/lit_index.asp?HREF=guzzetti2/index.html

Haggard, M. R. (1982). The vocabulary self-collection strategy: An active approach to word learning. *Journal of Reading, 26*, 203–207.

Haggard, M. R. (1986). Vocabulary self-collection strategy: Using student interest and word knowledge to enhance vocabulary growth. *Journal of Reading, 29*, 634–642.

Harmon, J. M. (2002). Teaching independent word learning strategies to struggling readers. *Journal of Adolescent and Adult Literacy, 54*, 606–625.

Harmon, J. M., & Hedrick, W. B. (2005). Research on vocabulary instruction in the content areas: Implications for struggling readers. *Reading and Writing Quarterly, 21*, 261–268.

Harste, J., Short, K., & Burke, C. (1988). *Creating classrooms for authors*. Portsmouth, NH: Heinemann.

Hart, B., & Risley, T. (1995). *Meaningful differences in everyday experiences of young children*. Baltimore: Paul H. Brookes.

Harvey, S., & Goudvis, A. (2000). *Strategies that work*. York, ME: Stenhouse.

Haskell, R. E. (2001). *Transfer of learning: Cognition, instruction, and reasoning*. San Diego, CA: Academic Press.

Henderson, M. T., & Mapp, K. L. (2002). *A new wave of evidence: The impact of school, family, and community connections on student achievement*. Austin, TX: National Center for Family and

Community Connections with Schools and Southwest Educational Development Laboratory. Retrieved April 5, 2008, from http://www.sedl.org/connections/resources/evidence.pdf

Hennings, D. G. (2000). Contextually relevant word study: Adolescent vocabulary development across the curriculum. *Journal of Adolescent and Adult Literacy, 44*, 268–279.

Herman, W. (1969). Reading and other language arts in social studies instruction: Persistent problems. In R. Preston (Ed.), *A new look at reading in the social studies* (pp.1–20). Newark, DE: International Reading Association.

Hickman, P., Pollard-Durodola, S., & Vaughn, S. (2004). Storybook reading: Improving vocabulary and comprehension for English-language learners. *Reading Teacher, 57*, 720–730.

Higashi, C. (1998). Planning a movable poetry feast. *American Libraries, 29*(2), 52–54.

Hoffner, H. (2003). Writing a movie. *The Reading Teacher, 57*, 78–81.

Hopkins, G., & Bean, T. W. (1998–1999). Vocabulary learning with the verbal-visual word association strategy in a Native American community. *Journal of Adolescent and Adult Literacy, 42*, 274–281.

Hunsberger, P. (2007). "Where am I?" A call for "connectedness" in literacy. *Reading Research Quarterly, 42*, 420–424.

Ivey, G. (2003). "The teacher makes it more explainable" and other reasons to read aloud in the intermediate grades. *The Reading Teacher, 56*, 812–814.

Jocson, K. M. (2006). "There's a better word": Urban youth rewriting their social worlds through poetry. *Journal of Adolescent and Adult Literacy, 49*, 700–707.

Johns, J. L., Lenski, S. D., & Bergland, B. L. (2003). *Comprehension and vocabulary strategies for the primary grades*. Dubuque, IA: Kendall/Hunt.

Johnson, D. (2002). Web watch: Picture book read-alouds. *Reading Online, 5*(9), 19–24. Retrieved March 28, 2008, from http://www.readingonline.org/electronic/elec_index.asp?HREF=webwatch/picturebooks/index.html

Johnson, D. D., & Pearson, P. D. (1984). *Teaching reading vocabulary*, 2nd Ed. New York: Holt, Rinehart and Winston.

Johnson, D. L. (2001). *Vocabulary in the elementary and middle school*. Boston: Allyn and Bacon.

Karwoski, G. L. (2003). Making history come alive. *Knowledge Quest, 32*(1), 41–42.

Kaszyca, M., & Krueger, A. M. (1994). Collaborative voices: Reflections on the I-Search project. *English Journal, 83*(1), 62–65.

Keehn, S. (2003). The effect of instruction and practice through readers theatre on young readers' oral reading fluency. *Reading Research and Instruction, 42*(4), 40–61.

Kelly, L. (2006). Reading allowed. *Education Week, 25*(33), 41.

Kieffer, M. J., & Lesaux, N. K. (2007). Breaking down words to build meaning: Morphology, vocabulary and reading comprehension in the urban classroom. *The Reading Teacher, 61*, 134–144.

Knopper, K. J., & Duggan, T. J. (2000). Writing to learn across the curriculum: Tools for comprehension in content areas. *The Reading Teacher, 59*, 462–470.

Kornfeld, J., & Leyden, G. (2005). Acting out: Literature, drama, and connecting with history. *The Reading Teacher, 59*, 230–238.

Krehel, S. (2003). Poetry performance in the elementary classroom. *Michigan Reading Journal, 35*(3), 20–23.

Kucan, L. (2007). "I" poems: Invitations for students to deepen literary understanding. *The Reading Teacher, 60*, 518–525.

Kuhn, M. R., & Stahl, S. A. (1998). Teaching children to learn word meanings from text: A synthesis of some questions. *Journal of Literacy Research, 30*, 119–138.

Lansdown, S. (1991). Increasing vocabulary knowledge using direct instruction, cooperative grouping, and reading in junior high school. *Illinois Reading Council Journal, 19*(4), 15–21.

Lawson, M. J., & Hogben, D, (1998). Learning and recall of foreign-language vocabulary: Effects of keyword strategy for immediate and delayed recall. *Learning and Instruction, 8*, 179–194.

Levin, J. R. (1988). Elaboration-based learning strategies: Powerful theory = powerful application. *Contemporary Educational Psychology, 13*, 191–205.

Lieberman, A. (2005). *Word origins . . . and how we know them: Etymology for everyone*. New York: Oxford University Press USA.

Liu, J. (2000). The power of readers theater: From reading to writing. *ELT Journal, 54*, 354–361.

Lloyd, S. L. (2004). Using comprehension strategies as a springboard for student talk. *Journal of Adolescent and Adult Literacy, 48*, 114–124.

Lowry, L. (1993). *The giver*. New York: Laurel Leaf.

Lyman, H. (2006). I-Search in the age of information. *English Journal, 95*(4), 62–67.

MacGillivray, L., & Curwen, M. S. (2007). Tagging as a social literacy practice. *Journal of Adolescent and Adult Literacy, 50*, 354–369.

MacQuarrie, L. L., Tucker, J. A., Burns, M. K., & Hartman, B. (2002). Comparison of retention rates using traditional, drill sandwich, and incremental rehearsal flash card methods. *School Psychology Review, 31*, 584–595.

Macrorie, K. (1988). *The I-search paper*. Portsmouth, NH: Boynton/Cook Publishers.

Marzano, R. J. (2004). *Building background knowledge for academic achievement: Research on what works in schools*. Alexandria, VA: Association for Supervision and Curriculum Development.

Mastropieri, M. A., Scruggs, T. E., & Fulk, B. J. M. (1990). Teaching abstract vocabulary with the keyword method: Effects on recall and comprehension. *Journal of Learning Disabilities, 23*, 92–96.

McCrudden, M. T., Schraw, G., & Hartley, K. (2006). The effect of general relevance instruction on shallow and deeper learning and reading time. *Journal of Experimental Education, 74*, 293–310.

Meehan, J. (2006). Generating excitement for reading in the middle grades: Start with nonfiction read-alouds! *Illinois Reading Council Journal, 34*(4), 3–16.

Milligan, J. L., & Ruff, T. P. (1990). A linguistic approach to social studies vocabulary development. *Social Studies, 81*, 218–220.

Moore, D. W., & Moore, S. A. (1986). Possible sentences. In E. K. Dishner, T. W. Bean, J. E. Readence, & D. W. Moore (Eds.), *Reading in the content areas* (pp. 174–178). Dubuque, IA: Kendall/Hunt.

Moore, D. W., & Readence, J. E. (1984). A quantitative and qualitative review of graphic organizer research. *Journal of Educational Research, 78*, 11–17.

Moran, K. J. K. (2006). Nurturing emergent readers through readers theater. *Early Childhood Education Journal, 33*, 317–323.

Nagy, W. E. (1988). *Teaching vocabulary to improve reading comprehension*. Newark, DE: International Reading Association.

Nagy, W. (2005). Why vocabulary instruction needs to be long-term and comprehensive. In E. H. Hiebert & M. L. Kamil (Eds.), *Teaching and learning vocabulary: Bringing research to practice* (pp. 27–44). Mahwah, NJ: Lawrence Erlbaum Associates.

Nagy, W., & Anderson, R. C. (1984). How many words are there in printed school English? *Reading Research Quarterly, 19*, 304–330.

Nagy, W., Herman, P., & Anderson, R. C. (1985). Learning words from context. *Reading Research Quarterly, 20*, 233–253.

Nagy, W. E., & Scott, J. A. (2000). Vocabulary processes. In M. L. Kamil, P. D. Mosentahal, P. D. Pearson, & R. Barr (Eds.), *Handbook of reading research* (Vol. 3, pp. 269–284). Mahwah, NJ: Lawrence Erlbaum Associates.

National Center for Education Statistics. (2006). *Public elementary and secondary students, staff, schools, and school districts: school year 2003–04*. Retrieved March 23, 2008, from http://nces.ed.gov/pubs2006/2006307.pdf

National Center for Education Statistics. (2007). *Table 20: Household income and poverty rates, by state: 1990, 2000, and 2003–2005*. Retrieved March 23, 2008, from http://nces.ed.gov/programs/digest/d06/tables/dt06_020.asp?referrer=list

National Institute of Child Health and Human Development. (2000). *The report of the National Reading Panel: Teaching children to read* (NIH Publication No. 00-4754). Washington, DC: U.S. Government Printing Office.

National Research Council. (2000). *How people learn: Brain, mind, experience, and school* (J. Bransford, A. L. Brown, & R. R. Cocking, Eds.). Washington, DC: National Academy Press.

Nilson, A. P., & Nilson, D. L. F. (2006). Latin revived: Source-based vocabulary lessons courtesy of Harry Potter. *Journal of Adolescent and Adult Literacy, 50*, 128–134.

Noden, H., & Moss, B. (1995). Nurturing artistic images in student reading and writing. *The Reading Teacher, 48*, 532–534.

O'Hanlon, C. (2008). They get the picture. *T H E Journal, 35*(1), 20–21.

Painter, D. D., Whiting, E., & Wolters, B. (March 2005). *The use of an interactive whiteboard in promoting interactive teaching and learning*. Paper presented at the VSTE Conference, Norfolk, VA. Retrieved April 9, 2008, from http://www.techlearning.com/showArticle.php?articleID=169400643

Pappas, M. L. (2003). My America in poetry and pictures. *School Library Media Activities Monthly, 19*(8), 21–24, 26.

Park, L. S. (2001). *A single shard*. New York: Dell Yearling.

Partnership for 21st Century Skills. (2002). *Learning for the 21st century*. Retrieved March 23, 2008, from http://www.21stcenturyskills.org/images/stories/otherdocs/p21up_Report.pdf

Pearson, P. D., & Fielding, L. (1991). Comprehension instruction. In R. Barr, M. L. Kamil, P. B. Mosenthal, & P. D. Pearson (Eds.), *Handbook of reading research* (Vol. 2, pp. 951–983). White Plains, NY: Longman.

Pearson, P. D., Hiebert, E. H., & Kamil, M. L. (2007). Vocabulary assessment: What we know and what we need to learn. *Reading Research Quarterly, 42*, 282–296.

Pearson, P. D., & Johnson, D. D. (1978). *Teaching reading comprehension*. New York: Rinehart and Winston.

Peck, S. M., & Virkler, A. J. (2006). Reading in the shadows: Extending literacy skills through shadow-puppet theater. *Reading Teacher, 59*, 786–795.

Pederson, C. H. (2008). Anchors of meaning-helpers of dialogue: The use of images in production of relations and meaning. *International Journal of Qualitative Studies in Education, 21*(1), 35–47.

Pehrsson, R. S., & Robinson, H. A. (1985). *The semantic organizer approach to writing and reading instruction.* Rockville, MD: Aspen Systems.

Pflaum, S. W., & Bishop, P. (2004). Perceptions of reading engagement: Learning from the learners. *Journal of Adolescent and Adult Literacy, 48*, 202–213.

Pittleman, S. D., Heimlich, J. E., Berglund. R. L., & French, M. P. (1991). *Semantic feature analysis.* Newark, DE: International Reading Association

Poe, E. A. (January, 1843). The Tell-Tale Heart. *The Pioneer, 1*, 29–31.

Pressley, M., Levin, J. R., & Delany, H. D. (1982). The mnemonic keyword method. *Review of Educational Research, 52*, 61–91

Raikes, H., et al. (2006). Mother–child book reading in low-income families: Correlates and outcomes during the first three years of life. *Child Development, 77*, 924–953.

Ranker, J. (2007). Using comic books as read-alouds: Insights on reading instruction from an English as a second language classroom. *Reading Teacher, 61*, 296–305.

Readence, J. E., Bean, T. W., & Baldwin, R. S. (1998). *Content area literacy: An integrated approach* (6th ed.). Dubuque, IA: Kendall/Hunt.

Richardson, J. S. (1994). Great read-alouds for prospective teachers and secondary students. *Journal of Reading, 38*(2), 98–103.

Richardson, J. S. (2000). *Read it aloud! Using literature in the secondary content classroom.* Newark, DE: International Reading Association.

Richek, M. A. (2005). Words are wonderful: Interactive, time efficient strategies to teach meaning vocabulary. *The Reading Teacher, 58*, 414–423.

Rinehart, S. D. (2001). Establishing guidelines for using readers theater with less-skilled readers. *Reading Horizons, 42*(2), 65–75.

Roberts, J. E., Burchinal, M., & Durham, M. (1999). Parents' report of vocabulary and grammatical development of African American preschoolers: Child and environmental associations. *Child Development, 70*, 92–106.

Roe, B. D., Stoodt-Hill, B. D., & Burns, P. C. (2004). *Secondary school literacy instruction: The content areas, English edition.* Boston: Houghton Mifflin.

Rosenblatt, L. M. (2003). From "The Poem as Event." *Voices from the Middle, 12*(3), 48–50.

Rosenblatt, L. M. (2005). From "What Facts Does This Poem Teach You?" *Voices from the Middle, 12*(3), 43–46.

Ross, W. D., Hunter, A., & Chazanow, L. (2006). Reading aloud: The *Moby-Dick* marathon. *English Journal, 95*(3), 39–43.

Rubenstein, R. N., & Schwartz, R. K. (2000). Word histories: Melding mathematics and meanings. *Mathematics Teacher, 93*, 664–669.

Rubinstein-Avila, E. (2006). Connecting with Latino learners. *Educational Leadership, 63*, 38–43.

Ruddell, M. R., & Shearer, B. A. (2002). "Extraordinary," "tremendous," "exhilarating" "magnificent": Middle school at-risk students become avid word learners with the vocabulary self-collection strategy (VSS). *Journal of Adolescent and Adult Literacy, 45*, 352–363.

Rycik, J. A. (1998). From information to interaction: Involving parents in the literacy development of their adolescent. *NASSP Bulletin 82*(600), 67–72.

Saint-Laurent, L., & Giasson, J. (2005). Effects of a family literacy program adapting parental intervention to first graders' evolution of reading and writing abilities. *Journal of Early Childhood Literacy, 5*, 253–278.

Santaro, L. E., Chard, D. J., Howard, S., & Baker, S. K. (2008). Making the very most of classroom read-alouds to promote comprehension and vocabulary. *The Reading Teacher, 61*, 396–408.

Schippert, P. (2005). Read alouds and vocabulary: A new way of teaching. *Illinois Reading Council Journal, 33*(3), 11–16.

Schnur, S. (1999). Building a father-daughter bridge—out loud. *Christian Science Monitor, 91*(140), 15.

Scholfield, P. (1982). Using the English dictionary for comprehension. *TESOL Quarterly, 16*, 185–294.

Schwartz, D. M. (1989). *If you made a million.* New York: Lothrop, Lee, and Shephard Books.

Schwartz, R. M., & Raphael, T. L. (1985). Concept of definition: A key to improving students' vocabulary. *The Reading Teacher, 39*, 198–205.

Scott, J., & Nagy, W. (1997). Understanding the definitions of unfamiliar verbs. *Reading Research Quarterly, 32*, 184–200.

Scott, J. A., & Nagy, W. (2004). Developing word consciousness. In J. Baumann & E. Kame'enui (Eds.), *Vocabulary instruction: Research to practice* (pp. 201–217). New York: Guilford.

Sénéchal M. (2006). Testing the home literacy model: Parent involvement in kindergarten is differentially related to grade 4 reading comprehension, fluency, spelling, and reading for pleasure. *Scientific Studies of Reading, 10*(1), 59–87.

Sénéchal, M., & LeFevre, J. A. (2002). Parental involvement in the development of children's reading skill: A five-year longitudinal study. *Child Development, 73*, 445–460.

Shapiro, A. M. (2004). How including prior knowledge as a subject variable may change outcomes of educational research. *American Educational Research Journal, 41*, 159–189.

Shira, L., & Smetana, L. (2005). Effects of comprehensive vocabulary instruction on Title I students' metacognitive word-learning skills and reading comprehension. *Journal of Literacy Research, 37*, 163–200.

Short, K. G., & Harste, J. (1996). *Creating classrooms for authors and inquirers*. Portsmouth, NH: Heinemann.

Siegel, M. (1984). Sketch to stretch. In O. Cochran (Ed.), *Reading, writing and caring* (p. 178). New York: Richard C. Owen.

Siegel, M. (1995). More than words: The generative power of transmediation for learning. *Canadian Journal of Education, 20*, 455–475.

Smith, G. E., & Throne, S. (2007–2008). Using I-Search to differentiate by interest. *Learning and Leading with Technology, 35*(4), 33–34.

Smith, J. B. (1983). "Pigue": A group dictionary assignment. *Exercise-Exchange, 29*, 35.

Smith, L., & Fershleiser, R. (2008). Not Quite What I Was Planning: Six-Word Memoirs by Writers Famous and Obscure. New York: Harper Perennial.

Smolik, L. (2006). How to speak Arabic and not know it. *Take Our Word for It*, 208, 1. Retrieved March 23, 2008, from http://www.takeourword.com/current/page1.html

Snow, C. E., & Beals, D. E. (2006). Mealtime talk that supports literacy development. *New Directions for Child and Adolescent Development, 111*, 51–66.

Spencer, B. H., & Guillaume, A. M. (2006). Integrating curriculum through the learning cycle: Content-based reading and vocabulary instruction. *The Reading Teacher, 60*, 206–221.

Stahl, S. A. (1983). Differential word knowledge and reading comprehension. *Journal of Reading Behavior, 15*, 33–50.

Stahl, S. A. (1986). Three principles of effective vocabulary instruction. *Journal of Reading, 29*, 662–668.

Stahl, S. A. (1999). *Vocabulary development*. Cambridge, MA: Brookline Books.

Stahl, S. A. (2005). Four problems with teaching word meanings (and what to do to make vocabulary an integral part of instruction). In E. H. Hiebert & M. L. Kamil (Eds.), *Teaching and learning vocabulary: Bringing research to practice* (pp. 95–114). Mahwah, NJ: Lawrence Erlbaum Associates.

Stahl, S. A., & Clark, C. H. (1987). The effects of participatory expectations in classroom discussion on the learning of science vocabulary. *American Educational Research Journal, 24*, 541–555.

Stahl, S., & Fairbanks, M. (1986). The effects of vocabulary instruction: A model-based meta-analysis. *Review of Educational Research, 56*, 72–110.

Stahl, S. A., & Kapinus, B. A. (1991). Possible sentences: Predicting word meanings to teach content area literacy. *The Reading Teacher, 45*, 36–43.

Stairs, J. (2007). Word wall connections. *Science Scope, 30*(5), 64–65.

Standerfer, L., (2006). Working vocabulary. *Principal Leadership (High School Ed.), 7*(1), 43–44.

Stanovich, K. E., & Cunningham, A. E. (1993). Where does knowledge come from? Associations between print exposure and information acquisition. *Journal of Educational Psychology, 85*, 211–229.

Stephens, E. C., & Brown, J. E. (2000). *A handbook of content literacy strategies: 75 practical reading and writing ideas*. Norwood, MA: Christopher Gordon.

Stetson, E. G., & Williams, R. P. (1992). Learning from social studies textbooks: Why some students succeed and others fail. *Journal of Reading, 36*, 22–30.

Stoller, F., & Grabe, W. (1995). Implications for L2 vocabulary acquisition and instruction from L1 vocabulary research. In T. Huckin, M. Haynes, & J. Coady (Eds.), *Second language reading and vocabulary learning* (pp. 24–45). Norwood, NJ: Ablex.

Stone, C. L. (1983). A meta-analysis of advanced organizer studies. *Journal of Experimental Education, 51*, 194–199.

Swanborn, M. S. L., & de Glopper, K. (1999). Incidental word learning while reading: A meta-analysis. *Review of Educational Research, 69*, 261–285.

Taba, H., Durkin, M. C., Fraenkel, J. R., & McNaughton, A. H. (1971). *A teacher's handbook in elementary social studies: An inductive approach* (2nd ed.). Reading, MA: Addison-Wesley.

Tabor, K. S. (2001). When analogy breaks down: Modelling the atom on the solar system. *Physics Education, 36*, 222–226.

Tallman, J. I., & Joyce, M. Z. (2006). *Making the writing and research connection with the I-Search process: A how-to-do-it manual* (2nd ed.). New York: Neal-Schuman.

Tan, A., & Nicholson, T. (1997). Flashcards revisited: Training poor readers to read words faster improves their comprehension of text. *Journal of Educational Psychology, 89*, 276–288.

Terrell, M. C., Scruggs, T. E., & Mastropieri, M. A. (2004). SAT vocabulary instruction for high school students with learning disabilities. *Intervention in School and Clinic, 39*, 288–294.

Thompson, D. R., & Rubenstein, R. N. (2000). Learning mathematics vocabulary: Potential pitfalls and instructional strategies. *Mathematics Teacher, 93*, 568–574.

Thornbury, S. (2002). *How to teach vocabulary.* Upper Saddle River, NJ: Pearson.

Tobin, K., & Tippins, D. J. (1996). Metaphors as seeds for conceptual change and the improvement of science teaching. *Science Education, 80*, 711–730.

Tompkins, G. E. (2004). *Literacy for the 21st century: Teaching reading and writing in grades 4 through 8.* Upper Saddle River, NJ: Prentice Hall.

Tortello, R. (2004). Tableaux vivants in the literature classroom. *The Reading Teacher, 58*, 206–208.

Uberti, H. Z., Scruggs, T. E., & Mastropieri, M. A. (2003), Keywords make the difference. *Teaching Exceptional Children, 35*, 56–62.

Vallejo, B. (2006). The word wall. *The Science Teacher, 73*(2), 58, 60.

van Steensel, R. (2006). Relations between socio-cultural factors, the home literacy environment and children's literacy development in the first years of primary education. *Journal of Research in Reading, 29*, 367–382.

Wade, S. E. (1992). How interest affects learning from text. In K. A. Renninger, S. Hidi, & A. Krapp (Eds.), *The role of interest in learning and development.* (pp. 255–278). Hillsdale, NJ: Lawrence Erlbaum Associates.

Walsh, B. A., & Blewitt, P. (2006). The effect of questioning style during storybook reading on novel vocabulary acquisition of preschoolers. *Early Childhood Education Journal, 33*, 273–278.

Wentink, H. W. M. J., van Bon, W. H. J., & Schreuder, R. (1997). Training of poor readers' phonological decoding skills: Evidence for syllable-bound processing. *Reading and Writing: An Interdisciplinary Journal, 9*, 163–192.

Werner, M. J. (1993). Library access for all limited English proficient students: One school's approach. *Emergency Librarian, 20*(5), 20–23

White, T. G., Sowell, J., & Yanigihara, A. (1989). Teaching elementary students to use word-part clues. *The Reading Teacher, 42*, 302–308.

Whitehurst, G. J., Zevenberg, A. A., Crone, D. A., Schultz, M. D., Velting, O. N., & Fischel, J. E. (1999). Outcomes of an emergent literacy intervention from Head Start through second grade. *Journal of Educational Psychology, 91*, 261–272.

Whitfield, J. (1993). "Dictionary skills" is not a four-letter word. *English Journal, 82*, 38–40

Whitin, P. W. (2002). Leading into literature circles through the sketch-to-stretch strategy. *The Reading Teacher, 55*, 444–450.

Wilkinson, J. R., & Minter, S. (2004). Bringing poetry to life in the high school. *Library Media Connection, 22*(6), 40–41.

Wilton, D. (2004). *Word myths: Debunking linguistic urban legends.* New York: Oxford University Press USA.

Wolf, S. A. (1998). The flight of reading: Shifts in instruction, orchestration, and attitudes through classroom theatre. *Reading Research Quarterly, 33*, 382–415.

Worthy, J., & Prater, K. (2002). "I thought about it all night": Readers theatre for reading fluency and motivation. *Reading Teacher, 56*, 294–297.

Wyra, M., & Hungi, N. (2007). The mnemonic keyword method: The effects of bidirectional retrieval training and of ability to image on foreign language vocabulary recall. *Learning and Instruction, 17*, 360–371.

Wysocki, K., & Jenkins, J. R. (1987). Deriving word meaning from morphological generalization. *Reading Research Quarterly, 22*, 66–81.

Yopp, R. H., & Yopp, H. K. (2002). Ten important words: Identifying the big ideas in informational text. *Journal of Content Area Reading, 2*, 7–13.

Yopp, R. H., & Yopp, H. K. (2007). Ten important words plus: A strategy for building word knowledge. *The Reading Teacher, 61*, 157–160.

Young, A. (2003). Writing across and against the curriculum. *College Composition and Communication, 54*, 472–485.

Young, L. (2007). Portals into poetry: Using generative writing groups to facilitate student engagement with word art. *Journal of Adolescent and Adult Literacy, 51*, 50–55.

Young, S. (1994). Teacher voices, student voices: An EJ reader responds. *English Journal, 83*(4), 98–100.